The Death Penalty Beyond abolition

Introduction by Roger Hood
Preface by Robert Badinter

Council of Europe Publishing

b 25484011

French version:

ISBN 92-871-5332-9

ZZ
CE
2004D26

Cover design: Mediacom
Layout: Pre-press unit, Council of Europe

Edited by Council of Europe Publishing
http://book.coe.int

Council of Europe Publishing
F-67075 Strasbourg Cedex

ISBN 92-871-5333-7
© Council of Europe, April 2004
Printed in Germany

Contents

Foreword

Europe is a highly diverse continent which survived the extreme brutality of two world wars and several totalitarian regimes and dictatorships over the last century. Europe is today a continent firmly committed to universal values, partly owing to its history.

Today the Council of Europe is proud that the 800 million inhabitants of its 45 member countries live in a de facto death penalty-free zone.

The abolition of the death penalty did not come about easily. The death penalty is a very sensitive subject which touches upon our deepest instincts and provokes a multitude of emotions which influence our opinions. In this book, we invite you to analyse these opinions and to reflect, in a rational manner, on the core arguments that have convinced European leaders to abolish the death penalty – from the "utilitarian" arguments (lack of dissuasive force, risk of mistakes, cost in terms of image...) to the ethical arguments (death penalty versus human rights).

In countries where the death penalty is still in force, it gives rise to very serious concerns:

> Can a system, based on the rule of law, run the risk of killing an innocent person?

> Is it acceptable to apply the death penalty when there is an alternative?

> Is it really humane to keep a person on death row for years, not knowing if the next day will be his/her last?

> Is it acceptable to execute a person with a mental disorder?

> Can this definitive punishment be applied to a person who was a minor at the time of the crime?

> Does the death penalty serve a real purpose?

For the Council of Europe of today, there is no right way to apply the death penalty, because the death penalty itself is wrong. Our ambition is to further contribute to speeding up the unstoppable movement towards universal abolition.

I am convinced that the information contained in this book will help its readers to understand our commitment to this cause. I trust that it will convince those who still have doubts that capital punishment has no place in a society founded on universal values.

I wish also to thank the authors of the texts for joining us in our endeavours towards the abolition of the death penalty, – a key objective of the Organisation and a concern very close to my heart.

Walter Schwimmer
Secretary General of the Council of Europe

Preface – Moving towards universal abolition of the death penalty

Robert Badinter

The death penalty – Beyond abolition is a fundamental work which bears witness to the strategic role of the Council of Europe's institutions in the move towards the universal abolition of the death penalty. The credit given is only fair, so vital has their action been in this enduring campaign, and so vital does it remain. The book also throws up some exciting ideas for increasing the effectiveness of the efforts to achieve abolition in those democratic countries which still apply the death penalty. It is clear that, as we move towards universal abolition, this work can play a useful role.

The whole continent of Europe freed from the death penalty

In not much more than fifty years, the continent of Europe has been turned into a death penalty-free area. When the Council of Europe was set up, in 1949, most member states still had the death penalty on their statute book. The prevailing mindset in Europe at the time is clear to anyone who reads the Convention for the Protection of Human Rights and Fundamental Freedoms, which was adopted in 1950. Paragraph 2 of Article 2, on the right to life, reads: "Deprivation of life shall not be regarded as inflicted in contravention of this article when it results from the use of force which is no more than absolutely necessary". This tolerance, however, could only be temporary, as the articles by Roger Hood and Eric Prokosch show.

Certain European states decided to take the first steps, then the process of eliminating capital punishment accelerated. The death penalty was abolished in Finland and Germany in 1949, in Austria in 1968, in the United Kingdom in 1969, in Sweden in 1972, in Portugal in 1976, in Luxembourg in 1979 and in France in 1981.

Backing up the efforts of most of its member states, the Parliamentary Assembly of the Council of Europe took the initiative of drafting a Protocol to the Convention concerning the abolition of the death penalty. After years of discussions, the now celebrated Protocol No 6 was adopted on 28 March 1983. For abolitionist Europe, this was a watershed. Article 1 of the Protocol reads: "The death penalty shall be abolished.

No one shall be condemned to such penalty or executed". The protocol came into force as early as 1985, enabling western Europe to close the door on capital punishment. As it takes precedence over member states' domestic law, the option of reversing their relevant legislation has no longer been available to them since that date.

The fundamental political changes which occurred after the Berlin Wall came down led to a second campaign against the death penalty, directed towards the new member states of the Council of Europe in central and eastern Europe. This presented a test for the superior values upheld by the Council of Europe, first and foremost the right to life. It was precisely at that juncture that the organisation had to make a new "profession of faith" in favour of abolition, looking beyond the already precious instrument which existed in the form of Protocol No 6. The Parliamentary Assembly again shouldered its responsibilities when, in 1994, it adopted Resolution 1044, linking membership of the Council of Europe to abolition of the death penalty, firstly de facto (obligation for any acceding state to adopt a moratorium on executions) and then de jure (signature, followed by ratification, of Protocol No 6 within three years). This second stage of the campaign for abolition was as productive as the first – and more rapid – and the Russian Federation is the only one of the forty-five current member states which has not yet de jure abolished capital punishment. But it has de facto dropped the death penalty, and abolition seems inevitable in the next few years. Thus we have, in a period of barely ten years, seen the disappearance of statutorily imposed death for ordinary crimes throughout the continent of Europe, a fact to which Hans Christian Krüger's splendid article bears witness.

Thus one last stage remained, that of the abolition of capital punishment in all circumstances. This is the purpose of a recent addition to the Convention, Protocol No 13, signed by thirty-six member states in Vilnius on 3 May 2002. It came into force on 1 July 2003 and has, to date (start February 2004), been ratified by twenty-two countries.

In a stronger position thanks to its own progress, Europe can make its voice heard well beyond its own borders, and it is doing so by every possible means, particularly through the case-law of the European Court of Human Rights and the untiring efforts of the Parliamentary Assembly. Thus, while numerous states which still carry out the death penalty regard the issue as an exclusively internal matter, the Parliamentary Assembly of the Council of Europe has always advocated a different interpretation: where the death penalty is concerned, the principle which must be applied is that any person under a state's jurisdiction must benefit from human rights and fundamental freedoms, which have had an international dimension for many years now. Caroline Ravaud has written an outstanding article on this aspect.

The Parliamentary Assembly continues to try to turn Europe and its institutions into a "death penalty-free zone", so it has tried to persuade the non-member states which enjoy observer status with the Council of Europe as a whole, and the national parliaments which hold observer status with just the Assembly itself, that they, too, should engage in discussions with a view to abolition of the death penalty. On the basis of a report of the Committee on Legal Affairs and Human Rights, the Assembly, on 25 June 2001, adopted Resolution 1253 (2001) on the abolition of the death penalty in the countries enjoying observer status with the Council of Europe. Combining, as is its wont, an educational role and a firm stance, the Parliamentary Assembly is thus engaged in a dialogue with MPs of the two states concerned, the United States and Japan, trying to persuade them to abolish capital punishment. What is more, the Assembly has decided that it will not, in future, recommend that the Council of Europe grant observer status to any states which have not abolished the death penalty. Renate Wohlwend's article takes a very detailed look at the subject.

The march towards universal abolition

Fortunately, it is not only in Europe that this irresistible movement towards the universal abolition of the death penalty is under way.

The countries which have abolished capital punishment are now in the majority. As of 1 January 2003,[1] 112 countries had abolished capital punishment de facto or de jure. Abolition applied to all crimes in 76 of these, but only to ordinary crimes in another 15, and the other 21 were no longer implementing death sentences. On the same date, there were 83 countries where executions were still carried out.

Over the past ten years, in particular, an average of more than three countries a year have been abolishing the death penalty. Since 1990, over 30 countries worldwide have abolished it for all crimes. Among them are African states such as Angola, Ivory Coast, Mauritius, Mozambique and South Africa, countries of the Americas, including Canada and Paraguay, Asian representatives such as Hong Kong and Nepal, and east European and Caucasian countries including Azerbaijan, Bulgaria, Estonia, Georgia, Lithuania, Poland, Turkmenistan, Yugoslavia, Serbia and Montenegro, Turkey and, most recently, Armenia.

We must not ignore the particularly dark clouds which hang over some areas, with certain countries having a dreadful record where the death penalty is concerned, foremost among these being China.

---

1. Source: Amnesty International, 2002 report, Internet publication: www.amnesty.org

The figures are eloquent: at least 1 526 executions were carried out in some thirty-one countries in 2002,[2] with 81% of these taking place in China (1 060), Iran (113), Saudi Arabia and the United States (71). Since 1990, seven of the countries which still make use of capital punishment have executed persons who were minors when they committed their offence,[3] the sorry record in this respect being held by the United States, with 17 such executions since 1990.

The continuing use of the death penalty in the United States undeniably constitutes a longstanding obstacle to the final phase of universal abolition, in which the democracies which respect fundamental rights would present a united front against the totalitarian states. For, in the last analysis, once public opinion within the various democratic systems has finally been won over, the death penalty will remain inextricably linked to dictatorship and totalitarianism alone. It should be remembered that 877 people have already been executed since 1976 in the thirty-eight US states which have reinstated the death penalty, with almost 3 700 people still on death row. Yet opinions are changing in the United States, too, with 107 prisoners since 1976 already having succeeded in proving their innocence after being sentenced to death. And the death row cells of Illinois have been completely emptied following Governor Ryan's decision to commute all death sentences. The Supreme Court is again becoming more rigorous in its interpretation of the prohibition under the US Constitution of "cruel and unusual punishments" (8th Amendment). Hundreds of convictions are now being set aside by federal Courts of Appeal as the Supreme Court's case-law evolves. Therefore it is now vital to continue to support America's pro-abolition movements. In this context, Peter Hodgkinson's article about associations of victims and their families and Hugo Adam Bedau's about the situation in respect of the death penalty in the United States provide valuable food for thought.

Japan also occupies a particular place on the sad list of countries committed to capital punishment. It is another great democracy which not only continues to make use of the death penalty, but also treats those who have been sentenced to death with particular inhumanity. The oldest subject of a death sentence, for instance, died in July 2003 at the age of 86, having spent thity-three years in solitary confinement on death row, not knowing as each day dawned whether it would be his last, and aware that neither his family nor his lawyers would be informed in advance of his execution date. Since a de facto moratorium came to

---

2. These figures only include cases of which Amnesty International was aware for that year. According to Amnesty, the actual figures are certainly higher.
3. Saudi Arabia, United States, Iran, Nigeria, Pakistan, Democratic Republic of Congo and Yemen.

an end in 1993, forty-three people have been executed, mostly outside the period of parliamentary sessions, to avoid a reaction from parliament and a public backlash. Anyone who reads Yoshihiro Yasuda's article on the subject will gain deeper insight into Japan's specific situation.

Among all the other states of the world, none now carries out the death sentence with such intensity as the People's Republic of China. More people are executed there than anywhere else in the world, following trials which are parodies of justice, supposedly conducted to combat corruption or drugs trafficking, but looking more like part of a social cleansing process.

Islamic states such as Iran and Saudi Arabia also make assiduous use of the death penalty, readily invoking Koranic law, Sharia, as justification. They are clearly trying to conceal under the cloak of religion a barbaric practice. Of course the Koran's message of peace, like that of other religions' holy books, does not consider the death penalty to be a necessary part of the justice system.

Truth to tell, all these states are in fact subjected to totalitarian regimes which impose an official political, and sometimes religious, ideology. There is an indissoluble link between dictatorship and death penalty. All dictatorships make use of the death penalty, because it is the ultimate expression of the absolute power that the rulers wield over their subjects. The pale light cast by dictatorship is enough to reveal the true features of the death penalty, which is intrinsically totalitarian.

Thus the fight for universal abolition takes on a doubly liberating dimension: the elimination of the death penalty will be conducive to the promotion of human rights and the rule of law, for respect for life is both universal and indivisible. The cause of abolition will progress inexorably until its victory is complete, because it is the cause of humanity.

Introduction – The importance of abolishing the death penalty

Roger Hood
Professor Emeritus of Criminology, University of Oxford and an Emeritus Fellow of All Souls College, Oxford. Hood is currently Distinguished Visiting Professor, Department of Sociology, University of Hong Kong

Europe is in practice a capital punishment free zone. In none of the 45 member states of the Council of Europe nor in any of the 15 member states of the European Union or the 13 candidate countries is the death penalty now enforced. Altogether, by November 2003, 92 countries worldwide were abolitionist: 77 for all crimes and 15 for ordinary crimes. In a further 33 retentionist countries there have been no executions for at least ten years.[1]

It is always worth restating what the main objections are to capital punishment being used as an instrument of state punishment. They are so well known, of course, that a brief summary will suffice:

- The death penalty is an extreme example of torture, a form of punishment that violates human rights. It is therefore an illegitimate mode of punishment for a state to employ.

- There is no convincing evidence that the rate of murder (or any other crime threatened with the death penalty) is consistently lower when the death penalty is on the statute book and enforced by executions. When all the circumstances surrounding the way in which capital punishment can be used in democratic states and under the rule of law are taken into account, it has not proved to be a more effective deterrent than the alternative sanctions of life or long-term imprisonment.

- In countries which abide by the rule of law and take into account mitigating as well as aggravating circumstances, capital punishment is, in practice, inflicted only in a relatively small proportion of the

---

1. See United Nations, "Status of the international covenants on human rights: question of the death penalty", E/CN.45/2003/106, 2003. Also, more generally, Roger Hood, *The death penalty: a worldwide perspective*, (3rd edn), Oxford University Press, Oxford, 2002. Amnesty International lists 76 countries as completely abolitionist, and 16 for ordinary offences, because, unlike the United Nations, it counts Bolivia as abolitionist for ordinary crimes only, rather than for all crimes.

cases which could legally fall within its scope. Experience has shown that it cannot be administered without an unacceptable degree of arbitrariness, inequity and discrimination even when it is retained only for a restricted category of murders.

• It is counterproductive in the moral message it conveys, for it legitimises the very behaviour – killing – which the law seeks to repress. This is especially true when those executed appear as scapegoats and excite pity, and even more so when occasionally the innocent are executed – an inevitable consequence of capital punishment. It therefore undermines the legitimacy and moral authority of the whole legal system.

Europe in the abolitionist vanguard

While the first attempts by enlightened European rulers at the end of the eighteenth century to abolish capital punishment were soon reversed, the movement to restrict it to murder had been successful in many countries by the mid-nineteenth century. In 1846, the mid-American state of Michigan, and in 1853 Wisconsin, abolished the death penalty completely for murder and have remained abolitionist ever since, a fact that should be recalled every time that the United States is quoted as a country where the death penalty holds sway. Venezuela became the first country to abolish capital punishment for all crimes as long ago as 1863.

Portugal (where there had been no executions since 1843), the first European country to abolish capital punishment for murder in 1867, was soon followed by the Netherlands, Romania, Italy, and Norway. After the first world war they were joined by Sweden, Denmark and Switzerland. With the end of fascist tyranny, capital punishment was abandoned first by Italy in 1944 (it had been restored by Mussolini) and then by the Federal Republic of Germany in 1949. In 1962 executions were being carried out in western Europe – usually quite rarely – only in the United Kingdom, France, Greece, the Irish Republic, Spain and Turkey. It was on the statute book but unused in Belgium and Luxembourg. All of these countries have now abandoned capital punishment for all crimes whether against the person, against the state, in peacetime or in time of war, with the exception of Turkey (which keeps it in case of time of war). The last execution in western Europe took place in France in 1977, a quarter of a century ago as Anne Ferrazzini and Michel Forst recount, and Turkey has not carried out an execution since 1984.

However, it must be remembered that several countries have signalled their complete rejection of capital punishment only since the mid-1990s, the United Kingdom being one of them when, as late as 1998, it abolished capital punishment for treason and piracy as well as for military offences some thirty years after it had been abolished for murder. Capital punishment had been endemic in all the countries of eastern Europe which formed the former Soviet bloc, although in some of these countries it was used more as a tool for suppressing political dissent than for punishing common offenders. Executions were still being carried out in east European countries until less – and in some instances much less – than twenty years ago: in Croatia until 1987, Hungary 1988, Poland 1988, Bulgaria 1989, Moldova 1989, Estonia 1991, Armenia 1991, Azerbaijan 1993, Georgia 1994, Lithuania 1995, and finally in Ukraine in 1997. Indeed nine member states of the Council of Europe did not abolish the death penalty until 1997 or later. The Russian Federation, moreover, has imposed a moratorium on all executions since 1996. Despite strong pressures from various quarters to re-instate it – vividly described in Anatoly Pristavkin's article – President Putin remains committed to eventual de jure abolition, and since 1999 all death sentences have been commuted to life imprisonment.

Thus, the near-complete abolition of capital punishment in Europe is quite a recent achievement. It reminds us that the debate is still fresh and must be pursued with vigour if countries outside the European human rights domain are to be persuaded to abandon the death penalty and those within European countries who still at times press for its re-introduction are to be assuaged. This is why this book includes essays by Peter Hodgkinson both on the reactions and needs of victims of homicide and on the development of satisfactory alternatives to the death penalty.

How has this change been achieved? What marks out the modern period from the past, when abolition was very much regarded as an internal "national" criminal justice issue, is the development of a trans-European political movement to make abolition of the death penalty the touchstone of acceptable national standards of respect for human rights. European countries are not only anxious to consolidate their achievement, but to spread the gospel to as many countries as possible in other parts of the world. As Hans Christian Krüger points out, it was towards the end of the 1970s that the Committee of Ministers of the Council of Europe first began to consider the question of capital punishment as a human rights issue. And Eric Prokosch reminds us that it is only twenty years ago, in 1983, that Protocol No. 6 to the Convention for the Protection of Human Rights and Fundamental Freedoms (the European Convention on Human Rights – ECHR) calling for the abolition of the death penalty in peacetime, was opened for signature. So far forty-three countries have ratified the protocol and there are only two member states of the Council of Europe, having signed the protocol, who have yet to ratify it: the Russian Federation, which has suspended the use of capital punishment and Serbia and Montenegro, which has in fact, abolished the death penalty for ordinary crimes.

The European commitment to total abolition has now been endorsed by the adoption of Protocol No. 13 to the ECHR, which was opened for signature in May 2002 and came into force on 1 July 2003.

The most important political decision came in the wake of the 1st Summit of the Heads of State and Government of the member states of the Council of Europe held in Vienna in 1993, which laid down that applicant states should, among other things, undertake to sign and ratify the ECHR. Nine years ago, following the influential report in 1994 by Hans Göran Franck on "The abolition of the death penalty", the Parliamentary Assembly made it a condition that any country which wished to become a member of the Council of Europe should agree to implement an immediate moratorium on executions and then sign and ratify, within a set number of years, Protocol No. 6 to the ECHR. As Renate Wohlwend so vividly recounts, the desire to be a member of the Council of Europe played a vital role, along with the pressure exerted by human rights lawyers, in persuading Ukraine – despite the initial serious breaches of its obligation to honour the moratorium – to embrace finally the abolitionist cause.

The European Union (EU) has similarly made the abolition of capital punishment a precondition for membership and in 1998 it embarked on a diplomatic policy to persuade other nations through the adoption of *Guidelines for EU policy towards third countries on the death penalty.* These stressed that "the death penalty has no place in the penal systems of modern civilised societies" and "abolition of the death penalty contributes to the enhancement of human dignity and the progressive development of human rights". Indeed, the European stance is not to accept the argument that capital punishment can be defined in relativistic religious or cultural terms or as a matter purely for national sovereignty. Rather it has become transformed into a prospective international human rights norm. This is reflected in the Charter of Fundamental Rights, adopted by the EU in Nice in December 2000, which prohibits the extradition of offenders to any country where the death penalty might be imposed unless a firm guarantee is given that it will not be imposed. The European stance has been influential in persuading both the Canadian Supreme Court and the South African Constitutional Court to take the same position: in effect announcing a policy of non-co-operation with governments that maintain capital punishment unless they accept the integrity of the anti-capital punishment argument. Following the Council of Europe delegations to Japan and the United States, the Parliamentary Assembly of the Council of Europe adopted Resolution 1253 (2001) calling on Japan and the United States, among other things, to institute a moratorium on executions and to take necessary steps to abolish the death penalty as well as to improve conditions on death row immediately. A decision was made to review the observer status at the Council of Europe of these two countries should no significant progress be made to implement the resolution by 1 January 2003. Caroline Ravaud discusses all these significant developments.

The European Union now regularly makes approaches to state governors in the United States whenever an execution is imminent and individual European countries, such as the United Kingdom, have pleaded strongly for its own citizens to be spared execution. Yet the attitude of the authorities has, so far, remained resistant to such pleas. For example, in relation to the execution by the State of Texas of a British national, John (Jackie) Elliott on 5 February 2003, who insisted that he was innocent but was refused the benefit of further DNA testing of evidence, the Deputy Chief of the US Mission to the OSCE Permanent Council in Vienna stated on 23 January 2003:

> We take note of the statement by The European Union concerning the death penalty in the United States and the pending execution of Mr. John Elliott ... [but note]... that in a democratic society the criminal justice system, including the punishments prescribed for the most serious crimes, should reflect the will of the people, freely expressed and appropriately implemented. In the United States, the use of the death penalty is a decision left to democratically elected governments at the federal level and at the level of each individual state, which in this case is the State of Texas.

Persuading the others

It has to be recognised that many countries share the view of the United States Government. For example, a representative of Libya declared at the 57th session of the UN Commission on Human Rights in 2001, that "the death penalty concerns the justice system and is not a question of human rights". Similarly, as Yoshihiro Yasuda informs us: "The government [of Japan] views the death penalty as a matter relating to the penal system, not as a human rights issue ... the death penalty is regarded ... as a means of accepting responsibility and thereby atoning for one's sin."

In support of their view that "there is no international consensus that capital punishment should be abolished",[2] some countries have appealed to the wording of Article 6(2) of the International Covenant on Civil and Political Rights (ICCPR) which states that "the sentence of death may be imposed only for the most serious crimes", meaning "intentional crimes with lethal or extremely grave consequences". But, as Sir Nigel Rodley points out, this is by no means a declaration that capital punishment is, in principle, acceptable. Indeed, Article 6(6) declares that: "Nothing in this article shall be invoked to delay or to prevent the abolition of capital

2. Statement drawn up by Saudi Arabia at the 57th session of UN Commission on Human Rights, April 2001.

17

punishment by any State Party to the present Covenant". Clearly Article 6(2) is not meant to support the use of the death penalty, but to limit its scope until abolition is achieved.

There is no doubt that abolition is the goal. Indeed, it has be argued that, notwithstanding Article 6(2) the case for abolition is supported by Article 7 of the ICCPR, which states categorically that "no one shall be subject to torture or cruel, inhuman or degrading punishment".[3] This is because even those who favour capital punishment "in principle" have had to face the fact that in recent years more and more evidence has accrued to support the view that capital punishment does not have a uniquely powerful deterrent effect in comparison with lesser punishments, and that in practice it is inevitably accompanied by arbitrariness in its infliction, racial and social discrimination, mistakes, and inhumanity in its administration. Thus the same values which retentionists proclaim to protect the rights of victims of crime can also be invoked to protect the rights of the accused when threatened with state-inflicted death, especially when it can be shown that there is a risk that innocent persons will be subject to the death penalty or that the system as a whole inflicts capital punishment on persons who are undeserving of it for various reasons. In other words, there remains a large gap between the belief that some persons may "deserve to die" for the crimes they commit, and believing that a state system for the administration of capital punishment can be devised which meets the high ideals of equal, effective, procedurally correct, and humane justice that civilised societies seek to implement. The article on the situation in the United States where, as Hugo Adam Bedau points out, so many errors in the administration of the death penalty have occurred, and the essay on Japan which describes the way prisoners are mistreated in an inhumane environment as "barbarous and uncivilised torture", both amply illustrate this message.

It is precisely when there are strong reactions to serious crimes that the use of the death penalty as an instrument of crime control is most dangerous. Pressure on the police and prosecutors to bring offenders to justice, especially those suspected of committing outrages, is likely to lead to shortcuts, breaches of procedural protections, and simple myopia in investigation once a suspect is identified. Thus, the situation described in Japan, where "almost half of death row inmates were indicted after interrogation without the presence of a counsel at the police investigation stage" is nothing short of scandalous. As Professor Bedau reminds us, researchers in the United States have shown that two-thirds of death

---

3. See Manfred Nowak, "Is the death penalty an inhuman punishment?", in Theodore S. Orlin, Allan Rossas and Martin Sheinin (eds), *The jurisprudence of human rights law. A comparative interpretive approach* (2000), pp. 27-45 at p.44.

sentences have been reversed by appeal courts on the grounds of error. Yet investigative journalists have still uncovered cases that have passed through all the lengthy appeal processes without such errors being spotted, and in which, with the aid of DNA, convincing evidence of innocence has been forthcoming. The problem appears to be endemic to the systematic use of capital punishment, and not simply a reflection of this or that fault in the administration of criminal justice in a particular country. One only has to think of what the consequences would have been had the United Kingdom still had the death penalty on its statute books. Those convicted of terrorist murders during the IRA bombing campaign would undoubtedly have been executed, yet many of them were exonerated of responsibility for these crimes years later by the Court of Appeal. It was this that persuaded Michael Howard, the then Conservative party Home Secretary, renowned for his tough approach to crime, to change his stance from seeking the re-introduction of capital punishment to embracing abolition.

In the face of such evidence, there are positive signs that more and more countries are willing to accept the view that the imposition of capital punishment is incompatible with a political culture based on human rights. Although some Islamic scholars maintain that Islamic Law "demands" the death penalty, a substantial number of Muslim countries rarely carry out executions. They appear to recognise that, in practice, death is too harsh a penalty for many murders, and of course they have the opportunity to avail themselves instead of *kisas* (recompense) if the victim's family agrees. It is encouraging to the abolitionist cause that Bosnia and Herzegovina, Azerbaijan and Turkmenistan, all countries with large Muslim majorities among their populations, have abolished the death penalty, and others such as Tajikistan and Uzbekistan have substantially reduced the scope of capital punishment and the incidence of its infliction.

Many retentionist countries, including India and Japan, hang on to capital punishment with apparently little commitment to use it as a vigorous means of crime control. Indeed, there were only nine or ten countries in the world that appeared to have judicially executed as many as 100 people over the whole of the five-year period between 1996 and 2001. Having forgone the crime control justification, countries will become more open to the human rights argument. In this regard it is notable that, despite its continuing widespread use of capital punishment, in recent years China has been willing to discuss the death penalty under the umbrella of human rights dialogues with European countries.

However, it has to be recognised that the European initiative to influence so-called third countries will prove difficult for as long as the United States continues to reject human rights arguments on the death penalty

19

as defined by international consensus or treaty unless they are endorsed by its own Supreme Court. The challenge for Europe is to find a way to persuade the United States, with which it shares so many values and beliefs, that the European view of the death penalty is both morally right and free from social danger.

The demand for capital punishment in the United States is often said to rest on the popular belief that it is an essential defence against, and an appropriate reaction to, what has undoubtedly been a high rate of homicide. But that rate has been falling, not it seems because of the use of executions, but to a considerable extent to changes in the demographic structure of the population. The annual number of executions has also fallen from its highpoint of 98 in 1999 to 71 in 2001 – carried out in thirteen states, 33 of the 71 executions being carried out in Texas alone. This meant that in addition to the thirteen wholly abolitionist states, twenty-five of those with capital punishment on their statute books carried out no executions. In 2002 only three non-Southern states carried out any executions: Missouri (6), Ohio (3) and California (1). Moreover, those executed still account for only a tiny fraction of all homicides.

Indeed, since the first edition of this book in 1999, there have been several other encouraging developments. The institution of a moratorium on executions in Illinois and the setting up of a Commission of Inquiry by Governor Ryan has acted as a beacon. The commission concluded unanimously "that no system given human nature and frailties could ever be devised or constructed that would work perfectly and guarantee absolutely that no innocent person is ever sentenced to death". Because so few of the safeguards that it regarded as essential had been in place, the commission considered that many of those on death row must be worthy of clemency. On his last day in office the governor took the unprecedented action of granting clemency to all those under sentence of death.

Several leading figures have started to voice their opposition to the death penalty. Thus, the former Chief Justice of Illinois, Justice Moses Harrison joined a roster of judges, including former Supreme Court Justices Blackmun and Powell, as well as the former Chief Justice of Florida, Judge Gerald Kogan, in declaring that the system is immoral because it can never be made infallible. In an extraordinary judgment in June 2002, a federal judge, Judge Rakoff, held in the federal district court in Manhattan that the death penalty was unconstitutional as it "not only deprives innocent people of a significant opportunity to prove their innocence, and thereby violates procedural due process, but also creates an undue risk of executing innocent people, and thereby violates substantive due process". Although this view was overturned in December 2002 by a federal appeals court for the 2nd Circuit in New York on the grounds that "binding precedents of the Supreme Court prevent us from finding capital punishment unconstitutional based solely on a statistical or theoretical possibility that a defendant might be innocent", the argument remains powerful.

At the same time there is evidence that the US Supreme Court has begun (although as yet tentatively) to look beyond American shores in interpreting its judgment of whether capital punishment violates "evolving standards of decency". Thus, in the judgment reached in the case of *Atkins v Virginia* that it was a violation of the American Constitution to impose the death penalty on a mentally retarded person, the Supreme Court referred not only to the number of American states that had abolished the death penalty for the mentally retarded, but also to international opinion on the matter. *Atkins v Virginia* awoke many Americans to the fact that it had been one of the few countries in the world to breach international human rights standards in this unacceptable way. It led swiftly to a challenge to the constitutionality of executing persons who had committed a capital offence when under the age of 18; another breach of international standards. And although this challenge was not successful, four of the nine Supreme Court justices declared in October 2002 that the execution of such offenders "is a relic of the past and is inconsistent with evolving standards of decency in a civilized society. We should put an end to this shameful practice". Undoubtedly the weight of international opinion is being felt, as is evident in the judgments of the International Court of Justice against the United States in relation to its failure in the cases of the Paraguayan citizen Angel Breard and the German citizens Karl and Walter La Grand (and in cases currently under review of Mexican prisoners on death row), to fulfil its obligations under Article 36 of the Vienna Convention on Consular Relations to ensure that consular assistance is provided to foreign nationals arrested for serious crimes in the United States. As a distinguished American law professor and former Assistant Secretary of State for Democracy, Human Rights and Labor, Harold Koh has put it: "the death penalty has become America's Achilles heel ... in almost every multilateral human rights forum".[4]

The death penalty remains in the United States, and in far too many other countries, as a cruel penal symbol comparatively rarely enforced, applied in an unacceptably arbitrary way, often in flagrant violation of international standards for the protection of prisoners, and for no demonstrable gain in the diminution of murder. There is little doubt that

---

4. See Harold Hongju Koh, "Paying 'decent respect' to world opinion on the death penalty". *UC Davis Law Review*, 2002, vol. 35, pp. 1085-131, at p. 1105. Quoted in Roger Hood, *The death penalty: a worldwide perspective*, (3rd edn), Oxford University Press, Oxford, 2002, p. 73.

the supporters of capital punishment are on the defensive.[5] It is to be hoped that political and judicial leaders will emerge in the United States with the courage, whatever opinion polls may show, to declare capital punishment to be incompatible with a political culture which values human rights.

---

5. See, Franklin E. Zimring, *The contradictions of American capital punishment,* Oxford University Press, New York, 2003, Chapter 8, "The beginning of the end".

The death penalty versus human rights

Eric Prokosch
Theme Research Co-ordinator, Amnesty International

Half a century after the adoption of the United Nations Universal Declaration of Human Rights, the trend towards worldwide abolition of the death penalty is unmistakable. When the declaration was adopted in 1948, eight countries had abolished the death penalty for all crimes; as of May 2003, the number stands at seventy-six. More than half the countries in the world have abolished the death penalty in law or practice, and the number continues to increase.

In Europe the trend is especially remarkable: the Parliamentary Assembly of the Council of Europe now requires a commitment to abolition as a condition of entry into the Organisation, and the European Union has adopted a far-reaching policy governing the promotion of abolition in non-member states. Within the United Nations, the Commission on Human Rights has called on states that still maintain the punishment "to establish a moratorium on executions, with a view to completely abolishing the death penalty".[1] Yet there are still calls for the use or extension of the death penalty, often in response to public concern about crime.

What do these matters have to do with human rights?

Understanding the death penalty as a human rights violation

Amnesty International opposes the death penalty as a violation of fundamental human rights – the right to life and the right not to be subjected to cruel, inhuman or degrading treatment or punishment. Both of these rights are recognised in the Universal Declaration of Human Rights, other international and regional human rights instruments and national constitutions and laws.

Defence of life and defence of the state may be held to justify, in some cases, the taking of life by state officials; for example, when law-enforcement officials must act immediately to save their own lives or those of

---

1. Resolution 2003/67 of 24 April 2003, co-sponsored by seventy-five countries and adopted by a vote of 24 for and 18 against, with 10 abstentions.

others, or when a country is engaged in armed conflict. Even in such situations the use of lethal force is surrounded by internationally accepted standards of human rights and humanitarian law to inhibit abuse.

The death penalty, however, is not an act of defence against an immediate threat to life. It is the premeditated killing of a prisoner for the purpose of punishment – a purpose that can be met by other means.

The cruelty of torture is evident. Like torture, an execution constitutes an extreme physical and mental assault on a person already rendered helpless by government authorities. The cruelty of the death penalty is manifest not only in the execution but in the time spent under sentence of death, during which the prisoner is constantly contemplating his or her own death at the hands of the state. This cruelty cannot be justified, no matter how cruel the crime of which the prisoner has been convicted.

If it is impermissible to cause grievous physical and mental harm to a prisoner by subjecting him or her to electric shocks and mock executions, how can it be permissible for public officials to attack not only the body or the mind but the prisoner's very life?

Threatening to kill a prisoner can be one of the most fearsome forms of torture. As torture, it is prohibited. How can it be permissible to subject a prisoner to the same threat in the form of a death sentence, passed by a court of law and due to be carried out by the prison authorities?

The cruelty of the death penalty extends beyond the prisoner to the prisoner's family, to the prison guards and to the officials who have to carry out an execution. Information from various parts of the world shows that the role of an executioner can be deeply disturbing, even traumatic. Judges, prosecutors and other officials may also experience difficult moral dilemmas if the roles they are required to play in administering the death penalty conflict with their own ethical views.

The right to life and the right not to be subjected to cruel, inhuman or degrading treatment or punishment are the two human rights most often cited in debates about the death penalty. But the death penalty also attacks other rights.

As indicated by the annual reports to the United Nations Commission on Human Rights by its Special Rapporteur on Extrajudicial, Summary or Arbitrary Executions and by Amnesty International's own information, in many cases prisoners are sentenced to death in trials which do not conform to international norms for a fair trial. Prisoners facing a possible death sentence are often represented by inexperienced lawyers, and sometimes by no lawyer at all. The defendants may not understand the charges or the evidence against them, especially if they are not conversant with the language used in court. Facilities for interpretation and translation of court documents are often inadequate. In some cases prisoners are unable to exercise their right to appeal to a court of higher jurisdiction or exercise their the right to petition for clemency or commutation of the death sentence. In some jurisdictions, capital cases are heard before special or military courts using summary procedures. Such practices undermine the right to a fair trial and are in violation of standards recognised in international human rights instruments.

Unlike imprisonment, the death penalty entails the risk of judicial errors that can never be corrected. There will always be a risk that some prisoners who were innocent will be executed. The death penalty will not prevent them from repeating a crime that they did not commit in the first place.

In the United States a statistical study released by the Columbia University Law School of death sentences passed between 1973 and 1995 found that they were "persistently and systematically fraught with error". The study concluded that courts had found serious errors in 68% of the 4 578 cases reviewed, and expressed "grave doubt" as to whether the courts catch all such errors.[2]

Since 1973 more than 100 prisoners have been released from US death rows after evidence of their innocence emerged.

The then governor of the US State of Illinois, George Ryan, announced on 31 January 2000 that he would suspend executions pending a special investigation into the state's capital punishment system. His decision followed the exoneration of the thirteenth death row prisoner found to have been wrongfully convicted in the state since the United States resumed executions in 1977. In January 2003, Governor Ryan pardoned four death row prisoners and commuted all 167 other death sentences in Illinois. The death penalty is often used disproportionately against members of disadvantaged social groups, and thus in a discriminatory fashion, contrary to Articles 2 and 7 of the Universal Declaration of Human Rights. It is the ultimate denial of the dignity and worth of the human person, affirmed in the preamble to the Universal Declaration of Human Rights.

There is no criminological justification for the death penalty that would outweigh the human rights grounds for abolishing it. The argument that the death penalty is needed to deter crime has become discredited by the consistent lack of scientific evidence that it does so more effectively than other punishments. The death penalty negates the internationally accepted penological goal of rehabilitating the offender.

---

2. James S. Liebman, Jeffrey Fagan and Valerie West, "A broken system: error rates in capital cases, 1973-1995", Columbia University Law School, New York, June 2000.

Restriction through international standards

International human rights standards have developed in a way that favours ever-tighter restrictions on the scope of the death penalty. This progressive narrowing of the death penalty is mirrored by actual practice in most states that still use the punishment.

Progressive restriction as a goal

In a resolution on capital punishment, the United Nations General Assembly in 1971 affirmed that:

> in order fully to guarantee the right to life, provided for in Article 3 of the Universal Declaration of Human Rights, the main objective to be pursued is that of progressively restricting the number of offences for which capital punishment may be imposed, with a view to the desirability of abolishing this punishment in all countries.[3]

The goal of progressive restriction of capital offences was reiterated by the General Assembly in 1977 (resolution 32/61 of 8 December 1977), by the United Nations Commission on Human Rights in resolution 2003/67 of 24 April 2003, and by the European Union in the Guidelines for EU policy towards third countries on the death penalty (EU Guidelines), adopted in 1998.

Restriction to the most serious offences

The International Covenant on Civil and Political Rights (ICCPR), adopted by the United Nations General Assembly in 1966, states in Article 6(2):

> In countries which have not abolished the death penalty, sentence of death may be imposed only for the most serious crimes...

In a general comment on Article 6 of the ICCPR, the Human Rights Committee established under that treaty stated that "the expression 'most serious crimes' must be read restrictively to mean that the death penalty should be a quite exceptional measure" (general comment 6, adopted in 1982).

The United Nations Economic and Social Council, in the Safeguards guaranteeing protection of the rights of those facing the death penalty (ECOSOC Safeguards), adopted in 1984, reiterated that the death penalty should be imposed only for the most serious crimes and stated that the scope of these crimes "should not go beyond intentional crimes with lethal or other extremely grave consequences".

---

3. UN General Assembly resolution 2857 (XXVI) of 20 December 1971.

There have been various specific standards and statements about the crimes for which the death penalty should not be used. Article 4(4) of the American Convention on Human Rights (ACHR) states that the death penalty shall not be inflicted "for political offences or related common crimes". The Human Rights Committee has stated that "the imposition... of the death penalty for offences which cannot be characterised as the most serious, including apostasy, committing a third homosexual act, illicit sex, embezzlement by officials, and theft by force, is incompatible with Article 6 of the Covenant".[4] The United Nations Special Rapporteur on Extrajudicial, Summary or Arbitrary Executions has stated that the death penalty should be eliminated for: economic crimes; drug-related offences; other so-called "victimless" offences (activities of a religious or political nature including acts of treason, espionage and other vaguely defined acts usually described as "crimes against the state" or "disloyalty"); actions primarily related to prevailing moral values, such as adultery and prostitution, and matters of sexual orientation, and that the death penalty should under no circumstances be mandatory by law, regardless of the charges involved.[5] The United Nations Commission on Human Rights has urged that the death penalty not be imposed for "non-violent acts such as financial crimes, non-violent religious practice or expression of conscience and sexual relations between consenting adults."[6]

The international standard of restricting the death penalty to the most serious crimes, in particular to those with lethal consequences, is broadly reflected in practice. Most states that continue to carry out executions today do so only for murder, although they may retain the death penalty in law for other crimes. Moreover, the rate of executions in most such countries has declined to a point where it represents only a tiny fraction in relation to the number of reported murders. (The most outstanding exception is China, which carries out more executions than all other countries combined, and continues to execute prisoners for non-violent offences including theft and embezzlement.)

A further development in the restriction of capital offences was the adoption by an international conference in Rome in July 1998 of the Statute of the International Criminal Court, in which the death penalty is not provided for what are arguably the most heinous crimes of all: genocide, other crimes against humanity and war crimes. Similarly, the United Nations Security Council excluded the death penalty for these

---

4. United Nations Document No. CCPR/C/79/Add.
5. United Nations Document Nos. E/CN.4/1997/60, 24 December 1996, paragraph 91; E/CN.4/1999/39, 6 January 1999, paragraph 63.
6. Resolution 2003/67 of 24 April 2003.

grave crimes in 1993 and 1994 when it established the International Criminal Tribunals for the former Yugoslavia and for Rwanda. If these decisions are read together with the well-established standard that the death penalty should be used only for the most serious crimes in countries that have not abolished it, the implication is that the death penalty should not be used at all. If the use of the death penalty is excluded for the most serious international crimes, it can hardly be countenanced for lesser crimes.

Restriction of applicable offenders

International standards have also developed in such a way as to exclude more and more categories of people from those against whom the death penalty might be used in countries that have not abolished it.

*   The exclusion of child offenders, that is those under 18 years of age at the time of the offence, is so widely accepted in law and practice that it can be considered a norm of customary international law, binding on all states. The prohibition on sentencing child offenders to death has been set out in the ICCPR (Article 6(5)), the ACHR (Article 4(5)), the ECOSOC Safeguards, the 4th Geneva Convention of 1949 relative to the Protection of Civilian Persons in Time of War and the two Additional Protocols of 1977 to the Geneva Conventions of 1949 and, more recently, in the Convention on the Rights of the Child (Article 37(a)), which has been ratified by all but two United Nations member states. The prohibition is widely observed in practice. Between January 1994 and April 2003 Amnesty International documented only twenty executions of child offenders worldwide, carried out in five countries. More than half of the executions were carried out in just one country, the United States of America. The UN Sub-Commission on the Promotion and Protection of Human Rights has affirmed that "the imposition of the death penalty on those aged under 18 at the time of the commission of the offence is contrary to customary international law." (resolution 2000/17, adopted on 17 August 2000).[7]

*   The exclusion of pregnant women, new mothers, and people over 70 years of age, set out variously in the ICCPR, the ACHR and the ECOSOC Safeguards, are also widely observed in practice. The Human Rights Committee established under the ICCPR has referred to the prohibition on executing pregnant women and children as a rule of general international law (general comment 24, adopted in 1994).

---

7. See Amnesty International, *Children and the death penalty: executions worldwide since 1990*, AI Index: ACT 50/007/2002, September 2002.

- The ECOSOC Safeguards also state that executions shall not be carried out on "persons who have *become* insane" (emphasis added), and in Resolution 1989/64, adopted on 24 May 1989, ECOSOC recommended that United Nations member states eliminate the death penalty "for persons suffering from mental retardation or extremely limited mental competence, whether at the stage of sentence or execution".

Procedural safeguards

Procedural safeguards to be followed in all death penalty cases have been set out in Article 6 of the ICCPR and Article 4 of the ACHR and reiterated and elaborated upon in the ECOSOC Safeguards and in other United Nations' resolutions. They include all international norms for a fair trial, including the right of appeal to a higher court, and the right to petition for clemency. By its General Assembly resolution 2393 (XXIII) of 26 November 1968 and successive resolutions, the United Nations has repeatedly stated its wish to ensure the most careful legal procedures and the greatest possible safeguards for those accused in capital cases in countries where the death penalty has not been abolished. The need to respect minimum standards in death penalty cases is also reflected in the EU Guidelines.

Although the safeguards exist in principle in many countries that retain the death penalty, they are often not fully observed in practice, and even where an effort is made to observe them, the use of the death penalty often remains arbitrary. Factors such as inadequate legal aid and prosecutorial discretion result in some defendants being sentenced to death and executed while others convicted of similar crimes are not. The safeguards have failed to prevent the arbitrary use of the death penalty or to preclude its use against people innocent of the crimes of which they were convicted.

The emergence of abolition as a human rights norm

International bodies have increasingly made statements and adopted policies favouring abolition on human rights grounds. These statements and policies are beginning to be backed up by national court decisions ruling out the death penalty because it is a violation of human rights.

Statements and policies

In resolution 2857 (XXVI) of 20 December 1971, cited above, the United Nations General Assembly affirmed the desirability of abolishing the death penalty in all countries. The desirability of abolishing the death penalty was reiterated in General Assembly resolution 32/61 of 8 December 1977 and, most recently, by the United Nations Commission on Human Rights in resolution 2003/67 of 24 April 2003.

In its general comment on Article 6 of the ICCPR, cited above, the Human Rights Committee stated that Article 6 "refers generally to abolition [of the death penalty] in terms which strongly suggest... that abolition is desirable. The Committee concludes that all measures of abolition should be considered as progress in the enjoyment of the right to life... "

In resolution 1997/12 of 3 April 1997, the United Nations Commission on Human Rights expressed its conviction "that abolition of the death penalty contributes to the enhancement of human dignity and to the progressive development of human rights". This statement was reiterated by the Commission on Human Rights in resolution 2003/67 of 24 April 2003.

The United Nations Special Rapporteur on Extrajudicial, Summary or Arbitrary Executions has emphasised that "the abolition of capital punishment is most desirable in order fully to respect the right to life" (United Nations Document No. E/CN.4/1997/60, paragraph 79) and has urged governments of countries where the death penalty is still enforced "to deploy every effort that could lead to its abolition."[8]

In Resolution 727 (1980) of 22 April 1980, the Parliamentary Assembly of the Council of Europe stated that "capital punishment is inhuman" and appealed to the parliaments of member states which retained the death penalty for peacetime offences to abolish it. It widened the appeal in its Resolution 1044 (1994) of 4 October 1994, calling:

> upon all the parliaments in the world which have not yet abolished the death penalty, to do so promptly following the example of the majority of Council of Europe member states.

In Resolution 1253 (2001) of 25 June 2001 it stated that the application of the death penalty "constitutes torture and inhuman and degrading punishment within the meaning of Article 3 of the European Convention on Human Rights".

The EU Guidelines, cited above, state that "abolition of the death penalty contributes to the enhancement of human dignity and the progressive development of human rights". The guidelines establish a European Union objective "to work towards universal abolition of the death penalty as a strongly held policy view agreed by all EU member states".

---

8. United Nations Document No. A/51/457, paragraph 145.

National court decisions

On 24 October 1990 the Hungarian Constitutional Court declared that the death penalty violates the "inherent right to life and human dignity" as provided under Article 54 of the country's constitution. The judgment had the effect of abolishing the death penalty for all crimes in Hungary.

On 6 June 1995 the South African Constitutional Court declared the death penalty to be incompatible with the prohibition of "cruel, inhuman or degrading treatment or punishment" under the country's interim constitution.[9] Eight of the eleven judges also found that the death penalty violates the right to life. The judgment had the effect of abolishing the death penalty for murder.

On 9 December 1998 the Constitutional Court of the Republic of Lithuania declared that the death penalty for murder as provided under the Lithuanian Criminal Code contradicts provisions of the Constitution of the Republic of Lithuania stating that the right to life shall be protected by the law and prohibiting torture, injury, degradation and maltreatment and the establishment of such punishments.

On 29 December 1999 the Constitutional Court of Ukraine declared the death penalty under the country's laws to be unconstitutional and the laws providing for it void. The court stated that the death penalty is incompatible with articles of the Constitution of Ukraine that provide for the right to life and prohibit torture and cruel, inhuman or degrading treatment or punishment that violates a person's dignity. It noted that, unlike the ICCPR, the Ukrainian Constitution does not explicitly allow for the death penalty as an exception to the right to life.

On 11 November 1999 the Constitutional Court of the Republic of Albania abrogated the death penalty in peacetime as being incompatible with the Constitution of the Republic of Albania, Article 21 of which states: "The life of a person is protected by law". The court stated that the death penalty "is a denial of the right to life and constitutes an inhuman and cruel punishment". The court noted that, unlike previous Albanian constitutional provisions, Article 21 of the Constitution of 1998 does not explicitly allow for the death penalty as an exception to the right to life.

International abolitionist treaties

The community of nations has adopted four international treaties providing for the abolition of the death penalty; one is of worldwide scope, the other three are regional. In order of adoption, they are Protocol No. 6

---

9. "Makwanyane and Mcbunu v. The State (1995)", *Human Rights Law Journal,* vol. 16, pp. 154-208 paragraphs 95, 146.

to the Convention for the Protection of Human Rights and Fundamental Freedoms (the European Convention on Human Rights) concerning the abolition of the death penalty, adopted by the Council of Europe in 1982; the Second Optional Protocol to the International Covenant on Civil and Political Rights, aiming at the abolition of the death penalty, adopted by the United Nations General Assembly in 1989; the Protocol to the American Convention on Human Rights to Abolish the Death Penalty, adopted by the General Assembly of the Organisation of American States in 1990; and Protocol No. 13 to the European Convention on Human Rights, concerning the abolition of the death penalty in all circumstances. The first of these treaties provides for the abolition of the death penalty in peacetime; the second and the third provide for the total abolition of the death penalty but allow states parties to retain the death penalty in time of war if they make a declaration to that effect at the time of ratification or accession; while Protocol No. 13 provides for total abolition in all circumstances with no exceptions.

Protocol No. 6 is the most widely ratified of the four in comparison to the number of states parties to the parent treaty; as of mid-May 2003 it had been ratified by forty-one states and signed by another four. The Second Optional Protocol to the ICCPR had been ratified by forty-nine states as of the same date and signed by another seven; the Protocol to the American Convention on Human Rights to Abolish the Death Penalty had been ratified by eight states and signed by another one; while Protocol No. 13 had been ratified by thirteen states and signed by another twenty-seven. The numbers of signatories and states parties continue to grow.

The road to abolition

The pace of abolition has accelerated since the middle of the twentieth century, and especially in the past twenty years. At the beginning of the century, only three states had permanently abolished the death penalty for all crimes: Costa Rica, San Marino and Venezuela. In 1948, the number stood at eight. By the end of 1978 it had risen to nineteen. Since then the number has quadrupled.

Seventy-six countries and territories today have abolished the death penalty for all crimes. Another fifteen countries have abolished the death penalty for all but exceptional crimes such as wartime crimes.

Alongside the countries which have abolished the death penalty for all crimes or for ordinary crimes only, there are twenty-one which can be considered abolitionist in practice, in that they retain the death penalty in law but have not carried out any executions for the past ten years, or have made an international commitment not to do so. As Roger Hood has stated,[10] the death penalty in these countries "appears to have a far greater symbolic than practical significance".

These figures make for a total of 112 countries that have abolished the death penalty in law or practice. Eighty-three other countries and territories could be said to retain the death penalty, but the number of countries which actually executes prisoners in any one year is much smaller. In 2002, for example, Amnesty International recorded 1 526 executions in thirty-one countries worldwide. The vast majority of reported executions, 81%, were carried out in just three countries: China, Iran and the United States.

As indicated above, these developments in law and practice nationally have been mirrored by the development of international standards restricting the application of the death penalty and affirming the desirability of abolition on human rights grounds. As William A. Schabas has observed:[11]

> Given the enormous and rapid progress in the development of international norms respecting the death penalty since the end of the second world war, the general acceptance of abolition and its elevation to a customary norm of international law, perhaps even a norm of *jus cogens*, may be envisaged in the not too distant future.

The trend to abolition seems inexorable, yet the battle has to be fought over and over again. Each country has to go through a process that is often long and painful, examining for itself the arguments for and against, before finally, we hope, rejecting the death penalty.

Even after abolition, there may be calls to bring the death penalty back. If the calls are serious enough, the arguments have to be gone through again.

The decision to abolish the death penalty has to be taken by the nation's government and the legislators. This decision can be taken even though the majority of the public favour the death penalty. Historically, this has probably almost always been the case. Yet when the death penalty is abolished, usually there is no great public outcry, and once abolished, it almost always stays abolished.

This must mean that although the majority of the public in a given country favours the death penalty, it is also the case that a majority of the public is willing to accept abolition. This is a feature of public opinion that is not usually revealed by polls asking respondents to state their

---

10. Roger Hood, *The death penalty: a worldwide perspective*, (3rd edn), Oxford University Press, Oxford, 2002, p. 96.
11. W.A. Schabas, *The abolition of the death penalty in international law* (2nd edn), Cambridge University Press, Cambridge, 1997, p. 20.

position on the death penalty. If the questions were more sophisticated, the polls would probably give a better sense of the complexities of public opinion and the extent to which it is based on an accurate understanding of the actual situation of criminality in the country, its causes and the means available for combating it.

The assertion that the death penalty deters crime more effectively than other punishments is now largely discredited by the lack of scientific evidence despite the many studies that have been made. Yet many members of the public believe that it is a deterrent. Their belief flies in the face of the scientific evidence. In other words, the public does not have a scientific understanding of the deterrent effect of the death penalty.

As the United Nations secretariat suggested as long ago as 1980, governments should take on the task of educating the public as to the uncertainty of the deterrent effect of capital punishment.[12] A better public understanding of crime prevention and criminal justice would produce more support for anti-crime measures that are genuine and not merely palliative. At the very least, politicians should not make demagogic calls for the death penalty, misleading the public and obscuring the need for genuine anti-crime measures.

For Amnesty International, the human rights argument is paramount. But in practice, it is only one of several powerful arguments against the death penalty that needs to be part of the national debate.

While Amnesty International is making the human rights argument, others need to make the other arguments. Statements from religious leaders, other respected public figures, influential organisations and the news media can create a moral climate in which the legislators will be more willing to vote in a way which they know will be unpopular with many of their constituents.

Often the national debate on the death penalty is conducted in purely national terms. The international dimension needs to be brought in. Countries can learn from other countries' experience.

Over the centuries, laws and public attitudes relating to torture have evolved. It is no longer permissible to use thumbscrews or the rack as legally sanctioned means of interrogation and punishment. Attitudes toward the death penalty are also changing and, as an increasing number of countries abolish capital punishment, the guillotine, the garrotte and the noose are being relegated to the museums, alongside the medieval instruments of torture.

---

12. United Nations Document No. A/CONF87/9, paragraph 68.

Bringing about abolition requires courageous political leadership, leadership that will be exercised in the defence of human rights. The requirement of respect for human rights has to include the abolition of the death penalty. It is not possible for a government to respect human rights and retain the death penalty at the same time.

Capital punishment – The families of the homicide victim and the condemned[1]

Peter Hodgkinson
Director of the Centre for Capital Punishment Studies, School of Law, University of Westminster

Crime victims are too often ignored and when remembered too often exploited in the interest of political expediency. They are a constituency almost universally overlooked by the traditional abolitionist movement and this I believe has proved a significant obstacle to the process of replacing the death penalty. Politicians the world over justify the retention of the death penalty, in part, because of their concerns about crime victims though frequently, in my experience, little or no provision for them has been made by the state.

In common with the bulk of materials published about capital punishment much of the information that has developed around victims and the death penalty is based on the scholarship and experience of the United States. It is especially important therefore when evaluating the experience of the United States with regard to victims that one takes care to distinguish between what does and does not "work" and its relevance or otherwise to influencing victim-services models worldwide. I cannot do justice in this article to the wealth of scholarship dedicated to the issue of crime victims in general so I will restrict my review and analysis to the literature dedicated to the issues of victims and their relationship to the death penalty and punishments in general.

There has been an exponential growth in victim research and services over the past two to three decades with international and regional bodies such as the United Nations[2] and the European Commission[3] dedicating research and resources to improved practice and guidelines. These have

1. This chapter builds on the paper I wrote for the Council of Europe's earlier publication *The death penalty – abolition in Europe*, Council of Europe Publishing, Strasbourg, 1999. ISBN 92-871-3874-5. It appears in a forthcoming volume, *Capital punishment – strategies for abolition* edited by Peter Hodgkinson and William Schabas, Cambridge University Press, Cambridge, 2003, and is reproduced here with their kind permission.
2. United Nations Victim Charter, www.odccp.org/crime_cicp_sitemap.html
3. Commission of the European Communities, "Crime victims in the European Union: reflections on standards and action",: European Commission, Brussels, 1999. COM (1999) 349 Final. http//europa.eu.int/comm/justice_home/pdf/com1999-349-en.pdf

developed largely through the improvement in understanding of the issue initiated by International Victimology,[4] the World Society of Victimology[5] and the European Forum for Victims Services.[6] An excellent text produced by Paul Rock,[7] provides a wealth of information in a very sympathetic format about how homicide affects individuals and the range of responses that have been developed to address the pain and suffering experienced by the families and friends of homicide victims. The United Kingdom and the United States differ in that the latter retains and uses the death penalty but in many aspects of penal policy the United Kingdom, to its cost, bases much of its recent criminal justice practice on imports from the United States so one might have expected the development of victim services in the UK to be heavily influenced by the current pro-punishment approach in the US. Thankfully this is not the case and the mainstream response to victims' needs continues to mirror the approach imported from California, some thirty years ago.

Victims' issues are crucial to any debate about capital punishment though paradoxically the attention given to this topic and therefore to homicide victims and their families frequently exacerbates the anger, hurt and confusion felt by many who have been victimised. Where victim initiatives exist they seem increasingly to manifest themselves by lobbying for procedural rights and harsher penalties at the expense of their more traditional needs-based origins. The most vociferous of these are to be found in the United States where such groups have made considerable inroads into shaping the agenda in legal and penal policy. My experience thus far has not identified similar fundamentalist groups elsewhere even in countries such as Taiwan and the Philippines, where the United States continues to have a significant influence in shaping political

---

4. The International Victimology website (IVW) was launched in June 1999 as a resource for all those interested in improving justice for victims of crime and abuse of power. Through IVW, the UN Centre for International Crime Prevention, the Research and Documentation Centre of the Netherlands Ministry of Justice and the World Society of Victimology aim to promote the UN Declaration of Basic Principles of Justice for Victims of Crime and Abuse of Power. www.victimology.nl (revised 17 December 2002).
5. World Society of Victimology (WSV). The purposes of the WSV are to promote research on victims and victim assistance; advocacy of their interests throughout the world; to encourage interdisciplinary and comparative research in victimology; to advance the co-operation of international, regional, and local agencies, groups, and individuals concerned with the problems of victims.
www.world-society-victimology.de/frameset.html
6. European Forum for Victim Services, "Statement of victims' rights in the process of criminal justice." Victim Support, London (1996).
www.victimology.nl/onlpub/eurforvicrts96a.html
7. Paul Rock, *After homicide – practical and political responses to bereavement*, Clarendon Press, Oxford, 1998.

and popular culture. Groups such as Justice for All[8] and Parents of Murdered Children[9] characterise the pro-punishment victim movement in the US and both enjoy considerable political support. Of the two, Houston-based Justice for All, a comparative newcomer, adopts a particularly virulent line on punishment, especially the death penalty. Its views represent a failure of the political system to responsibly address the legitimate feelings of pain and anger many crime victims and their families experience. There is of course a contrary view that it suits populist politicians to have such aggressive emotions aired as it provides ammunition for their platform on the extremes of law and order policy.

The victim issue – rather like the offence issue – receives too little attention in both the scholarship and the debate, given that both have developed to a great extent around the paradigm offence of murder, its victims and their families. We need to remind ourselves when considering victims' needs that for many crimes that attract the death penalty there is some difficulty in identifying just exactly who has been victimised, as in most countries where the death penalty is available it is not reserved for the offence of murder alone. For example the Philippines has a mandatory death sentence for twenty-one offences none of which is specifically for murder, and of those currently on death row the largest proportion (45%) are there for offences stemming from the offence of rape, of which number only six persons (8%) have been sentenced to death for rape followed by murder.[10] A further twenty-six offences attract a discretionary death sentence.[11] It is difficult to know quite how to formulate a victims' services strategy for offences such as bribery, arson, drug use and trafficking.

In the modern era of the death penalty, rape is not an offence that typically attracts the death penalty and rape victims who escape death manifest different needs from those who are killed during the assault, the most obvious being the capacity to articulate those needs, which

---

8. Justice for All announces on its website that it is a criminal justice reform organisation that "shall act as an advocate for change in a criminal justice system that is inadequate in protecting the lives and property of law-abiding citizens." www.jfa.net. Other sites supported by Justice for All – www.prodeathpenalty.com (revised 2 January 2003) and www.murdervictims.com

9. National Organisation of Parents of Murdered Children, Incorporated www.pomc.com

10. On the 20 April 2002 there were 969 men and 25 women sentenced to death in the Philippines. Of the 20 executions scheduled for 2002, 11 were sentenced for qualified rape (incest), 5 for rape, 2 for robbery with homicide and 2 for kidnap for ransom. Examples of other crimes attracting the death penalty on death row are: 40 for drug-related offences, 1 for illegal possession of firearms, 1 for carjacking with homicide, 10 for qualified bribery and 125 for kidnap offences. See Flag (Free Legal Assistance Group) link on the website of the Centre for Capital Punishment Studies, www.wmin.ac.uk/ccps

11. See Flag link in previous footnote.

occasionally include some reference to the issue of punishment. However, I hasten to add that I am not advocating that punishment should be influenced by individual victims; in fact the very premise on which this article is based is to avoid victim sentencing.

A case could be made for saying that there is no need or place for a separate victim service as the state prosecutes not on behalf of individuals but of society as a whole and the "victim" loss or suffering is already factored into the decision to prosecute and the final sentence. Whilst this may be an argument for not including the victim's perspective in the trial process it should not replace the development of services to meet the material and psychological needs of individuals who are primary or secondary victims of crime.

An ongoing discussion in the literature is about the issue of what to name the friends and families of homicide victims. One might wonder why it should make any difference? Should one restrict this association to immediate family, to non-married live-in partners, to heterosexual and homosexual relationships, to intimate friends? Who decides? Unlike other types of victims, homicide victims have no further involvement in the process of criminal justice, as this function is assumed by the state and occasionally by their nearest and dearest. Terms that have been adopted and used interchangeably are "secondary victim", "invisible victim", "co-victim" and more recently "survivor". I use the terms "primary", meaning the actual crime victim and "secondary", to describe others, not necessarily restricted to the family and immediate friends of the homicide victim. It also has to be recognised in this context that "secondary victims" should be a title conferred on the family and friends of the condemned. The family of the victim and the accused are usually innocent parties and should be treated as such.

The explanation for the need for this debate is that in the current political climate of the victims' movement, especially in the United States, a label can affect status and influence the ensuing debate about victims' needs and rights that flow from this official recognition. For example the right to:

- economic and emotional support;
- be informed about the progress of the police investigation;
- be present at trial;
- provide information at the sentencing phase (Victim Impact Statement (US)/Victim Personal Statement (UK)),
- receive compensation from the state and/or from the condemned;
- be consulted about the sentence – life or death;
- be consulted at clemency and parole hearings;
- be present at the execution.

Crime victim issues in the United Kingdom

The United Kingdom has experienced a sea change in the victims' movement with a multiplicity of groups competing with Victim Support, the founding victim group in the UK,[12] competing, not just for funds but for public and government support of their ideologies. A criticism levelled at Victim Support by some of these new arrivals is that the organisation must inevitably compromise its position and therefore the needs and rights of victims because it is largely dependent on the government for funding. Victim Support for its part has always taken the line of not campaigning in the area of punishment, in fact its constitution bars it from so doing save in the area of compensation. Moreover, Victim Support does not make public statements on the punishment and sentencing of offenders, except when discussing issues that directly involve the victim; for example compensation or protection.

In contrast, some of the new organisations, aping their US counterparts, campaign aggressively for stiffer penalties and the establishment of procedural rights for victims. These rights include victim personal statements, active participation in the sentencing process, involvement in any decision-making forum where early release is being considered, and finally the right to know when "their" offender is being released from prison and where s/he is living. This is a far cry from the days when the needs of victims were provided by local volunteers who helped with such "mundane" activities as providing a sympathetic ear, contacting builders to repair damage to property, helping to allay fear of revictimisation, contacting friends and relatives, and finding temporary accommodation.[13] Victim Support continues to concentrate on these fundamental needs, supporting and initiating schemes directed at making the criminal justice system less frightening and more accessible to victims; projects such as the witness service to help witnesses at Court, victim relations with the prosecuting authorities, separate facilities for victims and their families at court.[14] It has also promoted research

---

12. The National Association of Victim Support Schemes (NAVSS, now Victim Support) had its origins in the initiative prompted by the National Association for the Care and Resettlement of Offenders [Nacro], which founded the Bristol Victim-Offenders Group in 1969. This group developed strategies to work with the victims of personal crime referred to them by the police. They established a multidisciplinary team of professionals who trained volunteers. This group eventually formed into the Bristol Victim Support Scheme in 1974. Similar groups began to form countrywide and the NAVSS was formed in 1979. www.victimsupport.com

13. C. Holtom and P. Raynor, "Origins of victim support: philosophy and practice" in M. Maguire and J. Pointing, (Eds). *Victims of crime: a new deal?* Milton Keynes, Open University Press, 1988.

14. Paul Rock, "The Victim in Court Project at the crown court at Wood Green." Howard Journal, 1991, vol. 30 No.4, pp 301-10.

into victim needs and effective measures to meet those needs. For example, special projects have been established to respond to families of murdered children and to the victims of rape. On the whole Victim Support has been successful in meeting its objectives over the last three decades without needing to engage in aggressive political campaigns demanding "rights" for victims.[15] Undoubtedly the decision to produce a Victim's Charter in 1990 and 1996 was directly the result of the quiet, behind the scenes lobbying that characterises the approach of Victim Support[16] though the 1996 version did owe much of its rhetoric to the influence of the more vocal lobbyists and the populist tendency of the then Home Secretary, Michael Howard.[17]

Many decades of research have improved our knowledge of the experiences and needs of victims.[18] From von Hentig's[19] work in the 1940s, which raised the notion of victim precipitation, arguing that there were characteristics inherent to some who became victims, which led to their victimisation – subsequent research in this area suggested that victims were in some way to "blame" for their predicament. The 1960s saw the arrival of "victim survey"[20] research in the US and the UK, which in turn spawned the British Crime Surveys[21] that have in recent years provided valuable information about the perceptions victims have of the criminal justice process. The core effects identified by such research that are experienced by the families of homicide victims

---

15. Paul Rock, *Helping victims of crime: the Home Office and the rise of victim support in England & Wales.* Clarendon Press, Oxford, 1990.

16. Home Office *Victim's Charter: a statement of the rights of victims.* London, 1990.

17. Home Secretary Michael Howard launched this document in June of 1996. The byword was "giving victims a voice" and it was set out to make quite specific undertakings to victims – perhaps more "rights orientated" than "needs oriented". The main tenets of the charter are: provision of information to victims; taking victims' views into account; treating victims with respect and sensitivity at court; and providing support to victims.

18. J. Shapland, J. Willmore, and P. Duff, *Victims and the criminal justice system.* Gower, Aldershot, 1985: Also, M. Maguire and C. Corbett, *The effects of crime and the work of victim support schemes.* Gower, Aldershot, 1987.

19. H. Von Hentig, *The criminal and his victim.* Archon Books, New York, 1948.

20. R. Sparks, H. Genn, and D. Dodd, *Victims and the criminal justice system.* Wiley Press, Chichester, 1977.

21. The first British Crime Survey was undertaken in 1982 and then bianually until 2000 and annually since 2001. The original conception was an attempt to provide an alternative and, it was hoped, a more accurate picture of the nature and volume of crime than that provided by the official statistics collected by the police forces. Over the years it has evolved and in addition to refining its statistical accuracy it has established an agenda of data collection and research which highlights the experiences and perceptions of victims which has led to initiatives which attempt to meet the identified needs of victims. This model has also been used in discrete local areas where its results have directly influenced crime prevention and victims' needs policies. www.homeoffice.gov.uk/rds/bcs1.html

include fear of crime,[22] fear of strangers,[23] over-protectiveness of their other children,[24] anger,[25] and isolation.[26]

At the extremes there are victims whose suffering is so intense as to be disabling both physically and psychologically thus amounting to a clinical condition. There is evidence too that such bereavement affects members of the same family in different ways and that family members may adopt different coping or survival mechanisms. According to some claims in the United States as many as 70% of such families end in separation of some form or other and Paul Rock[27] recalls the views of a number of family members:

> we've split into two now and there are three or four daughters that I don't see and seven grand children because we were too close and because our opinions varied so much – "hang them", "don't hang them", and all things around it. (member of Survivors of Murder and Manslaughter, SAMM).

Another member of SAMM said:

> I mean I couldn't even look at my husband for three years. I hated him, I didn't want him near me because I couldn't cope with his ... I couldn't recognise his pain. It was only me that was in pain. I didn't even want my other son. All I wanted was ...

If this incomplete catalogue of "effects" teaches us anything it is that there is one myth that needs debunking immediately and that is the perception among some researchers and policy makers that victims of crime are a homogeneous group with identical needs susceptible to similar solutions.

---

22. C. Murray-Parkes, "Psychiatric problems following bereavement after homicide", *British Journal of Psychiatry*, 1993, vol. 162.

23. Robert Kilroy-Silk, "The suffering continues", Police Review, 20 May 1988; A. Burgess, "Family reactions to homicide", *American Journal of Orthopsychiatry*, April 1975, vol. 45, No. 3.

24. Daphne Vaughan, "Death by murder". Paul Rock (see fn.7) quotes an extract from this personal paper written by the mother of a murdered child: "A certain fear envelopes you. You become paranoid over your surviving children going out and wait anxiously for their return. You become fearful of facing people and to hear someone walking behind you fills you with dread."

25. "I was so angry I sometimes didn't know what to do with myself, I used to take the car out into Derbyshire, drive into some remote area and scream. I would hear this terrible demented screaming like a madwoman or someone possessed and realised that it was me." Quote in Paul Rock (see fn.7) from Irene Ivison, *Fiona's story*, Virago, London, 1997, pp. 270-71.

26. "Everyone expects you to be 'all right', but you feel that you will never be 'normal' again. The world goes on much the same as before, while inside you feel alone, isolated and no-one really understands the pain, emptiness and anger, which you are suffering." Quoted in Paul Rock (see fn.7) from a Support After Murder and Manslaughter (SAMM) leaflet..

27. See Paul Rock, *After homicide – practical and political responses to bereavement*, Clarendon Press, Oxford, 1998, p.46.

Over the past decade or so there has been a growth of victims groups in the UK, many of which have developed in response to the plight of individual victims or particular crimes. The Suzy Lamplugh Trust and the Zito Trust were both established by family members in the hopes that others may learn from the mistakes that led to their loved ones suffering. They set out to create a climate of understanding through which change could be encouraged – the change achieved in the case of the Lamplugh Trust was to the procedures of estate agents[28] to ensure that no female staff should attend such appointments unaccompanied. Jayne Zito's husband Jonathan was killed, whilst waiting at a railway station, by Christopher Clunis who had recently been discharged from mental health care, it later transpired without support or medication. Her campaign for a public enquiry[29] was successful and the trust she founded has become active and influential on such issues as community care for the mentally ill and the needs of the victims of assault by the mentally ill. I use these two examples to illustrate the capacity to divert the pain of bereavement in such circumstances from destructive outcomes into creative outcomes, believing that such an approach has benefits for the families of victims and society in general, although Rock's volume and other writings about crime victims reveal that amongst the pain and confusion of individuals bereaved by murder there is occasionally conflict and dissent about means and ends leading to fractures and the emergence of new groupings.

The abolitionist community might attract some sympathy for their agenda if they promoted policies that helped to establish a climate where respect for victims and their families is at least of equal importance to ensuring the legal and civil rights of the accused and the condemned. Jayne Zito, drawing on her background in mental health coupled with a working knowledge of the criminal justice system, was able to put this to use and this helped in her words, to avoid "a destructive pattern of grief". Parents of Murdered Children, POMC[30] and Support After Murder and Manslaughter, SAMM[31] are two groups that developed in response to the needs of the families of murder victims and they in turn have spawned other groups such as Justice for Victims.

---

28. In 1986, Suzy Lamplugh disappeared after keeping an appointment alone with a male client, who had ostensibly arranged to view a property – there has been no trace of her since then.

29. North East and South East Thames Regional Health Authorities, "The report of the inquiry into the care and treatment of Christopher Clunis", HMSO, London ,1994.

30. Parents of Murdered Children was established in 1990 as a separate group which had its origins in The Compassionate Friends set up in 1969. In 1980, The Compassionate Friends and POMC became a joint organisation. Out of POMC sprang the Victims of Crime Pressure Group (1993) and Families of Murder Victims (1993).

31. SAMM, which was formed out of POMC in 1994, experienced some conflict of direction in its early days when a sub-group, Justice for Victims (1994), formed from among its membership. Justice for Victims had and continues to have some antipathy towards Victim Support, which harmed the relationship SAMM had with them. The current relationship is more positive as SAMM has an office in Victim Support premises and they collaborate on a number of issues.

This brief review has been undertaken to set the context for the discussion of the development of responses to the needs of victims of murder and to their families and the influence they have on the debate about punishment, in this instance capital punishment. Rock's enquiry charts the development of the victims movement, its relationship to its constituents, to other group members, to the general public and finally to central government. Whilst his work focuses on the United Kingdom it is obvious to see the influence that the victim movement in the US has had and continues to have on some in the movement in the UK. At the risk of oversimplifying the debate, it appears that the principal thrust of many new groups is concern for severe punishment and more procedural rights for victims to influence the outcome of actions against offenders. This approach has struck a rich vein of approval amongst the public, the tabloid press and politicians on the right (and some on the left) and there is evidence that it is having an impact shaping policy on the ground locally and centrally. This, despite the fact that there is little evidence to suggest that longer sentences lead to a more effective sentencing policy or that victims benefit – the only people to benefit from this approach would appear to be politicians and lobbyists at the expense of victims' vulnerability being further exposed and exploited.

An example of this is the public concern expressed when individuals convicted of sexual offences against children are released from prison. Specifically, demands are made for the resettlement plans and locations of such offenders to be disclosed and on those occasions when such information has been leaked it has led, predictably, to the formation of vigilante groups, which hound out such individuals. This shifts the "problem" to the police who are obliged to take the former offender temporarily into protective custody whilst more permanent and suitable plans are devised. This development is in itself deeply worrying but more so is the evidence that legislators are being persuaded to contemplate new legislation placing more restrictions on the movements and therefore individual rights of people who have formally paid their debts to society. Whilst adequate safeguards are essential to ensure public safety a balance has to be struck between the needs and rights of potential future victims and the needs and rights of former offenders. Such public disclosure will have the effect of driving such individuals underground where they will escape any supervision. This particular victims' "right" has been influenced by developments in the United States and[32] there is

---

32. Megan's Law is legislation named after Megan Kanka, the 7-year-old girl who was raped and killed by Jesse Timmendequas. On 29 July 1994, Timmendequas lured Megan into his house across the street from her house to see his puppy, where he killed her. The next day he led police to the body in a nearby park. After the murder it was disclosed to her parents and neighbours that he had two previous sex convictions against children and had been moved into that area after being released from prison. Her parents campaigned for laws to require that neighbours be notified when sex offenders move into an area. New Jersey passed legislation, which came into effect on 31 October 1994, followed by most other states. President Clinton enacted a federal law in 1996. CNN Plus website.

little doubt that Michael Howard's decision [33] in principle and in practice to consign a number of life-sentenced prisoners to a natural life sentence was in direct response to the lobbying of certain victim groups. In the view of some, the rise in retributive punishment is directly the responsibility of the modern victims movement, an outcome mirroring the developments in the United States. Pat Carlen for one believes that:

> The final strand in the new punitiveness is the rise and rise of the crime victim. Since the mid-1970s there has been a growing emphasis on the neglect and invisibility of the victim of crime in the administration of justice. The trumpeting of crime victim wrongs has been useful to anyone wishing to make an electoral appeal on law and order issues. Although at a common-sense level one might have thought that it is because crimes do have victims that anyone ever cared about crime in the first place, the 1970s rediscovery of the victim has certainly fed into the 1990s punitiveness – and with a vengeance! The results? A greatly increased fear of crime, daily demands for stiffer sentences, and a steep increase in levels of criminological nonsense...[34]

Victims and capital punishment – the United States

The major co-ordinating group in the United States for homicide victims, the National Organisation of Parents of Murdered Children (NOPOMC)[35] had its beginnings in the early 1970s and like many such groups in the US is rooted in the rights-based model unlike Victim Support in the UK. NOPOMC and Justice for All owe their origins to the political right and consider that an important need of victims is the right to procedural intervention in the criminal justice system including the determination of sentence. Many such groups, which are allied with movements to

---

33. Michael Howard MP, was the former British Conservative Home Secretary who identified seventeen life-sentenced prisoners for whom he would not exercise his discretion for early release, implying that they would serve whole of life sentences. He also increased the tariff from 8 to 15 years for the two 10-year-old boys convicted of the murder of 2 1/2 year-old Jamie Bulger. This decision has been successfully challenged in the domestic and European courts.

34. P.Carlen, *Jigsaw: a political criminology of youth homelessness.* Open University Press, Milton Keynes 1996, p. 53.

35. The National Organisation of Parents of Murdered Children (POMC) was founded in 1978 and now co-ordinates a confederation of 300 groups across the USA and receives over 100 000 requests for assistance annually. It publishes, nationally, a newsletter *Survivor*, which informs its membership about the activities of the national and state branches. Reports of changes to legislation and practice that affect victims, updates on personal stories of victimisation, a letters page, the Parole Block campaign and MINE (Murder Is Not Entertainment) are regular features. Recent issues have addressed support for the campaign to introduce a victims' rights amendment to the US Constitution. Parole Block is a campaign to support friends and families of homicide victims objecting to the release on parole of "their" murderer. MINE is a campaign to persuade the entertainment industry to treat the topic of murder with sensitivity. Some state variations include in their brief "other survivors of homicide victims". POMC, 100 East Eighth St., B-41 Cincinnati, Ohio 45202, Tel: (513) 721-5683 - www.pomc.com

impose the death penalty, benefit from their connections with politicians and prosecutors and, given the populist nature of American politics, are well placed to influence penal policy at the ballot box. This "power" is significant given that many decision makers in the legal system are elected officials and many victim groups have representatives located in offices adjacent to attorneys general and district attorneys whose confidence and support they enjoy. They are, in a word, very influential in shaping some aspects of penal policy and their power rests not only in influencing particular pieces of legislation but more insidiously in dictating the agenda and the rhetoric about capital punishment, shamelessly exploiting their status as relatives of murder victims – a very strong emotional pull.

By many accounts Justice for All (JFA) has a hugely disproportionate and alarming influence on the shape of the political and criminal justice industry in Texas especially when one considers its youth as an organisation and its membership estimated to be about 4 000. Despite its ambitions to become a national organisation along the lines of POMC, the bulk of its members are Houstonian and Texan. Given their activities and their agenda we should be grateful for small mercies!

Crime victim Pam Lychner was attacked by a parolee William Kelley at the home she and her husband were selling. It was only when Kelley was being considered for parole just two years into a 21-year sentence and when he sued the Lychners for "mental anguish" for locking him in a cupboard at the time of the assault, that Mrs Lychner became active and founded JFA in 1993. It is suggested that JFA became and remains a major force through the patronage of the crime victims' advocate in Houston, Andy Kahan. This partnership flourished for several years and Lychner's influence can be measured through the fact that a federal statute requiring the registration of sexual offenders carries her name as does a bronze statue of her in her home town and uniquely the renaming of a Texas department of criminal justice prison – an honour usually reserved for prison staff.

The current president of JFA, Dianne Clements, took over in 1996 and has taken the organisation to new heights of punitiveness.

More alarming to me than the catalogue of political intrigue and abuse of power recounted in Nowell's article[36] is the evidence of destructive hostility shown by Clements and therefore one assumes JFA towards another victims' organisation. The essence of my concern is illustrated by the following passage taken from his article where he describes an

---

36. S. Nowell, "Just who is a victim?" *Houston Press* 3 October 2002. Mr. Nowell provides an interesting insight into the development of the victims' movement with particular scrutiny of Justice for All and the politics of the victims' movement in Texas.

incident that took place at the 2002 National Organisation of Victim Assistance conference:

> The session was called "Healing the wounds of murder" and most of the audience seemed attentive. However workshop hosts noticed a middle-aged woman who took a back row seat in a far corner.... The woman was Dianne Clements, president of the Houston-based victims' rights group JFA. She soon began interrupting the speakers. According to some attendees, these exchanges followed: Cushing asked Clements to hold her questions until after the presentation. She refused, demanding answers. "I want you to tell us," Clements angrily insisted, "what are you? Are you an abolitionist group or a victim support group?"
> "We're both," replied Bishop. That answer was unacceptable to Clements. She repeated her line of questioning, then stunned listeners when she told Cushing and Bishop. "You're really a bunch of abolitionists who just happened to have family members killed."

I suspect that Ms Clements views both Murder Victims' Families for Reconciliation (MVFR)[37] and the Journey of Hope[38] with the same distaste as they take altogether different positions on the issue of the death penalty; both organisations share similar beliefs and constituents, the latter having evolved from the former, as all are families or friends of victims of homicide and passionately opposed to the death penalty. MVFR's opposition to the death penalty is based on the fact that "Most criticism of the death penalty focuses on how it affects the person on death row. Our concern is how the death penalty affects the rest of us in society. Our opposition to the death penalty is rooted in our direct experience of loss and our refusal to respond to that loss with a quest for more killing. Executions are not what will help us heal." The founder of MVFR, Marie Deans, believes that "after a murder, victims' families face two things: a death and a crime. At these times families need help to cope with their grief and loss, and support to heal their hearts and rebuild their lives. From experience, we know that revenge is not the answer. The answer lies in reducing violence, not causing more death. The answer lies in supporting those who grieve for their lost loved ones, not creating more grieving families. It is time we break the cycle of violence. To those who say society must take a life for a life, we say: 'not in our name'".

---

37. Marie Deans following the murder of her mother-in-law founded Murder Victims Families for Reconciliation (MVFR) in Virginia. MFVR was founded to provide a national forum for murder victims' family members, including family members of those executed by the state, who are opposed to the death penalty. Later with the help of Marietta Jaeger, whose daughter was murdered, MFVR expanded its movement throughout the states. In Indiana in 1993 the first Journey of Hope was staged and this has been followed with marches throughout a variety of states every year since. www.mvfr.org
38. Journey of Hope – www.journeyofhope.org

Since 1993 the Journey of Hope has taken this message onto the road in a different state of the US each year, holding meetings in the local communities through which the "journey" passes.

The National Organisation for Victim Assistance (NOVA) offered as a foil to these "partisan" groups was founded in 1975 and is the oldest national group of its kind worldwide providing authoritative and objective information for victims. It is a private, non-profit organisation for victims and witnesses offering programmes for "practitioners, criminal justice agencies and professionals, mental health professionals, researchers, former victims and survivors, and others committed to the recognition and implementation of victim rights and services."[39] As part of its contribution to the death penalty issue it has produced an information video for those secondary victims faced with the choice of witnessing an execution [40] – a difficult task at the best of times but, as MFVR points out, NOVA's non-partisan position is called into question by the fact that this documentary portrays only the experiences of secondary victims who support the death penalty. Furthermore the funding for this project was drawn from the provisions in the 1984 Victims of Crime Act "that directly or indirectly provides financial support to public and non-profit institutions serving the needs of victims. What message is sent when these public funds are used to support only one subset of the victims' population?".[41]

The issue of victims and the death penalty provides a chilling illustration of the relationship between politicians and victims in support of the death penalty aligning themselves against those homicide victims' families who are opposed to the death penalty. For some years it has been apparent to such families that their access to victim services is being frustrated throughout the process and from time to time their adverse experiences have formed the basis of uncomfortable anecdotes. Recently, MVFR has conducted a thorough review of as many of these anecdotes as it was possible to corroborate and their findings are so worrying as to warrant close examination, especially by those institutions that purport to be concerned by the needs of crime victims and their families and friends as the evidence from this report begs the question whether such groups and individuals are pro-victim or pro-death penalty. A question that should be posed to Ms Clements of JFA.

---

39. National Organisation for Victim Assistance – www.try-NOVA.org
40. "Finding resolution: the stories of crime victims as witnesses to an execution", Candee Productions, www.candeeproductions.com
41. R. R. Cushing and S. Sheffer, "Dignity denied – the experience of murder victims' family members who oppose the death penalty", published by Murder Victims' Families for Reconciliation, August 2002, pp 17-18.

The experiences of Gus Lamm and his daughter Audrey illustrate the injustice and discrimination faced by the families of murder victims that oppose the death penalty. Victoria Lamm, wife of Gus and mother of Audrey, was together with Janet Mesner, murdered by Randy Reeves in 1980 who was subsequently sentenced to death. In 1998 as an execution date loomed the Lamms were contacted by the family of Janet Mesner and all travelled to the state legislature in Nebraska to present an account of their experiences. "It pains me to think that in some indirect way, my mother's death could cause another person to lose his life", said Audrey, now 21 years-old. "Killing another person doesn't do any honor to her memory." In 1999 when the Nebraska Board of Pardons met to consider commuting Reeves's death sentence only one of the three family members of Victoria Lamm present was permitted to speak and that was Victoria's sister who supported the death penalty. The Nebraska Constitution had been amended, as it had in another thirty-one states, giving rights to victims, including the right "to be informed of, present at, and make an oral or written statement at sentencing, parole, pardon, commutation, and conditional release proceedings". Gus and Audrey Lamm having been denied those rights brought an action against the Nebraska Board of Pardons claiming that their equal right to speak had been denied because of their views on the death penalty.

At the district court hearing the judge found that "the Lamms are not victims as that term is commonly understood" and went so far as to characterise the Lamms as "agents of Randy Reeves". All this because they opposed the death penalty. The Lamms appealed to the Nebraska Supreme Court at which hearing MVFR filed an *amicus curiae* brief.[42] The Supreme Court [Nebraska] chose not to comment on the issue of victim discrimination but to concentrate on the issue that the Constitution "requires that the legislature enact laws for implementing and enforcing those rights. The legislature had not yet done so, and so the Court ruled that such laws should now be enacted. To date, this has not taken place".[43] I have listened to MVFR members relate their experiences on a number of occasions and many state that when they declare their opposition to the death penalty prosecutors and other criminal justice agents accuse them of not really loving their murdered relatives. It is to be hoped that the compelling evidence of injustice revealed in this report

---

42. *State of Nebraska ex rel. Gus Lamm and Audrey Lamm v Nebraska Board of Pardons et al.* 620 North Western Reporter, 2nd Series. 763. The lawyer representing the Lamms stated, "The District Court's callous declaration, that [Gus and Audrey Lamm] are not victims does not obviate the loss they have endured. Rather, the ruling...adds insult to injury when their public plea not to desecrate the memory of their loved one by the taking of another life is met with a legal pronouncement that they are persona non grata under the Nebraska law..." Footnote 40 at page 10.
43. See fn.42 above, op.cit. Footnote 40 at page 10.

and the accompanying recommendations will not go unnoticed. Aside from the obvious violations of the victim legislation, what this report shows is the wholesale contamination and politicisation of the process when the death penalty is an issue.

Victim-driven criminal justice

An inherent contradiction and injustice in a victim-driven criminal justice system is illustrated by the two approaches reflected above with respect to those convicted of capital murder. If all victims' wishes are to be respected then prosecutions for capital murder will become even more inconsistent than at present – one simply cannot have a prosecution policy based on the wishes of the families and friends of homicide victims, where some are for and some against capital punishment. There is evidence that prosecutors do take the wishes of victims' families into account, though it appears that the majority of such families and such wishes are pro-death penalty.[44] There is also evidence that irrespective of their individual inclinations the agenda of such groups, actively supported by the prosecution industry, is pro-punishment and pro-revenge: they survive on anger and hate. This practice of a victim-driven prosecution and sentencing policy is evident in many other parts of the world, none more so than in those countries where Sharia law applies. Depending on local variations in interpretation and practice, victims' families have the right to determine whether the condemned is sentenced to death, choose the mode of execution (beheading or stoning – though in some jurisdictions the mode is determined by the offence), demand financial compensation as an alternative to choosing death and finally in some Islamic states the victim's family has the right to be or choose the executioner. Neither the United States nor the Islamic approach meets two essential elements of natural justice, namely consistency and proportionality. Another potential flaw in this process and one that bears on the importance of status is that all these negotiations are undertaken on behalf of the victim, by the state and by the secondary victims, begging the question as to whether the procedure of the "living

---

44. *Houston Chronicle*, 8 June 1998. Letter from Charles A. Sage whose sister Marilyn was murdered in 1993. He reflects on the meeting with prosecutors and family members before the trial when he suggested that acceptance of a life sentence for a defendant already dying of Aids was the sensible choice. "My view was dismissed by the prosecutors [part of the cottage industry of the death penalty] and by most, but certainly not all, members of the family. The entire process focuses attention on those survivors who favour the death penalty and dismisses opponents. Sanctimonious victim's rights groups court only supporters of the death penalty and ensure that theirs is the only viewpoint quoted by the press." What this letter also highlights is which view and which family member should represent the views of the deceased. Is there a hierarchy of family members and their influence?

51

will" should carry weight at the prosecution and the sentencing phases. There are numerous individuals in the United States who carry notarised declarations stating that in the event of their murder the state should not seek the death penalty. Should prosecutors respect that wish or should the state, or for that matter the family, have the right to override that wish?[45] If the move is towards a victim-driven system then it follows that the victim's view should be more influential than either that of the state or the friends and families of the victim.

Victim statements

In the United States since *Lockett v Ohio* in 1978[46] the defence team in a capital case has been allowed to introduce any information sympathetic to the defendant in mitigation whilst the prosecution was permitted to introduce evidence only relevant to one or other of the aggravating characteristics of the offence. Prosecutors and victims' groups, believing this led to an imbalance, sought to redress this by making similar provision for the deceased, the victim. Victim impact evidence was first raised in 1987 in *Booth v Maryland*[47] when information, showing the pain and loss suffered by surviving relatives and friends of a murder victim, offered in support of the prosecution's argument for a death sentence was declared inadmissible by the US Supreme Court. This judgment was overturned by *Payne v Tennessee* (1991)[48] when the Supreme Court ruled that the prosecution might now introduce evidence to show the victim in a favourable light. Inevitably this process is raw with emotion, antagonistic to the defendant, implicitly a demand for the death penalty and not subject to cross-examination by the defence. Hardly the ideal environment to tease fact from fiction, relevance from irrelevance or to ensure objectivity in sentencing especially when the prosecutor and the judge are likely to be elected officials. Hugo Bedau, critical of this development remarked:

> Criminal desert is supposed to be measured by the offender's culpability and the harm caused by the crime.... Now, however, it will be up to each capital

---

45. *Boston Globe*, 7 July 1998. Mario Cuomo, who was for three terms Governor of New York State, has attached such a notarised codicil to his will. It reads: "I hereby declare that should I die as a result of a violent crime, I request that the person or persons found guilty for my killing not be subject to or put in jeopardy of the death penalty under any circumstances, no matter how heinous their crime or how much I have suffered." The campaign in New York was started by Sister Camille D'Arienzo in 1994 during the governor's election when it seemed certain that the death penalty would be returning to New York State after an absence of some thirty years. She says that at least 10 000 people across the country have signed statements like Cuomo's.
46. *Lockett v Ohio*, 438 US 586 (1978).
47. *Booth v Maryland*, 482 US 496 (1987).
48. *Payne v Tennessee*, 501 US 808 (1991).

trial jury to decide for itself whether the murder of which the defendant has been found guilty is deserving of a death penalty because of some special features about the victim, features not defined by any statute, possibly not evident to the defendant at the time of the crime, and not specifiable by the trial court or in any uniform manner from case to case.[49]

The balance that has to be achieved is to give recognition to the victim in a respectful and dignified manner while still maintaining objectivity in the legal process. The trial is not the place to consider the very legitimate needs and rights of the families and friends of the victim; there should in effect be a separate victim justice system.[50] Here again the mainstream victim movement in the United Kingdom differs from its counterparts in the United States. Dame Helen Reeves, Chief Executive of the National Association of Victim Support Schemes (NAVSS) laid out its position with respect to the victim impact debate. Dame Helen's plans are:

> to ensure that victims have a voice and that the legitimate interests of the victim can be taken into account and acted upon by the police, the prosecution service, and the courts. She argues that the best interests of victims are not met by involving them directly in the sentencing process, or by raising expectations that their views will impact on the level of punishment of the offender. She argues that raising such expectations and involving the victim directly in the sentencing process can work against the best interests of the victims concerned.[51]

The UK experience of the victim statement is limited given that it was introduced nationwide only in October 2001[52] following a series of pilots around the country. An evaluation of both the One Stop Shop (OSS) project for crime victims and the Victim Personal Statement Initiative conducted by the Department of Law at Bristol University[53] found that less than 50% of eligible victims opted into the OSS and approximately 30% prepared victim personal statements (VPS). "Most victims prepared VPS for expressive reasons (getting it off their chests) and instrumental reasons (wanting to affect a decision). But approaching half did so for

---

49. Hugo Adam Bedau, "American populism and the death penalty: witnesses at an execution", *Howard Journal of Criminal Justice*, November 1994, vol. 33, pp. 289-303.
50. See Howard League proposals in their briefing paper "Victims of crime" available from the League's offices 708 Holloway Road, London N19 3NL.
51. Dame Helen Reeves and Edna Erez, Kent State University, USA debate the issue of the victim impact statement. 10th International Symposium on Victimology, Montreal, Canada, 2000.
52. Home Office Circular 35/2001: "Victim personal statements". This gives the option to all discernible victims to complete such a statement, which can include information about whether you would like to receive further information about the progress of the case; any concerns about bail; concerns or special needs related to being a potential witness; what compensation you are seeking, based on your financial loss and any physical or psychological injury you have suffered.
53. C. Hoyle, E. Cape, R. Morgan and A. Saunders, "Evaluation of the One Stop Shop and Victim statement pilot projects", A report for the Home Office, Research Development and Statistics Directorate, Department of Law, University of Bristol.

procedural reasons (for example wishing to back up evidential statements). Like most OSS participants, they also saw making a VPS as an expression of their rights and as an aid to their feeling in control of events. Both these schemes are staffed by police officers who are required to inform the victims that the VPS will form part of the case papers and can be disclosed to the defence if an offender is caught, meaning that the victim could be cross-examined on what has been said in the statement. Furthermore, "If it is in the public interest to do so, the VPS should be taken into account by all the criminal justice agencies who subsequently deal with a case but they are not obliged to act upon it. In relation to sentencing, the court can take into account the effect of the crime but cannot take account of any opinion about sentencing."[54]

It was clear from the start that the VPS would not imitate either the spirit or the process of the US victim impact statement and it would be emphasised that this was not a formula for influencing the sentencing process.

Victim offender mediation/dialogue (VOM/D)

My contribution to this chapter is based principally on my knowledge of the Texas experience though projects based on the restorative justice approach are to be found in other parts of the US that have capital punishment and in other parts of the world where it is applied to the generality of crime victims. The Texas VOM/D[55] is a programme for victims of violent crime including lethal crime so some of those who take part in this project are families of homicide victims whose murderers are on death row.

Figures available in April 2002 showed that 494 victims had requested to meet with their offenders, 62 were assigned to VOM/D staff, 42 were assigned to volunteers, 31 cases were resolved, 26 cases were completed in that the victim and offender had met face-to-face, 5 had been resolved by "creative alternatives" not requiring face-to-face meetings, 209 cases were described as closed, meaning that either contact with the victim had been lost or the victim had withdrawn or that the offender was deemed inappropriate or had refused. There were 150 pending cases. Of the 494 cases 244 involved murder victims (51 of the prisoners found guilty of murder were on death row). Of the offenders, 130 sought to initiate mediation through the VOM/D. In 2001, 22 mediations were completed.

---

54. The Liberty Guide to Human Rights – www.YourRights.org.uk

55. The Victim Offender Mediation/Dialogue is an initiative of the Victim Services Division of the Texas Department of Criminal Justice – www.tdcj.state.tx.us/victim/victim-vomd.htm. To paraphrase: The mission of the Victim Services Division is to provide a central mechanism for victims and the public to participate in the criminal justice system. Its philosophy is to strive to reduce victimisation through education within an environment of integrity, fairness, compassion, dignity and respect.

The important principle to be remembered is that this scheme is essentially for the crime victim and secondary victim unlike some earlier projects which brought together victims with their offenders where victims were clearly being "used" as part of the offender's therapy programme. The anecdotal evidence of the impact of this process is overwhelmingly positive in nature for both the victims and the offenders who have taken part. There is ongoing research at the Center for Restorative Justice & Peacemaking at the University of Minnesota, victim–offender mediation programmes are being examined in Texas, Ohio and in a number of other states work is being undertaken with serious violent crime including capital crimes. The evidence to date from interviews with victims and offenders indicates that both constituencies almost universally described the experience of all aspects of the programme as "very helpful". The briefing paper[56] reviewing the work in progress published by the School of Social Work refers to a number of earlier studies the outcomes of which mirrored those of the Minnesota study. Jon Wilson, another author on the subject writes about the growing movement that in his view "brings victims and offenders together in search of true justice" and how the Texas VOM/D "brings true healing to crime victims, and true accountability to their offenders".[57]

The overwhelming majority of those participating in a Training and Awareness Symposium in Austin, Texas in 2001[58] staged by the Victim Services Division of the Texas Department of Criminal Justice, which I attended, had personal experience of violent crime as primary or secondary victims, which was significant as no one felt the need to hide the pain of their experiences, nor justify the differing approaches they had adopted to cope with their individual circumstances. I was privileged to have been permitted to attend the conference though I frequently felt that I was intruding on the very private and painful reconstructions of their experiences.[59] Families of murder victims whose offenders were on death row constituted a minority in attendance at the meeting and I was able to meet with a number of them for private conversations. Interestingly, all those that I spoke to had participated in the VOM/D meeting "their" offenders and subsequently had also witnessed their execution. This is not always the experience of the Victim Services Division

---

56. Mark S. Umbreit, Robert B. Coates and Betty Vos, "Victim-offender mediation dialogue in crimes of severe violence", Center for Restorative Justice & Peacemaking, University of Minnesota, School of Social Work, 105 Peters Hall, St. Paul, MN 55108.

57. Jon Wilson, "Readings in restorative justice" *Hope Magazine*, www.hopemag.com. Jon Wilson is the publisher and Editor-in-Chief of *Hope Magazine*.

58. 2nd Annual Victim Offender Mediation/Dialogue Training and Awareness Symposium, Shepherd of the Hills Lutheran Church, Austin, Texas 20/21 April 2001.

59. I would like to thank all those who attended the symposium for allowing me to be present, especially those who allowed me to interview them.

which is also responsible for the scheme permitting victims' families to witness the execution of "their" offender. I say of interest because there appears to me to be an inherent contradiction between the objectives of the VOM/D and the Witness Execution project (of which more later). A contradiction supported by the testimony of the majority of those at the symposium indicating that the VOM/D programme provided lasting resolution and healing whereas no one I spoke to claimed such benefits flowing from the experience of witnessing the execution of "their" offender.

Most of those that I spoke to reflected on an aspect of their experience that they felt could have been/should have been addressed. One family nearly a decade on was still lobbying to meet with the parents of the condemned man responsible for their daughter's death as all their attempts to meet them and console them at the trial and subsequent court hearings had been aggressively thwarted by the prosecutors. This sharing of grief, exchanges of consolation and offerings of apologies is anathema to prosecutors and seen as undermining the anger and passion on which death penalty prosecution relies. These sentiments echo those that I have heard during my many discussions with the families of the condemned all of whom regret not being able, ever, to express their sorrows and apologies to the families of the victims. This is not a process that has time for anything that hints of healing – it prefers to tar all those associated with the defendant as being in some way culpable. Some of the counsellors in VOM/D share the regrets of their "clients" and believe such contact between the two sets of secondary victims to be crucial to the healing process for both parties.

The advocates of the VOM/D approach are very careful to point out that it is not an approach that will meet the needs of all victims or their families and I was introduced to families where the "one model fits all" approach had been quite counterproductive and had led to intermittent difficulties in their relationships. Possibly the main area of concern and dissent was about the issue of forgiveness and I was left with the uncomfortable impression that there was a strong covert pressure to forgive with the implication that it was not possible to "move on" without forgiving. One of the workshops addressed this issue and was staged by a husband and wife team who were both secondary victims – the husband had forgiven, the wife had not and furthermore could not envisage ever being able to.[60] Whilst this was the only workshop to formally address forgiveness the issue formed the basis of much emotive discussion in other workshops and plenary sessions. Literature on the subject provided

---

60. Don and Mary Streufert led a workshop on Issues of Forgiveness asking such questions as : "What is the nature of forgiveness? When is it an option and/or is it an option?".

by the International Forgiveness Institute based in Madison, Wisconsin[61] suggested definitions of forgiveness and the means through which to achieve it. Nikki Erickson, a secondary victim, described in a paper entitled "What does it mean to forgive" the murder of her mother by a 16-year-old boy who in the act of trying to steal her purse stabbed her to death. Ms Erickson was 6 years old at the time. She speaks warmly of her experience of the Texas VOM/D and of the personal steps she had taken since her mother's murder and of the decision that it was possible to forgive yet not forget and felt she was honouring her mother by so doing.[62]

I was left wondering whether this entire process owed more to the strong Christian principles that pervaded the meeting and many of the participants than to the theoretical fundamentals of restorative justice. When I challenged them about this I was assured, though not reassured, that the approach worked equally well with non-believers and with believers of all faiths. My concerns do not detract in any way from what are the proven benefits of this approach but do raise the question of whether it is as effective with secular and non-Christian groups and if not, what adjustments need to be made to the process to make it accessible to all.

Execution witness programme

At what I consider to be at the negative end of the continuum of victims' services there is a burgeoning practice of permitting the families and friends of homicide victims to witness the execution of "their" murderer. The decision to extend this "right" to those who survive the victim was arrived at after vigorous campaigning by the pro-punishment victims' lobby and is justified on the grounds that the condemned are allowed to invite witnesses to their execution and such a spectacle would provide an invaluable opportunity to the families and friends of victims for "closure".

At least thirteen states and the federal system have provision for victims' families to witness executions[63] with each state having different regulations governing numbers, status, age and dress code. In all states the victims'

---

61. R. Enright and G. Reed, "A process model of forgiving", Department of Educational Psychology, University of Wisconsin, Madison, USA.
62. Nikki Erickson, "What does it mean to forgive?", *The Crime Victims Report*, March/April 2001, vol. 5, No.1.
63. Oklahoma and Washington guarantee families the right to watch. In addition, California, Florida, Illinois, Louisiana, Montana, North Carolina, Ohio, Pennsylvania, Texas, Utah and Virginia hold hearings to determine access. Numbers permitted access varies from state to state, as does the family status of witnesses. Illinois allows families to watch only through closed-circuit television. It seems that not all states have the same minimum age for witnesses; Missouri does not permit those under the age of 21. Ironic really that one is not old enough to witness an execution at 21 but old enough at 16 to be executed.

witnesses are segregated from the witnesses for the condemned and practice is very varied between states as to the preparation and support, before, during and after, for all witnesses. Why the remaining twenty-five states do not currently have provision for victims' families to witness or why some states do not permit the family of the condemned to witness executions is unclear. Permitting, even encouraging, already pained and vulnerable people to watch while someone is put to death by hanging, lethal injection, lethal gas, firing squad or electrocution is a measure that should not have been implemented without extensive research into the reasons for and the effects of such an experience. I am not aware that there has as yet been much authoritative research conducted on the effects on all those who witness executions but the reason generally offered by politicians and some victims' lobbies for witnessing an execution is that the spectacle brings "closure".

The State of Texas is interesting in this respect because as well as being infamous for its enthusiastic support of the death penalty it has in place a number of projects worthy of further examination. When the state decided to permit the families of victims to witness executions it initiated a victim witness preparation process under the auspices of the Victim Services Division of the Texas Department of Criminal Justice. In addition to providing information by way of literature to victim witnesses, victim services staff visit prospective witnesses to discuss the execution process and to provide a personal point of contact for the family when they arrive for the execution. The "support room" for the victim witnesses is now housed within the Walls prison at Huntsville rather than in the administration offices in Huntsville, and it is here that they wait before and return to after the execution whilst the family of the condemned continue to be housed in the administration building across the road from the prison. It is a requirement for the assigned victim services representative to accompany the witness before, during and after the execution when the family meet with the post-trauma support team for a debriefing session and then at the press conference if they have indicated a wish to meet the press.[64]

Each witness is contacted several weeks after the execution to see if they have experienced any emotional or physical problems in the interim.[65] The literature provided by the Victim Services Division avoids any

---

64. Full details about the procedure are available on the Texas Department of Criminal Justice website, www.tdcj.state.tx.us/victim/victim-viewexec.htm

65. A report dated 28 August 1998 indicates that, "For the most part, the majority that have been interviewed have expressed no regrets in their decision to view and did not suffer any post-trauma symptoms." Dan Guerra, Assistant Director, Texas Department of Criminal Justice, Victim Services Division, PO Box 13401, Austin, Texas 78711. Tel: 512 406-5427.

comment about the purpose of this particular victims' right though the most frequently quoted justification is that it provides "closure" for the family and friends of victims and, more importantly, it is what they want. The data from the Victim Services Division suggests that it is becoming more common for executions to be attended, with 62% of executions attended in 1997 and 82% in 2001. The two most common complaints Texas victim witnesses have expressed about the execution process was that it took too long for the execution to take place after the sentencing, and that it was "too easy". And, while many were glad that the execution had transpired, *they did feel compassion and empathy for the inmate's family who were just starting their grieving process* (author's emphasis). This has resonance with my earlier comments about victims' families' wishes to meet with the offender's family, but through to the end every attempt is made to keep these parties separate including structural alterations to execution viewing chambers. The most important outcome for these families was some undefined but clearly felt sense of justice having been achieved. None claimed to have participated in the process for reasons of vengeance and none considered that witnessing the execution had in any way led to the much vaunted and promised "closure". They, in common with most informed commentators, were unclear as to what "closure" is.

My major difficulty with this initiative, notwithstanding the rights or wrongs in principle, is that such individuals should be protected from further suffering at the hands of the state and whilst I am satisfied that they have certain structural checks and balances in place I remain deeply sceptical as to the need for this provision, which I view as further political exploitation of a very vulnerable constituency – all this for the tenuous objective of "closure". The entire context of the debate is so contaminated by the politics of hate that I believe it is almost impossible to make a rational assessment of what the positive outcomes are for victim witnesses. It seems to me that by complying with this demand the state seeks to divest itself of further responsibility having already surrendered any remnants of political courage in capitulating to the demands of the pro-punishment victims' lobby.

It was not until victims' families were allowed to witness executions that the above measures were implemented despite the fact that the families of the condemned have been witnessing executions for decades. Thankfully this omission has now been addressed to some extent in the State of Texas where pastoral responsibility for these families has been delegated to the prison chaplains' department, which attempts to provide a similar service to that provided to the victim witnesses. It could be argued that the experiences of these "secondary victims" at the hands of the criminal justice system equals, perhaps exceeds, the suffering of the victim's family – exceeds because their experience is aggravated by a universally unsympathetic, even hostile, legal and penal system when compared to the experience of the family of the victim. Referred to above but worth mentioning again are the accounts by both sets of secondary victims that early contact should be facilitated where requested so that the beginnings of understanding and healing can begin. Marginalising the family of the condemned has to be avoided and their inclusion into the activities of MVFR is to be applauded.

The general question about how this experience affects all witnesses is also poorly researched but the anecdotal evidence and the testimony of numbers of prison personnel such as the former warden of Parchman penitentiary in Mississippi, Don Cabana[66] and abolitionists such as Sister Helen Prejean[67] would suggest that significant ill effects are experienced by many of those who have exposure to the raft of procedures involved in the process of capital punishment. Research conducted involving the media witnesses at the execution of Robert Alton Harris in California in 1992 indicated a range of psychological ill effects experienced by some of those witnesses. The researchers concluded that "the experience of being an eyewitness to an execution was associated with the development of dissociative symptoms in several journalists".[68] Evaluation of the effects on victim witnesses is being undertaken by the Social Work Programme of the University of Texas at El Paso but in my opinion this evaluation should be extended to include all those who have been exposed to this spectacle as many such witnesses are not there by choice but as part of the expectations of their employment. One such post is that of the prison chaplain and in Texas Chaplain Carroll Pickett,[69] over fifteen years of ministry, stood beside ninety-five inmates as they were put to death. His practice was to spend the last day with the condemned and with members of his family, some of whom stayed to watch the execution. Chaplain Pickett found this to be one of the most difficult aspects of his ministry as what he saw was a group of victims that nobody cared about. Five years after his retirement and five years trying to "ignore the awful memories of the death chamber Pickett has found a new calling as a vocal member of the anti-capital punishment lobby".[70]

66. Donald A. Cabana, *Death at midnight: the confession of an executioner*, Northeastern University Press, Boston, 1996.
67. S.R. Helen Prejean, *Dead man walking: an eyewitness account of the death penalty in the United States.:* Random House, New York, 1993.
68. A. Freinkel, C. Koopman and D. Spiegel, "Dissociative symptoms in media eyewitnesses of an execution", *American Journal of Psychiatry*, 1994, vol. 151, pp. 1335-39.
69. C. Pickett and C. Stowers, *Within these walls: memoirs of a death house chaplain.* St Martin's Press, New York, 2003.
70. *The Australian Magazine*, 20 July 2002.

Conclusions

"Closure" is a term imported into this debate from the world of psychiatry especially from the world of practice in the United States. It appears to have a fluid definition and application in the way it is applied to the issue of victims and the death penalty and provides yet another illustration of politicians' duplicity in offering painful and largely fictional solutions to the friends and families of homicide victims gained through witnessing the execution of "their" offender. If what is meant by "closure" is an end to pain and suffering then no victims' family I have talked to or authorities I have read can confirm such an outcome. In fact, "closure" as a means of "getting over it" is not recommended by bereavement counsellors such as Deborah Spungen.[71]

In the view of some observers an essential ingredient of "closure" is forgiveness and as discussed earlier this issue is very difficult to confront for many secondary victims. Spungeon's views on the issue of victim–offender mediation are that "the co-victim's acceptance of the notion of forgiveness for the defendant should not be made a prerequisite for participation. It may happen at a later time, or it may never happen. The decision to forgive or not forgive the defendant must always be the co-victims' choice. Achieving a sense of self-forgiveness, often an important issue for co-victims may be a surprising and beneficial outcome for the co-victim".

Scott Turow writing in *The Wall Street Journal* about his experiences on the commission set up by Governor Ryan in Illinois comments, "We found that survivors need enhanced support services and reliable communication about developments in a case. Compassionate services, rather than a determinative role in the penalty process, may be a better answer for survivors as well as for the system." In order to get to this position some radical reappraisal needs to be made by victims for and against the death penalty and especially by the traditional abolitionist movement.

The intellectual argument challenging the purpose and the effect of the death penalty has long been favourable to those opposed to capital punishment, as has the moral argument so far as international human rights treaties and the mainstream religious groups are concerned, save Islam and the Mormon Church. The emotional argument however, about the needs and rights of victims and their families and friends is definitely with the pro-punishment lobby – the emotional appeal is very compelling and even more compelling when it appears even to neutral observers that abolitionists and other penal reform groups are concerned only about the needs and rights of offenders.

---

71. D. Spungen, "Homicide: the hidden victims – a guide for professionals", in *Interpersonal violence: the Practice Series,* Sage Publications, California, 1998.

There is little doubt that the pro-punishment victim movement attracts significant public and political support in the United States contrasted with the United Kingdom where the public support for punishment is arguably as strong as in the US but crucially without the same support from mainstream political and victim groups. Death penalty abolitionists have a steep hill to climb if they hope to influence this emotionally charged debate and the ground they have to make up is largely of their own creation – crucial to their future strategy has to be an explicit recognition of the needs and rights of victims. I am not suggesting a cynical adoption of a victim-friendly strategy but the acceptance that homicide victims and those that survive them have inherent rights and that these should be recognised. The failure to do so has driven many moderate, perhaps even anti-death penalty victims' families, reluctantly into the arms of the pro-lobby who claim to offer succour and "solutions" to the hurt, anger and frustration experienced by such families. The menu of "rights" referred to earlier in this article represents the incline of the hill that has to be climbed.

This very full menu of rights that the bereaved have sought and won is an indication of how such families and friends can and have influenced the very philosophy that the state pursues in capital cases. For example, an issue once on the periphery of the debate, the mode of execution, is beginning to gain more attention from the pro-punishment victim lobby confirmed by the views of those victim witnesses in Texas who commented that "it was too easy". The mode of execution debate goes to the heart of the modern purpose of the death penalty – retribution. The move towards the more sanitised and clinical lethal injection represents an interesting dilemma – on the one hand it is an attempt to make the execution process more civilised and therefore more acceptable, whilst on the other it represents a dilution of the retributive justification. Those states that fought to retain the electric chair did so because they believed that the process had to appear to be painful but not so painful as to violate the Eighth Amendment to the Constitution [Cruel and unusual punishment].

Reform groups have to counter the advances made by the pro-punishment victim lobby and it is not enough for them to rely on the intellectual and academic argument that the death penalty serves no useful purpose or that it is a vehicle for a multitude of abuses of due process and human rights. Whilst all this is correct it fails to address the needs of even the moderate victim lobby and it is this failure historically that has led to the birth of the angry, frustrated and pro-punishment victims' groups in the United States. The dominant debate on victims' needs and rights is provided by those victims' groups that focus on influencing penal policy rather than, and some would say, at the expense of, the more traditional needs of crime victims. The crime victim movement has become a political movement typified by the vocabulary, rhetoric and aggressive tactics of the Pro-Life movement.

Abolition of the death penalty and penal reform in general is not to be gained at the expense of the inherent needs and rights of crime victims. The simple analysis provided by some politicians that money spent on offenders is money denied to victim services is a fallacy. Victims' needs and rights should not be met at the expense of humane, effective and proportional responses to offenders and their needs should not be confused with or influence the treatment of offenders.

The role of the Council of Europe's Parliamentary Assembly

Renate Wohlwend
Vice-President of the Council of Europe's Parliamentary Assembly

Of all the struggles for the development of human rights and for the respect of human dignity, the one to abolish the death penalty seems the hardest to win.

The Parliamentary Assembly of the Council of Europe has always taken a very firm position on the issue of the abolition of capital punishment. It considers that the death penalty has no legitimate place in the penal systems of modern civilised societies, and that its application may well be compared with torture and be seen as inhuman and degrading punishment within the meaning of Article 3 of the Convention for the Protection of Human Rights and Fundamental Freedoms (the European Convention on Human Rights), and thus as a violation of the most fundamental right, that to life itself. The Assembly believes that the imposition of the death penalty has proved ineffective as a deterrent and, owing to the possible fallibility of human justice, also tragic through the execution of innocent people.

Consequently, the willingness to institute an immediate moratorium on executions and to abolish the death penalty in the long term has become, since 1994, a precondition for accession to the Council of Europe.

As a result of the Assembly's position, Europe has become de facto a death penalty free zone, with all of the Council of Europe's forty-five member states either having abolished the death penalty, or having instituted a moratorium on executions.

This was not easy to achieve, and member states often needed repeated prodding by the Assembly. However, the momentum towards the abolition of the death penalty in Europe is growing ever more rapidly; Serbia and Montenegro has acceded as the forty-fifth member state of the Council of Europe, free of the death penalty.

The Parliamentary Assembly's first success: Protocol No. 6

The Parliamentary Assembly started its activities in this matter in 1973 when a motion for a resolution[1] on the abolition of capital punishment was presented by Miss Bergegren and others, which was referred to the Committee on Legal Affairs. There were prolonged discussions within the committee in 1974 and 1975 and the then appointed rapporteur had to revise his report, but when in January 1976 the Legal Affairs Committee decided to defer the question, Mr Lidgard resigned as rapporteur. It was not until the beginning of 1979 that the committee decided to take up the question again and to appoint another rapporteur who was Mr Lidbom.

Thanks to his report[2] together with the resolution[3] and recommendation[4] passed by the Parliamentary Assembly on 22 April 1980, the Council of Europe achieved Protocol No.6 to the Convention for the Protection of Human Rights and Fundamental Freedoms concerning the abolition of the death penalty, drawn up by the Steering Committee on Human Rights and adopted by the Committee of Ministers. The protocol was opened for signature by the member states of the Council of Europe on 28 April 1983. Twelve of then twenty-one member states signed it on this date: Austria, Belgium, Denmark, France, Germany, Luxembourg, Netherlands, Norway, Portugal, Spain, Sweden and Switzerland. The entry into force on 1 March 1985 was achieved with the essential five ratifications of Austria, Denmark, Luxembourg, Spain and Sweden.

Protocol No. 6 was the first agreement under international law containing the legal obligation of the parties to abolish the death penalty in peacetime.

To date forty-three of the forty-five members of the Council of Europe have ratified Protocol No.6: Albania (2000), Andorra (1996), Armenia (2003), Austria (1984), Azerbaijan (2002), Belgium (1998), Bosnia and Herzegovina (2002), Bulgaria (1999), Croatia (1997), Cyprus (2002), Czech Republic (1992), Denmark (1983), Estonia (1998), Finland (1990), France (1986), Georgia (2000), Germany (1989), Greece (1998), Hungary (1992), Iceland (1987), Ireland (1994), Italy (1988), Latvia (1999) Liechtenstein (1990), Lithuania (1999), Luxembourg (1985), Malta (1991), Moldova (1997), Netherlands (1986), Norway (1988), Poland (2000), Portugal (1986), Romania (1994), San Marino (1989), Slovak Republic (1992), Slovenia (1994), Spain (1985), Sweden (1984),

---

1. Parliamentary Assembly Document 3297 (1973).
2. Parliamentary Assembly Document 4509 (1980).
3. Parliamentary Assembly Resolution 727 (1980).
4. Parliamentary Assembly Recommendation 891 (1980).

Switzerland (1987), "the former Yugoslav Republic of Macedonia" (1997), Turkey (2003), Ukraine (2000) and the United Kingdom (1999); the ratifications of the Russian Federation and Serbia and Montenegro are still outstanding. These states do respect a moratorium on executions.

Making the abolition of the death penalty binding on new member states

The chronology of reports debated in several sittings of the Parliamentary Assembly is as follows.

In autumn 1994 Mr Hans Göran Franck submitted his report[5] on the abolition of capital punishment, on the basis of which, on 4 October 1994, the Parliamentary Assembly adopted Resolution 1044 (1994) and Recommendation 1246 (1994). The rapporteur had rightly discerned a strong abolitionist current in member states of the Council of Europe at the time. The Assembly followed his lead in recommending that the Committee of Ministers draw up an additional protocol to the European Convention on Human Rights (ECHR), abolishing the death penalty both in peace and wartime, and obliging the signatories not to re-introduce it under any circumstances. The Assembly also recommended the setting-up of a control mechanism under the Secretary General and the organisation of a conference on the abolition of the death penalty to take place in 1995.

Possibly even more important was the Assembly's decision that the willingness to sign and ratify Protocol No. 6 to the ECHR was to be a prerequisite for membership of the Council of Europe. Accordingly, since October 1994 all applicant states had to enter into commitments vis-à-vis the Assembly during the accession procedure to sign and ratify that protocol within a given period. States that were still executing prisoners condemned to death were furthermore obliged to introduce moratoria on executions with effect from the day of accession to the Council of Europe.

The great success in the aftermath of that debate was that Belgium, Italy, Moldova and Spain abolished the death penalty completely, but unfortunately other countries gave no heed to the Assembly's call and paid no respect to their commitments in this matter.

Having discovered that executions were still carried out in Latvia, the Russian Federation and Ukraine, and being convinced that some of the prisoners on death row could still be saved from certain death by timely Council of Europe intervention, the Committee on Legal Affairs and

---

5. Parliamentary Assembly Document 7154 (1994).

Human Rights asked that a debate be held under urgent procedure to follow up on Mr Franck's 1994 report. The current author submitted a report[6] and the Assembly's debate took place on 28 June 1996. In my report I described the positive and negative developments between October 1994 and June 1996. Further, I dealt with the futility of capital punishment. Many people are in favour of retaining the death penalty because they believe that this will bring down the crime rate. But this "deterrence" argument is simply wrong. A survey of research findings on the relation between the death penalty and homicide rates, conducted by the United Nations in 1988, concluded that "this research has failed to provide scientific proof that executions have a greater deterrent effect than life imprisonment. Such proof is unlikely to be forthcoming. The evidence as a whole still gives no positive support to the deterrent hypothesis".

The experience of abolitionist states should be convincing proof in and of itself. For example, the homicide rate in Canada has continued to fall since the abolition of the death penalty for murder in 1976, while the neighbouring United States, which resumed the use of capital punishment in 1977, has seen a continuing rise in the rate of violent crimes, including murder. No abolitionist country experienced a sudden and serious change in the curve of crime following the abolition of the death penalty; on the contrary, since executions brutalise society, the effect of abolition has on the whole been positive.

However, the strongest possible argument for abolition is probably the risk of executing the innocent.

According to an article (*Die Welt,* 11 November 1998) so many judicial errors occur in the United States that the "survivors of death row" have meetings. For instance in Chicago, organised by the North-Western University, twenty-nine people met in order to discuss their fate. Too many people are wrongly convicted. People who have been killed legally by the state can never be brought back to life, even if their innocence is later proven. Between 1976 and now there have been 111 exonerated death row inmates in the United States.

If this can happen in the United States, with its history of democracy and rule of law, how much higher must be the risk of executing the innocent in countries with criminal justice systems that have only just broken free of the totalitarian yoke and are still in need of reform?

Another reason sometimes given for retaining the death penalty is that public opinion demands it. Polls often show considerable support for

---

6. Parliamentary Assembly Document 7589 (1996).

capital punishment, especially in times of rising crime rates, or following a particularly heinous or violent crime. But history and research show that the population's attitude to the death penalty changes with more knowledge of the facts, and with the abolitionist experience. Besides, an opinion poll approach to politics may produce disastrous results for human rights – what if the public favoured the use of torture in certain circumstances: would torture be permissible then? This example alone illustrates why human rights must never be dependent on the whims of public opinion.

Whilst most of the paragraphs in the resolution[7] and in the recommendation[8] resulting from the Assembly's debate of June 1996 recalled previous decisions, an important step forward, supported by the Assembly, was contained in the respective order,[9] namely to instruct the Committee on Legal Affairs and Human Rights to organise one or two seminars on the abolition of the death penalty in Europe, and to report back on developments in due course.

The Assembly's efforts in the Russian Federation and Ukraine: a case study

The Assembly has been trying to help those countries that would like to abolish capital punishment or have committed themselves to do so. An example is the Seminar on the Abolition of the Death Penalty organised by the Committee on Legal Affairs and Human Rights in co-operation with the Ukrainian Ministry of Justice, which took place in Kyiv at the end of November 1996; its aim was to press ahead despite the opposition from public opinion, key ministries or senior officials. Over a hundred participants, most of them from central and eastern European countries, were present in the seminar. The debates were open to the press, and they really offered the opportunity for the ministers of justice, the ministers of the interior and the attorneys general, chairs of parliamentary legal committees, as well as for representatives from NGOs and international experts, to discuss such themes as capital punishment and human rights, the incidence of the death penalty relating to the crime rate and the influence of public opinion.

On the occasion of that seminar members of the Committee on Legal Affairs and Human Rights learned from Mr Anatoly Pristavkin, Chairman of the Russian Presidential Pardons Commission, as well as from Mr Serhiy Holovatiy, then Minister of Justice in Ukraine, that death sentences

---

7. Parliamentary Assembly Resolution 1097 (1996).
8. Parliamentary Assembly Recommendation 1302 (1996).
9. Parliamentary Assembly Order No. 525 (1996).

were still being carried out in both those countries, that the deputies were in principle powerless compared with their ministers, and that their governments were behaving as though they had never welcomed the moratorium and accepted it voluntarily.

Therefore, on 29 January 1997, the Parliamentary Assembly held another urgent debate on reports concerning the honouring of the commitments entered into by Ukraine[10] and Russia,[11] upon accession to the Council of Europe, to put into place a moratorium on the executions of death sentences. In Resolution 1112 (1997), the Assembly condemned Ukraine for having violated her commitment to put into place a moratorium on executions, and deplored the eighty-nine executions that had already taken place in the first half year of 1996. It declared itself particularly shocked by the information that executions in Ukraine were shrouded in secrecy, with apparently not even the families of the prisoners being informed, and that the executed were reportedly buried in unmarked graves. The Assembly warned the Ukrainian authorities that "it will take all necessary steps to ensure compliance with commitments entered into", including, if necessary, the non-ratification of the credentials of the Ukrainian parliamentary delegation at its next part-session.

The same warning was given to the Russian authorities, in Resolution 1111 (1997). During the debate the Assembly was informed that the Russian Federation had not executed anybody since August 1996, but it continued to hold hundreds of people on death row.

Concerning Ukraine, at the end of summer 1997 news of secret executions in 1997 started to leak out. Some NGOs were concerned that they had had no news from certain death row prisoners for a long time, prompting the fear that they had been executed. Even more worrying, the former Minister of Justice Mr Holovatiy, declared to the press that thirteen executions had taken place in the first half of 1997, even naming the precise regions where they had been carried out. Two deputy ministers of justice confirmed this information to deputies of the Verkhovna Rada (the parliament) and to NGO activists in August 1997 in writing. However, when these letters were made available to the public, an international outcry followed, in the wake of which the deputy ministers retracted their statements and blamed the "false" information on a statistical error. Confusion reigned until the beginning of October 1997 when the President of Ukraine informed the President of the Assembly during the 2nd Summit of the Heads of State and Government of the member states of Council of Europe that he had not refused mercy to any death row inmate since 29 November 1996.

---

10. Parliamentary Assembly Document 7745 (1997).
11. Parliamentary Assembly Document 7746 (1997).

However, he also stated that the last execution in his country took place in March 1997. Despite attempts by both the Assembly President and the Secretary General to obtain more precise official information on this matter, no further light was shed by officials on the alleged breaking of the moratorium.

Thus, the Committee on Legal Affairs and Human Rights instructed its rapporteur to go on a fact-finding mission to Ukraine from 5 to 7 November 1997. The programme was very well-organised by the Ukrainian authorities and I was able to meet the Minister of Justice, the Minister of the Interior, the Prosecutor General and the Ukrainian parliamentary delegation. I was also allowed to visit three pre-trial detention centres in different parts of the country and to meet death row inmates whom I had asked to see in two of these prisons. Senior officials confirmed that a de facto moratorium on executions was in place since 11 March 1997.

Below are some explanations of the procedure as to how death sentences used to be confirmed and carried out in Ukraine, and some impressions of the conditions on death row.

The court of first instance that could hand down sentences in Ukraine was the regional *(oblast)* court. According to information received even from death row prisoners, lawyers were usually present during the trials at regional court level, although they were not always present during the first days of police custody, interrogation and investigation. Few prisoners could, however, afford the services of a lawyer to help them draw up an appeal to the Supreme Court (the court of second instance in death penalty cases), so most prisoners seemed to draw up their appeals to the Supreme Court themselves.

If the Supreme Court confirmed the death sentence (which it did in most cases), the inmate had five days in which to appeal to the President of Ukraine for mercy. If the prisoner himself did not draw up an appeal for mercy, the prison governor was obliged to do so on his behalf. The President, advised by a special pardons commission, had the right to pardon the death row inmates and commute their sentences; most often to twenty years' imprisonment, life imprisonment not being an option in Ukraine's criminal justice system at the time.

If the President refused to pardon the prisoner, he informed the Supreme Court of this decision, which in turn instructed the Ministry of the Interior to carry out the death sentence. In practice, a special unit of the Ministry of the Interior (called the *convoi*) would arrive at the pre-trial detention centre where the prisoner was held. The prison governor was then obliged to turn over the inmate to the *convoi* (without prior notification of either the governor or the inmate). The inmate was then transferred to an unknown destination where he was shot dead.

The Ministry of the Interior then informed the Supreme Court in writing that the sentence had been carried out. It has five days in which to do so. The Supreme Court sent back the whole file to the (regional) court of first instance, which had the task of informing the relatives of the inmate of the execution within ten days of receipt of the file. The regional courts drew up statistics bi-annually on executions, which were sent to the Ministry of Justice, the Supreme Court and possibly, also to the Prosecutor General.

The whole procedure was shrouded in secrecy. The State Committee on Secrets, chaired by the Deputy Minister of the Interior, had declared the following data to be state secrets: information on management, conditions and supervision of places of imprisonment, including corrective medical institutions and other punitive institutions where sentenced persons worked; and information regarding executions of capital punishment; the organisation of the execution and burial; the place of execution; the place of burial; and the people who had carried out the execution. In conformity with these rules, relatives of executed prisoners were not informed where their relatives had been buried, an affront to human dignity. Even prison governors received their information on executions – including on the moratorium currently in force – from the media.

Conditions on death row, which I saw in three pre-trial detention centres, namely Donetsk No. 1, Simferopol and Khmelnitsky, varied slightly. The internal regulations of the Ministry of the Interior mandated the following orders; at the time death row inmates:

- must wear special clothing (black);
- may not leave their cells, except to have a shower;
- are not allowed to walk in the corridors or in the courtyards;
- may be kept in single or double cells;
- are not allowed to communicate with other inmates except their cell-mate, if they have one;
- are permitted one short visit a month by no more than two relatives. There is no limit to the amount of letters that can be written or received, but these are censored.

In November 1997 there were thirty-six death row inmates in pre-trial detention centre Donetsk No. 1. Two of these were kept in single cells, the rest in double cells. The cell I saw was a double cell, extremely small, with one bunk-bed, one other bed, one (open) toilet, one washbasin with cold water and one light which was left on day and night. There was some fresh air through a ventilation system, but no daylight, and practically no room to move around. Inmates are allowed to shower, once every ten days, and read books from the prison library. They were woken at 5 a.m. and given three meals a day through the hatch. They were constantly watched through a peephole in the door, allowing them not a minute's privacy. The inmate I spoke to had lived in these conditions since 19 November 1992.

There were twenty-eight death row inmates in Simferopol pre-trial detention centre, all kept in double cells. I saw one of those, which was of acceptable size, but with not a single piece of furniture. There were only three concrete platforms in the concrete floor that served as beds, and a toilet with cold water flowing into it constantly instead of a wash-basin. There was a shuttered window through which fresh air could get through, and a light that was on day and night. Inmates were allowed to a shower once every five days, and to read books, newspapers and magazines of their choice. Security seemed a little less tight.

In Khmelnitzky there were six death row inmates, all of whom were kept in single cells. The empty cell I saw was of acceptable size, had two bunk beds and was adequately furnished, it had a wooden floor, there was an open toilet and a washbasin. There was a shuttered window through which some fresh air filtered, but no daylight. Inmates, here, were allowed a shower once a week, and were allowed to read books, newspapers and magazines.

Three inmates of this pre-trial detention centre who had wished to meet with a representative of the Council of Europe declined, at short notice, to meet with me. One can only assume there must have been some pressure put on them; an assumption which relatives later confirmed.

Shocked to find that thirteen executions had taken place in Ukraine and equally shocked by the secrecy surrounding the death penalty and executions in the country, as well as by the living conditions of death row inmates I wrote another report[12] and suggested to the Committee on Legal Affairs and Human Rights that a debate should be held during the January 1998 Assembly part-session.

After a realistic, but also emotional debate on 27 January 1998, Resolution 1145 (1998) was adopted by the Assembly in which it recalled its Opinion No. 190 (1995) on the application by Ukraine for membership of the Council of Europe which noted that the country had committed itself to "put into place, with immediate effect from the day of accession, a moratorium on executions". So, the Assembly demanded – once again – that no more executions be carried out under any circumstances whatsoever. It demanded that the secrecy surrounding executions be lifted without further delay, and that a list of all those who

---

12. Parliamentary Assembly Document 7974 (1997).

have been under sentence of death, and their ultimate fate, since the accession to the Council of Europe on 9 November 1995 be made public. The Assembly also demanded that the death penalty be abolished by the Ukraine Parliament as soon as a new parliament had been elected and that the President pardon all current death row inmates. Further, it insisted that all death row inmates be allowed one hour's exercise outside, in fresh air, per day. Lights that can be turned down at night should be installed in death row cells; where possible, daylight should be allowed into the cells as well as fresh air.

With Order No. 538 (1998) the Assembly instructed the Committee on Legal Affairs and Human Rights to evaluate the proof, to be furnished by the Ukrainian authorities, that a moratorium on executions had been established.

The Ukrainian authorities and parliament carried out both undertakings. By her letter dated 31 March 1998, the Minister of Justice confirmed vis-à-vis the President of the Assembly that her ministry had abolished the secrecy rules concerning data on the execution of capital punishment, according to instructions given by the President and the Prime Minister of Ukraine. The moratorium on executions put into place by the President of Ukraine was respected. In September 1998 the parliament passed the first reading of the new Criminal Code abolishing the death penalty. In November 1999, the Committee on Legal Affairs and Human Rights organised a similar seminar to the one it had held in Kyiv in November 1996. This seminar directly preceded Ukraine's abolition of the death penalty: on 29 December 1999, the Ukrainian Constitutional Court ruled capital punishment unconstitutional in a landmark case for eastern Europe. The Ukrainian Parliament officially abolished the death penalty on 22 February 2000, which opened the way for ratification of the Council of Europe's Protocol No. 6 on 4 April 2000. The new Criminal Code, finally adopted in April 2001, abolished the death penalty in both peace and wartime: thus, Ukraine became one of the Council's success stories.

The Russian Federation, for its part, has respected a moratorium on executions since August 1996. It signed Protocol No. 6 on 16 April 1997. In February 1999, the country's Constitutional Court ruled the application of the death penalty unconstitutional until jury trials are available for capital cases throughout the Federation. As a consequence, in June 1997, President Yeltsin commuted the sentences of the over 600 inmates on Russia's death row to life imprisonment; a practice which has been continued by the new President whenever death sentences are passed. The Assembly is currently eagerly awaiting the ratification of Protocol No. 6, and with it the de jure abolition of the death penalty in the country.

In 1999, the Assembly took stock of its achievements. Already, the Council of Europe had become a death penalty free zone – there was only one caveat: the break-away Republic of Chechnya (in Russia) had re-introduced the death penalty as a consequence of a fundamentalist interpretation of the Sharia. Thus, in Resolution 1187 (1999), the Assembly had to condemn in the strongest possible terms the executions that had taken place in Chechnya. It called on the responsible authorities to fully respect the moratorium on executions instituted by the Russian Federation. At the same time, the Assembly decided – and called on the whole of the Council of Europe, including the Committee of Ministers to do likewise – to offer full assistance to member states experiencing difficulties in abolishing the death penalty, in particular by disseminating information and by organising awareness-raising seminars aimed at ensuring support from governmental and from non-governmental circles.

A new challenge for the Assembly: the death penalty in Council of Europe observer states

During the debates held in the Assembly on the abolition of the death penalty, some speakers made reference to the United States of America. Many American states, as well as American federal civilian and military law, still have capital punishment on their statute books, and some states are executing an ever-increasing number of prisoners. The speakers felt that it was unfair that the Assembly harried some Council of Europe member states such as the Russian Federation, Ukraine and the Baltic states to abolish the death penalty, while the United States was not penalised although it was an observer state. Convinced of the necessity to deal with the abolition of the death penalty in observer states such as the US I, together with twenty-eight colleagues representing a wide range of countries and political groups, tabled a motion for a resolution on 5 February 1998 on the abolition of the death penalty in the United States of America. The motion was referred to the Committee on Legal Affairs and Human Rights for report, which appointed me rapporteur on 23 March 1998.

According to Statutory Resolution (93) 26 on observer status:

> Any state willing to accept the principles of democracy, the rule of law and the enjoyment by all persons within its jurisdiction of human rights and fundamental freedoms,... may be granted... observer status with the Organisation.

observer status with the Council of Europe has been granted to Canada, Japan, Mexico, the Holy See and the United States. Of these five countries Japan and the United States still apply the death penalty. Since there should be no double standards with regard to observer states, I decided to extend my scrutiny of the death penalty system to Japan, as well.

observer states must be willing to accept the enjoyment by all persons within their jurisdiction of human rights and fundamental freedoms. While the European Convention on Human Rights (ECHR) still allows the application of the death penalty "in the execution of a sentence of a court following his conviction of a crime for which this penalty is provided by law", it does not permit torture, inhuman or degrading treatment or punishment.

As described above, subsequent texts in the Council of Europe have upheld the right to life more strictly: Protocol No. 6 of the ECHR abolishes the death penalty, and the case-law of the European Court of Human Rights (especially the landmark *Soering* case) finds the "death row phenomenon" to be inhuman and degrading treatment. The Assembly has gone even further, classifying the application of the death penalty itself as inhuman and degrading punishment, and thus a violation of the most fundamental human right, that of the right to life itself. Under these circumstances, the Assembly must consider observer states which still apply the death penalty to be violating human rights, and therefore to be in contravention of Resolution (93) 26 on observer status.

Having submitted introductory memoranda to the Committee on Legal Affairs and Human Rights, and having received comments from the Japanese Ministry of Justice, and the United States government, I was authorised to go on fact-finding missions to the USA and Japan, to find out more facts, hear the official position of the authorities, and attempt to explain the Council of Europe's position in the hope of finding ways of influencing the attitude of the authorities and public opinion.

Unfortunately, in the end, I could not go to Japan myself for personal reasons, so the Committee's Chairman, Mr Gunnar Jansson, was so kind as to replace me at very short notice. The visit, which had been very well organised by the Parliamentary League for the Abolition of the Death Penalty, took place from 19 to 24 February 2001. Also very much involved in the organisation were several NGO activists, including members of Amnesty International Japan and the Japanese NGO, Forum 90. The programme included a meeting with the Minister of Justice and high-ranking officials in his ministry, and a visit to Tokyo detention centre. Here, Mr Jansson was allowed to speak to the director, and was shown an empty cell, but his request (and that of the Japanese MPs accompanying him) to speak to detainees on death row was denied. Mr Jansson also met with the Parliamentary League, and the vice-president of one of the parties sponsoring a bill aimed at introducing life imprisonment without parole (as the first step to abolition), with the Japanese Federation of Bar Associations, several barristers defending inmates on death row, and ex-detainees of death row who had been acquitted; families of inmates on death row and NGO activists. The press covered Mr Jansson's visit very well.

I myself visited the United States from 28 March to 6 April 2001, travelling from Washington DC, via Virginia (a retentionist state) and Illinois (a moratorium state) to Wisconsin (an abolitionist state). The programme had been organised by the State Department in co-operation with a private firm, Delphi International. Unfortunately, the programme fell far short of my expectations. While I was able to have interesting and fruitful discussions with members of the NGO and academic community, unfortunately the level of the meetings arranged with federal and state officials, for the most part, made a meaningful dialogue impossible. I particularly regretted that no meetings with parliamentarians (on federal or state level) could be arranged. I was allowed to visit two prisons, Greensville Correctional Center in Virginia, and Columbia Correctional Institution in Wisconsin, and spoke to their directors, but my requests to visit a death row (in a different prison or pre-trial detention centre) and to speak to inmates there were denied. I was able to meet with one ex-detainee on death row now acquitted. The press coverage of my visit was very low key.

On the basis of these visits, I was able to make a comprehensive judgment of the death-penalty systems in the two observer states, which are both very worrying, but in different ways. In Japan, where the death penalty is imposed for aggravated murder, some 100 people are imprisoned under sentence of death, about half of whose sentences have been upheld by the Supreme Court (or became final in lower courts). The latter prisoners can therefore be executed at any time. The Code of Criminal Procedure stipulates that a death sentence is to be executed within six months of the final verdict upon an order from the Minister of Justice. In practice, however, most prisoners are under sentence of death for years, some for decades. Since the execution order must be signed by the Minister of Justice, it is, in fact, this minister who decides when the sentence is carried out, the execution having to take place within five days of his giving the execution order. The last two executions took place in December 2001 – on average, Japan puts to death two to three inmates per year.

There is considerable secrecy surrounding executions in Japan, to the extent that neither prisoners, nor their lawyers or family members, are told in advance of the pending execution. In general, executions (by hanging) are carried out early in the morning, with the prisoner being told just 45 minutes to 1 hour beforehand. The prisoner must thus expect every day to be his last, which exacerbates the mental anguish known as "death row phenomenon", ruled by the European Court of Human Rights in 1989 to be torture and inhuman treatment. The practice of keeping pending executions secret even from the prisoner himself further deprives him of the opportunity to say farewell to his family, and makes it impossible for lawyers to file last-minute appeals (for example on the basis of insanity). Since the Minister of Justice's choice of whom to execute seems quite arbitrary, following no discernible logic, the fear of the inmates on death row is even more acute.

Conditions of detention are extremely harsh for those sentenced to death. Japanese law states that prisoners sentenced to death shall be treated like unconvicted prisoners. In practice their fate depends on the policies imposed by the Ministry of Justice and detention centre directors. In most detention centres there are examples of very harsh treatment. Some prisoners sentenced to death have been held in almost complete isolation for years. Often, prisoners may be visited only by their immediate family (in some cases, adopted family does not qualify), and by their lawyers, provided that they are preparing an appeal, re-trial or pardon request. Many conservative families renounce murderers, so that there are many prisoners under finalised sentence of death who have no outside contact whatsoever, except perhaps spiritual guidance by a monk or priest. Contact with other prisoners or guards is forbidden in any case. In addition, some directors of detention centres impose further arbitrary restrictions: some death row inmates may not read newspapers, or write letters. Thus, in many cases, the isolation of the prisoners is so complete as to qualify as inhuman treatment in and of itself.

There is a specifically Japanese characteristic in the official position of the Japanese Ministry of Justice on the death penalty which is particularly cruel: the search for obtaining what the ministry calls "peace of mind" of death row inmates. In this way of thinking, a death row inmate is to find "peace of mind" before he is executed, that is to say he is to be "ready" for death, accepting, even welcoming of the execution. Inmates on death row are to stop believing – or even hoping – that they will live any longer; they are to resign themselves to death, to accept it as atonement for their crimes. This seems to be why they are isolated as much as possible from society: so that they may lose hope.

An added concern is, once more, the fallibility of human justice, which can lead to the execution of innocent people. In fact, four innocent people were freed from death row in the 1980s, some of them after having spent decades there. Many other death row inmates in Japan claim not to have had access to a lawyer after their arrest, to have been beaten and tortured and to have confessed under duress. It is very difficult for a convicted prisoner to obtain a judicial review of his or her sentence once it has been finalised, since new evidence indicating innocence must be uncovered first (or the evidence on which the original judgment was based must have been proved false). The Japanese Federation of Bar Associations (JFBA), not against the death penalty in principle, contends that the Japanese criminal procedure fails to meet the requirements of international standards in terms of protection of those facing the death penalty, raising, among other things, the following points: "no provision to guarantee an official defence counsel for suspects, no mandatory appeal system for death penalty cases, no guarantee of suspension of an execution procedure when the defendant appeals for re-trial or clemency." The JFBA concludes that the current system of execution is a violation of the International Covenant on Civil and Political Rights (ICCPR), and calls on the Japanese government to suspend all executions.

In the United States, approximately 3 500 persons are currently held on death rows and about 875 have so far been executed; thirty-two states have executed prisoners and prisoners have also been executed under federal death penalty statutes. The death penalty is provided for many different offences in different state jurisdictions, but is, in practice, most often applied to murder in aggravating circumstances. In contravention of international standards, the United States puts to death juvenile offenders, persons with mental retardation and illness, and foreign citizens who have been denied the right to contact their diplomatic representations in breach of international treaties ratified by the United States. The concern about the increased use and expanded scope of the death penalty in the US is compounded by serious allegations that the defendants are not always granted fair trials by the criminal justice system, and that the decision to apply the death penalty remains arbitrary, and often racially and class discriminative. In the words of the UN Special Rapporteur on Extrajudicial, Summary or Arbitrary Executions, "race, ethnic origin and economic status appear to be key determinants of who will, and who will not, receive a death sentence." Poor and minority defendants often receive inadequate legal assistance at state-trial and state-appellate stages – and even less assistance at state *habeas corpus* levels.

Conditions on death row in the United States seem to vary from state to state, but can be described as harsh in most cases, with small cells and often segregation. Especially harsh is what is called "death row phenomenon", the mental torture inmates have to suffer while waiting for years on death row for their sentence to be executed, while they go through various appeal and pardon procedures. Many death row inmates are scheduled for execution several times, receiving stays of execution virtually at the last minute – sometimes already strapped to the electric chair, or the needles for the lethal injection already inserted in their arms. As indicated above, the European Court of Human Rights has ruled this to be a form of inhuman and degrading treatment and punishment. The fallibility of human justice, which can lead to the execution of innocent people, is made blatantly clear in the United States, where 111 people have been released from death row since 1973 following evidence of their innocence.

On 20 June 2002, the US Supreme Court ruled that the execution of mentally retarded persons violated contemporary standards of decency. Some time later it ruled that sentences to the death penalty should be pronounced by a jury, not a single judge.

On 25 June 2001, the Assembly held a debate on the abolition of the death penalty in Council of Europe observer states, at the end of which it adopted a resolution[13] addressed to both the United States and Japan, a recommendation to the Committee of Ministers,[14] and an Order.[15] In the resolution, the Assembly noted that, when Japan and the United States were granted observer status with the Council of Europe, the Organisation's position on capital punishment was already clear, but had not yet been taken on board by all European states. It made clear that, today, the Council of Europe does not accept countries in its midst which carry out executions. Viewing the application of the death penalty as a violation of the most fundamental human rights, such as the right to life and the right to be protected against torture and inhuman or degrading treatment, the Assembly thus found Japan and the United States in violation of their obligations under Resolution (93) 26.

The Assembly therefore required Japan and the United States to:

- institute without delay a moratorium on executions, and take the necessary steps to abolish the death penalty;

- improve conditions on death row immediately, with a view to alleviating "death row phenomenon" (this includes the ending of all secrecy surrounding executions, of all unnecessary limitations on rights and freedoms, and a broadening of access to post-conviction and post-appeal judicial review).

The Assembly resolved to take all necessary measures to assist Japan and the United States in instituting moratoria on executions and abolishing the death penalty. To this end, the Assembly decided to promote dialogue with parliamentarians from Japan and the United States (both state and federal) in all forms, in order to support legislators in their endeavours to institute moratoria on executions and abolish the death penalty, and in order to engage the opponents of abolition in an informed debate.

At the same time, the Assembly deplored the fundamental difference in values regarding the abolition of the death penalty between the Council of Europe on the one hand and Japan and the United States on the other hand. It urged these observer states to make a serious effort to bridge this widening gap. Not content just with exhortations, the Assembly also decided to set a deadline for compliance: it decided to call into question the continuing observer status of Japan and the United States with the Organisation as a whole, should no significant progress in the implementation of this resolution be made by 1 January 2003. To avoid the

---

13. Parliamentary Assembly Resolution 1253 (2001).
14. Parliamentary Assembly Recommendation 1522 (2001).
15. Parliamentary Assembly Order No. 574 (2001).

situation recurring, the Assembly also decided to henceforth grant observer status with the Assembly only to national parliaments, and to recommend the granting of observer status with the Organisation as a whole only to states which strictly respect a moratorium on executions or have already abolished the death penalty.

In May 2002, the Committee on Legal Affairs and Human Rights, acting upon the Assembly's order of the year before, held a seminar on the abolition of the death penalty in Tokyo. This was followed by a similar seminar in the United States in April 2003.

The seminars

While I was greatly surprised by the activities of Japanese parliamantarians – they have a league for the abolition of the death penalty – I was disappointed that American politicians at federal level did not seem to be concerned by the death penalty issue.

The conference in Tokyo, between the league of Japanese parliamentarians and the Human Rights sub-committee, was extremely fruitful because we managed to foster debate on the topic, and both sides listened carefully to each other's arguments. However, ultimately we were unable to reach an agreement with the Japanese Minister of Justice.

The Human Rights sub-committee tried to encourage the Minister of Justice to adopt a de facto moratorium on the death penalty stressing the importance of human rights and human dignity; the sub-committee encouraged her not to sign the orders for execution, a part of her duties. However, agreement was not reached on this matter as the Minister of Justice considered signing the execution orders to be a part of her official responsibilities. Since the seminar, execution orders have continued to be signed by the Minister of Justice.

The conference entitled Justice and Human Rights in Council of Europe Observer States: the Abolition of the Death Penalty took place in Springfield (Illinois) and Washington DC from 9 to 11 April 2003. The seminar in Illinois, a state that already has a de facto moratorium, was highly promising. The state itself is already preparing a bill for abolition. Illinois would be a good example for other states to follow. The seminar in Washington was less successful with no politicians attending.[16]

On 1 October 2003, the Parliamentary Assembly debated the abolition of the death penalty in Council of Europe observer states once more in plenary session. Based on a report of the Committee on Legal Affairs and

16. There was a Parliamentary Assembly debate on the death penalty in Council of Europe observer states in September 2003.

Human Rights (Doc. 9908), the Assembly adopted Resolution No. 1349 (2003) and Recommendation No. 1627 (2003), both forward-looking texts aimed at engaging Japan and the United States of America in a constructive dialogue which yields results.

The Assembly took the opportunity to reaffirm its complete opposition to capital punishment, which it considers to be torture and inhuman and degrading punishment and thus a severe violation of universally recognised human rights. Taking its cue from the texts adopted in 2001, the Assembly, with regret, found Japan and the United States, once more, in violation of their fundamental obligation to respect human rights under Statutory Resolution (93) 26, due to their continued application of the death penalty. As a consequence, the Assembly required these two observer states to make more of an effort to take the necessary steps to institute a moratorium on executions with a view to abolishing the death penalty.

The Assembly asked the Japanese Parliament and Government to continue and deepen its constructive dialogue with the Council of Europe on this issue, and asked the United States Congress and Government, at federal and state level to enter into a more constructive dialogue. It encouraged American politicians to create abolitionist "caucuses" in their respective parliamentary assemblies, and to continue to engage opponents of abolition in informed debate. The Assembly decided to intensify its dialogue with parliamentarians from Japan with a view to encouraging rapid progress on the institution of a moratorium on executions and the abolition of the death penalty, and to continue its efforts to enter into a dialogue with parliamentarians from the United States (both state and federal) with a view to supporting them in their endeavours to institute moratoria on executions and abolish the death penalty. To this end, the Assembly will invite parliamentarians from both countries to a parliamentary conference to be held in 2004 on effective criminal justice in a human rights framework.

The Assembly also encouraged the Committee of Ministers to take more action on this issue with the two observer states in question. It reminded the Committee of Ministers that observer states have a moral obligation to engage in dialogue with the Council of Europe on matters of common concern, in particular the respect for human rights. "In fact, dialogue is only the first, minimum requirement, which must, eventually, bear fruit", the Assembly stated. It therefore recommended that the Committee of Ministers intensify its dialogue on the abolition of the death penalty with the governments of the countries concerned with a view to encouraging rapid progress on the issue, especially as it is becoming increasingly difficult for the Council of Europe to accept that observer states make use of the death penalty. The Assembly recommended that the Committee of Ministers take effective measures to encourage compliance by Japan and the United States of America with Assembly Recommendation 1522 (2001) and Resolution 1349 (2003) on the abolition of the death penalty in Council of Europe observer states. The issue of dialogue was essential to the Assembly: this is why it recommended that the Committee of Ministers make it a minimum requirement for existing Council of Europe observer states wishing to have their rights under Statutory Resolution (93) 26 extended to show their willingness to engage in a fruitful dialogue at parliamentary and governmental level with the Council of Europe on the abolition of the death penalty, if they have not yet abolished it, or put into place a moratorium on executions. The Assembly therefore did not recommend sanctions to be taken against Japan and the United States of America (although, at Committee level, the possibility of sanctioning the US for its lack of willingness to engage in dialogue was considered at first), but made it clear that dialogue is not a one-way street, and enjoying observer status with the Council of Europe also entails "observing" its most basic principles.

The Assembly will continue to deal with this question. It has asked the Committee of Ministers to report to it by January 2004 on the progress, since June 2002, of their dialogue on the issue of capital punishment with the countries concerned. In addition the Assembly has resolved to debate the abolition of the death penalty in Council of Europe member and observer states whenever the necessity arises, and, in any case, at the latest in the year 2005.

A personal note from the rapporteur: the experience of Liechtenstein

How did and does Liechtenstein deal with the death penalty? The last execution in Liechtenstein took place in 1785. The death penalty was struck off the Penal Code in Liechtenstein only in 1989. Since then the maximum punishment has been life imprisonment, which is imposed for murder and genocide. According to the Liechtenstein Constitution the prince has the prerogative of remitting, mitigating or commuting sentences that have been legally pronounced.

The Liechtenstein Constitution does not contain any provision with respect to capital punishment. However, according to the prevailing doctrine, Protocol No. 6 to the European Convention on Human Rights which Liechtenstein ratified on 15 November 1990, and the Second Optional Protocol to the International Covenant on Civil and Political Rights aiming at the abolition of the death penalty, to which Liechtenstein acceded on 10 December 1998, have at least the status of law. Upon its accession to the Second Optional Protocol, Liechtenstein did not make any reservation as to the application of the death penalty in time of war. The Liechtenstein Parliament ratified Protocol No. 13 on 5 December 2002.

Under the law on mutual assistance in criminal matters of 11 November 1992 the government, when examining a decision for extradition, has to make sure that existing obligations of the principality of Liechtenstein under international law have duly been taken into account. Among these obligations under international law is the provision of the European Convention on Extradition which stipulates that extradition may be refused if the offence for which extradition is requested is punishable by death under the law of the requesting party.

The conviction that the abolition of the death penalty contributes to the progressive development of human rights is also the basis of Liechtenstein's attitude towards this matter in international bodies. Thus, Liechtenstein was, for instance, a co-sponsor of Resolution 1997/12 and Resolution 1998/8 of the United Nations Commission on Human Rights, both of which aim at abolishing the death penalty worldwide.

In some reports presented to the Assembly from the beginning, and in some speeches of parliamentarians at the accompanying debates, the following sentence was very often quoted: "In the United Europe of tomorrow...the formal abolition of capital punishment should be the first article of the European Code for which we all hope."[17]

Concluding remarks

We are already very near the United Europe of tomorrow; today Europe is de facto a death penalty free zone, with all the Council of Europe's forty-five member states either having abolished the death penalty, or having instituted a moratorium on executions. In 2002, the Assembly's wish of 1994 that a protocol be drawn up to the European Convention on Human Rights to abolish the death penalty under all circumstances (both in peace- and wartime) became a reality: Protocol No. 13 was opened for signature in Vilnius (Lithuania) on 3 May 2002, and was immediately signed by thirty-three of the Council of Europe's forty-five member states. With the ratifictaion by fifteen member states of Protocol No. 13 it entered into force as of 1 July 2003.

Therefore, the parliamentarians and the Assembly as such will not cease their struggle before they reach their ultimate goal, the de jure abolition

---

17. Albert Camus, "Réflexions sur la guillotine", in Arthur Koestler and Albert Camus, *Réflexions sur la peine capitale*, Calmann-Lévy, Paris, 1978, p. 176.

of the death penalty in all Council of Europe member states. The Assembly will also not cease to try and convince the observer states which are meant to share the Council's values to live up to their obligations and put into place a moratorium on executions, in the hope of creating a better world for all of us to live in.

Protocol No. 6 to the European Convention on Human Rights

Hans Christian Krüger
Former Deputy Secretary General of the Council of Europe

This article presents a brief history of Protocol No. 6 to the European Convention on Human Rights and comments on its place in the framework of the human rights protection and political activities of the Council of Europe.

Three years after the second world war, leading politicians gathered in The Hague to launch a project of European reconciliation and re-unification. The declaration they adopted gave rise to the birth of the Council of Europe on 5 May 1949, when its Statute was signed by ten countries.

In what must be considered record time for international treaty making, the Convention for the Protection of Human Rights and Fundamental Freedoms (the European Convention on Human Rights) was adopted on 4 November 1950, that is, only sixteen months later. The Convention, which entered into force on 3 September 1953, is a catalogue of fundamental rights and freedoms, subject to the control of the European Court of Human Rights and the system of collective enforcement through the Committee of Ministers of the Council of Europe.[1]

Article 2, paragraph 1, of the European Convention on Human Rights specifies that everyone's life shall be protected by law and that no one shall be deprived of his life intentionally, save in the execution of a sentence of a court following his conviction of a crime for which this penalty is provided by law.

The Convention thus reserves the right of a state to impose capital punishment on condition that this punishment was foreseen in its national legislation and subsequently confirmed by a court of law.

But barely four years after the entry into force of the Convention, there was a move at expert level in the Council of Europe to "study the problems of capital punishment in Europe". For a long time, this work did not

---

1. Protocol No. 11 to the European Convention on Human Rights establishes the single Court. See also Article 46, paragraph 2 of the ECHR, as amended by Protocol No. 11.

yield results and it was only towards the end of the 1970s – following proposals from the Parliamentary Assembly of the Council of Europe – that the Committee of Ministers was invited to consider capital punishment as "inhuman" and to elaborate an additional protocol abolishing this punishment for crimes committed in times of peace.[2]

Similar proposals were also made by conferences of ministers of justice of the Council of Europe, which considered that Article 2 of the Convention no longer reflected public opinion in Europe.

As a result, the Committee of Ministers, in 1982, mandated its Steering Committee for Human Rights to "prepare a draft additional protocol to the European Convention on Human Rights abolishing the death penalty in peacetime". The text was prepared in approximately one year and was opened for signature on 28 April 1983.[3]

Protocol No. 6 of the European Convention on Human Rights entered into force on 1 March 1985, following the fifth ratification by a member state of the Council of Europe. (The full text of this protocol is reproduced in Appendix I.) The protocol includes features that are less common in international legal instruments.[4]

The wording of Article 1 is unique in the sense that it does not oblige states to act through the introduction of national legislation. Instead, it directly prohibits capital punishment. Second, states are not allowed to make reservations when ratifying the protocol.[5] Third, the protection against capital punishment under Protocol No. 6 is unconditional and cannot be suspended by Article 15 of the Convention, which otherwise allows contracting parties "in times of war or other public emergency threatening the life of the nation" to take "measures derogating from its obligations – to the extent strictly required by the exigencies of the situation".[6]

Finally, it should be mentioned that Protocol No. 6 is subject to the same formal conditions of denunciation as other articles of and protocols to the Convention; that is, only after the expiry of five years from the date on which it became a party to it and after six months' notice to the

---

2. See Parliamentary Assembly Resolution 727 (1980) and Recommendation 891 (1980).

3. See 1983 *Explanatory Report on Protocol No. 6 to the Convention for the Protection of Human Rights and Fundamental Freedoms concerning the abolition of the death penalty* (No. 114). Council of Europe Publishing, Strasbourg, ISBN-92-871-0216-3.

4. For further detailed comments, see Pettiti, Decaux and Imbert, "La Convention européenne des droits de l'homme", *Economica* (1955), pp. 1067 et seq.

5. That is other than interpretative reservations, see Article 64 of the ECHR (that is, Article 57 as amended by Protocol No. 11) and Article 4, Protocol No. 6 to the ECHR.

6. Article 3, Protocol No. 6 to the ECHR.

Secretary General of the Council of Europe.[7] The protocol has been invoked to refuse requests for extradition from a Council of Europe member state to third countries in which capital punishment still exists.[8]

The right to life is certainly among the most fundamental of human rights. It is protected also in other international human rights treaties, such as Article 3 of the Universal Declaration on Human Rights, Article 6 of the International Covenant on Civil and Political Rights and Article 4 of the African Charter on Human and Peoples' Rights. Furthermore, it is protected by Article 2, paragraph 1, of the Charter of Fundamental Rights of the European Union.

But it is clear from the foregoing that neither Article 2 of the European Convention on Human Rights, nor Protocol No. 6, provides an unconditional protection from execution since it is still authorised "in time of war or in imminent threat of war". Nor do these texts guarantee a certain quality of life. The main purpose is to protect the individual against arbitrary execution.

The fall of the Berlin Wall fundamentally changed the European political landscape. After forty years as a mainly western European organisation, the Council of Europe was finally able to play the pan-European role foreseen by its founding fathers and to fulfil the very raison d'être of the Organisation: the extension of democratic pluralism, human rights and the pre-eminence of law in a reunited Europe without dividing lines in which now more than 800 million people share the same values.

The 1st Summit of the Heads of State and Government of the member states of the Council of Europe (Vienna, 1993) acknowledged the Organisation as being the pre-eminent European political institution with a mission to include all democracies of Europe on an equal footing. The Vienna Summit also defined the political criteria for accession to the Council of Europe which presuppose that applicant states have brought their institutions and legal systems into line with the basic principles of democracy, the rule of law and respect for human rights; that the people's representatives have been chosen by means of free and fair elections, based upon universal suffrage and the freedom of expression, in particular of the media; that there is proper protection of national minorities and observance of international law and furthermore an undertaking to sign and ratify the European Convention on Human Rights and an acceptance of the Convention's supervisory machinery. Finally, the Vienna Summit also confirmed the responsibility of the Council of Europe in ensuring compliance with the commitments accepted by all member states.

---

7. Article 65 of the ECHR.
8. *Soering v the United Kingdom,* judgment of 7 July 1989, Series A No. 161.

What are these commitments? In the Council of Europe context we speak of three types of commitments. Looking at these in the order in which the applicant states encounter them, the first category is individualised commitments, entered into with varying degrees of explicitness, normally during the negotiations on accession to the Organisation, for example to sign and ratify a specific convention within a certain time limit. These commitments are incorporated in the opinions by which the Assembly has given its support for the admission of new members.

The second category is commitments made in the course of a member state's participation in Council of Europe activities, again often in the form of accepting conventions whose ratification entails legal obligations to comply with their basic provisions and to participate in their supervisory machinery where such exists.

The third and most obvious category covers commitments which follow from the Council of Europe's Statute, comprising principles which all members accept, namely the rule of law and the enjoyment by all persons within member states' jurisdiction of human rights and fundamental freedoms. Moreover, member states reaffirm their attachment to genuine democracy, which in itself is based on the foregoing values.

Since 1989, the Council of Europe has more than doubled its membership from twenty-one to forty-five states. In recent years, four states have also been granted observer status (Canada, United States, Japan and Mexico). The enlargement of the Council of Europe is almost completed. The challenge now is to ensure – in line with the Vienna Summit – that all member states comply with our standards and to assist them in the realisation of their legal, political and operational objectives.

To achieve these goals, the Council of Europe has established extensive programmes of co-operation and assistance, initially for the benefit of all new and potential member states. The overriding aim of these programmes is to safeguard and promote democratic reform and stability. Several of our 170 international conventions have paved the way for many European countries aspiring to membership of the European Union.

While the abolition of capital punishment has been envisaged for the last two centuries, the accelerating progress of the abolitionist movement traces its origins to the Universal Declaration of Human Rights of 10 December 1948.

The Council of Europe has been a pioneer in laying down the first binding legal instrument to outlaw capital punishment in peacetime. The Parliamentary Assembly and the Committee of Ministers have subsequently been able to exert political and other pressure to ensure that moratoria on executions have been put in place in countries that still keep the death sentence on their statute books. They have insisted that the states move towards abolition and ratification of Protocol No. 6 to the European Convention on Human Rights.

But the logical continuation of the tendency to restrict the application of the death penalty is total abolition. More recent political developments have facilitated our efforts in that direction. Indeed, on 3 May 2002, Protocol No. 13 to the European Convention on Human Rights, concerning the abolition of the death penalty in all circumstances, was opened for signature. It has now (February 2004) been signed by forty-two member states of the Council of Europe and has been ratified by twenty-two. This means that it will enter into force on 1 July 2003. (The full text of this protocol is reproduced in Appendix II.) By the end of the 1990s, international human rights law had significantly moved forward as far as abolition of the death penalty is concerned.

At the 2nd Summit of the Council of Europe (October 1997), the heads of states and governments reaffirmed their attachment to the fundamental principles of the Organisation: pluralist democracy, respect for human rights and the rule of law. They also called for the universal abolition of capital punishment and of the maintenance, in the meantime, of existing moratoria on executions in Europe.

The 102nd Session of the Committee of Ministers (May 1998) "stressed the conviction that priority should be given to obtaining and maintaining a moratorium on executions, to be consolidated as soon as possible by complete abolition of the death penalty". The Committee of Ministers also recognised the necessity of public awareness initiatives on the subject.

The international community has endowed itself with such legal instruments as the Second Optional Protocol to the International Covenant on Civil and Political Rights and Protocol No. 6 to the European Convention on Human Rights that outlaw capital punishment. But there has also been a progressive recognition that the use of capital punishment has no place in the overall human rights' scheme.

The abolition of capital punishment is at the top of the political agenda of organisations such as the Council of Europe to an extent that can be considered to be one of the major achievements of the international community since the 1993 United Nations World Conference on Human Rights, in Vienna.

Today, it is clear that a country seeking membership of the Council of Europe must subscribe to a firm commitment to put into effect an immediate moratorium on executions, to abolish capital punishment within a fixed time-scale, and to sign and ratify Protocol No. 6 – also within a specific time. The latter is required so as to provide an international guarantee against the re-introduction of capital punishment at the whim of whichever political tendency happens to prevail at a given point in time.

These conditions are now part of the core commitments which membership of our Organisation implies. They are relevant for old and new member states alike. Thus, a number of long standing member states that have abolished capital punishment have now also ratified Protocol No. 6 (for example Belgium and the United Kingdom). Several of the new member states, including Albania, Azerbaijan and Georgia, have already abolished capital punishment. Other countries that keep the death penalty on their statute books in one form or another, irrespective of whether or not death sentences continue to be handed down, will be expected to follow suit.

The Council of Europe's legal and political mechanisms have been put into effect to ensure that there is only one way ahead on this issue : forward. The process towards abolition within the Council of Europe is irreversible. This was emphasised again recently by the President of the Parliamentary Assembly and the Secretary General of the Council of Europe in a common statement made on 1 March 2003 on the occasion of the International Death Penalty Abolition Day.

From 1998 onward there has been an execution-free zone as far as the Council of Europe member states are concerned.

The Parliamentary Assembly of the Council of Europe has played a key role in securing the abolition of capital punishment. It is therefore most appropriate that a special article in this publication is devoted to the work of the Assembly that was at the origin of Protocol No. 6 in 1983. It has adopted successive proposals to outlaw the death penalty. More importantly, the Assembly has constantly brought pressure to bear on states in order to encourage abolition and, where necessary, insist on moratoria in individual countries.

It has done so not only in the framework of its examination of applicant countries but also by monitoring compliance of member states with commitments on joining the Organisation.

A view prevailing in the Assembly is that states with observer status with the Council of Europe should also adhere to the same principles, values and commitments as those which are required of member states. It is for this reason that the Assembly has turned its attention to the situation in Japan and the United States.[9]

---

9. See Resolution 1253 (2001) on the abolition of the death penalty in Council of Europe observer states, adopted by the Parliamentary Assembly of the Council of Europe on 25 June 2001 (17th Sitting) ; see also the Conference on Justice and Human Rights in Council of Europe observer states : the Abolition of the Death Penalty, organised by the Sub-Committee on Human Rights of the Parliamentary Assembly's Committee on Legal Affairs and Human Rights on 9 to 11 April 2003 in Springfield (Illinois) and Washington D.C.

The above demonstrates a convergence between the parliamentary and executive branches of the Council of Europe, which together have established a web of monitoring mechanisms to ensure that the abolitionist process is irreversible.

Generally speaking, the abolition of the death penalty is a natural and necessary step on the way towards full integration into European co-operation structures. It is not only the Council of Europe that requires prospective members to undertake the abolition of the death penalty. For its part, the European Union has made abolition a political precondition for membership. Indeed, the Charter of Fundamental Rights of the European Union provides in Article 2(2) that "No one shall be condemned to the death penalty, or executed". The Council of Europe and the European Union have agreed to work together to secure abolition.

The European approach to abolition is increasingly being echoed also at the global level. In March 1998, the United Nations Commission on Human Rights adopted a resolution, requesting states that still maintain the death penalty "to establish a moratorium on executions, with a view to completely abolishing the death penalty". This resolution was co-sponsored by many member states of the Council of Europe, including Lithuania, the Russian Federation and Ukraine and this text received positive votes of all Council of Europe member states represented on the United Nations Commission.

It is also significant that the statutes of the International Criminal Tribunals for the former Yugoslavia and for Rwanda, as well as those of the new International Criminal Court, do not provide for capital punishment among their range of sanctions. This is all the more remarkable considering the nature of the crimes that these tribunals are called upon to adjudicate.

For the Council of Europe, capital punishment is incompatible with accepted standards of human rights and dignity and has no place in a democratic society. Our objections are based on the fact that it is an arbitrary, discriminatory and irreversible sanction, and that the brutalisation of society that results from state institutions killing their citizens in the name of justice is a clear consequence of capital punishment.

The European and international communities have consolidated the position of abolition as one of the key human rights issues of the contemporary world and the abolitionist movement is expanding. But we continue to hear the old argument about public opinion against abolition.

The Council of Europe recognises that abolition of the death penalty may not be popular at a time when there is a perception in public opinion that crimes are committed on a scale and in forms unknown in recent history. All too often, the political elites in retentionist countries use such public opinion as an excuse for their own inaction concerning legal and penal reform. It cannot be denied that organised crime plays a very detrimental role, particularly in countries in transition, where the public at large suffers greatly both from direct and very violent crime and indirectly from the negative effects of widespread corruption which undermines confidence in democratic institutions. In these circumstances, popular opinion easily falls prey to populist messages of "getting tough" on criminals rather than accepting more sophisticated arguments such as the need to give proper thought to effective legal and social policies for the reduction of serious crime.

Many pro-death penalty opinions among the public are based on inaccurate information and/or false assumptions. This is why continuous attempts are being made to ensure public awareness of the negative aspects of the death penalty. This is also why the Council of Europe is offering assistance and support for governmental as well as non-governmental initiatives aimed at provoking public debate which allows the facts to be dissected rather than to advance simplistic emotional assumptions. In this way we seek to address common misconceptions about the death penalty. For example, the death penalty is still frequently seen as an effective measure to curb serious crime. The public should be made aware of the fact that all data and research on the subject show that abolition has no negative impact on crime rates. On the contrary, there is evidence to show that the re-introduction, or stepping up, of the death penalty has done nothing to curb serious crime. The so-called "deterrent" effect of the death penalty is a fallacy and should be presented as such.

It is often said that the death penalty is an important tool in the context of combating international organised crime. In fact the mere existence of the death penalty can constitute an obstacle to international co-operation. For example, countries that still impose the death penalty encounter serious problems when requesting the extradition of criminals from countries that have abolished the death penalty because the latter want guarantees that their prisoners would not be executed.

Another equally flawed pro-death penalty argument is its cost-effectiveness. It is claimed that recourse to the death penalty is less onerous than keeping criminals in jail. If the real issue is money one must consider the global prison situation. For example, before death sentences in the Russian Federation were commuted to life imprisonment, there were approximately 1 000 people on death row for which the total population of persons in prison or in other forms of incarceration was close to 1 million. Reference has also been made to the chronic problem of overcrowding in prisons and it is said that abolition of the death penalty would require the construction of new prisons.

However, if economics were the real issue, it would be more appropriate to look at the rate and duration of confinement of the vast number of persons detained for far less serious offences or who are awaiting trial. The introduction of a diversified sentencing policy – including alternatives to detention – as well as limited recourse to detention on remand, would certainly lead to much greater financial savings.

The death penalty is irreversible and the risk of judicial error can never be entirely ruled out. This is the reason why, in January 2003, George Ryan, then Governor of Illinois, commuted the death sentences of 156 prisoners to life imprisonment. Moreover, the representatives of the judiciary are particularly well placed to understand this risk. This is perhaps one reason why, increasingly, the judiciary has put a final stop to executions. In 1989, the Hungarian Constitutional Court ruled that the death penalty clashed with the human rights provisions of the constitution. In 1995, the Constitutional Court of South Africa, in one of its first judgments, declared the death penalty unconstitutional, thereby instantly saving the lives of 453 inmates on death row. Let us hope that these acts against the death penalty will be followed in other countries. The Human Rights Chamber for Bosnia and Herzegovina effectively barred an execution, ruling that the carrying out of a death sentence by a military court in Sarajevo in 1993 would violate Protocol No. 6 of the European Convention on Human Rights and thereby also breach Bosnia's obligations under the Dayton Peace Agreement.[10]

The courts in retentionist countries can play a potentially important role. They can set the tone by exercising self-restraint and by refraining from handing down capital sentences on the basis of existing Criminal Code provisions.

In our efforts to move towards full European abolition and taking Protocol No. 6 of the European Convention on Human Rights as the basis, it is extremely important to focus the debate on facts and on providing objective information. Indeed, there is a tendency among die-hard retentionists to dismiss arguments supporting abolition as emotional and even irrational. Rather than give in to cries for revenge – a death for a death – we must take one step back and work to make sure that, as the guilty are punished for their crimes, their punishment reflects the choices of a civilised, democratic society.

Our task is to make sure that abolition is part of a series of measures to develop a more humane penal system which will enable serious crime to be effectively tackled: to provide credible alternatives to the death

---

10. Decision of the Human Rights Chamber of Bosnia and Herzegovina (case of *Damjanovic v the Federation of Bosnia and Herzegovina*) of 5 September 1997, case No. CH/96/30.

penalty in a post-abolition context; to reduce the prison population and improve the material conditions of detention; to provide adequate assistance to victims of serious crime and to allow the rehabilitation of both victims and offenders.

The Council of Europe considers that there is no rationale behind, nor any justification for, the death penalty. It simply has no place in a society with a civilised penal system. No one has encapsulated this better than the Director General of Human Rights of the Council of Europe, Mr Pierre Henri Imbert, when he said:

> Revenge is kindred with our nature and our instincts but not with the law. The law cannot obey the same rules as human nature. Murder may come naturally to mankind, but the law is not made to imitate or reproduce nature. The law is crafted to correct nature.

Protocols Nos. 6 and 13 of the European Convention on Human Rights, the jurisprudence based on Protocol No. 6, and any future measure which the Council of Europe might take to ensure that the ban on capital punishment is respected, are all part of that law.

The case-law of the institutions of the European Convention on Human Rights

Caroline Ravaud
Former senior lawyer at the European Court of Human Rights

This article reviews the case-law of the Convention's organs with regard to the right to life, the prohibition on inflicting torture or inhuman or degrading treatment and abolition of the death penalty, specified in Protocol No. 6 to the European Convention on Human Rights.

The first paragraph of Article 2 of the Convention for the Protection of Human Rights and Fundamental Freedoms (the European Convention on Human Rights), which was signed in Rome on 4 November 1950 and entered into force on 3 September 1953 after having been ratified by ten states, provides:

> Everyone's right to life shall be protected by law. No one shall be deprived of his life intentionally save in the execution of a sentence of a court following his conviction of a crime for which this penalty is provided by law.

The second paragraph of Article 2 gives a restrictive list of cases where death is not considered to have been inflicted in violation of this article, because it results from the use of force rendered absolutely necessary either in order to defend a person from unlawful violence, or to effect a lawful arrest or to prevent the escape of a person lawfully detained, or, finally, to lawfully take action for the purpose of quelling a riot or insurrection.

This second paragraph does not primarily define instances where it would be permissible intentionally to kill someone, in contrast to the first paragraph; it merely describes situations where it is permitted to resort to force, which may result, as an unexpected outcome, in death. The use of force must be absolutely necessary for the achievement of one of the three purposes set out in paragraph 2 of Article 2, and therefore, when examining the cases brought before it, the European Court of Human Rights assesses the acts under consideration not only in themselves but also in the light of their planning and control.

The case-law established by the European Court of Human Rights as regards Article 2 of the Convention has mainly concerned cases involving possible exceptions to the right to life.[1]

The right to life and the ban on torture or inhuman or degrading treatment or punishment, contained in Article 3 of the Convention, are among the most fundamental rights which states must secure to everyone within their jurisdiction since, without respect for the right to life, enjoyment of all the other rights would be purely illusionary.

It should here be noted that the European Convention on Human Rights does not seek to protect individuals against other individuals' acts infringing their fundamental rights: no convention can prevent murder, incest, rape, armed robbery or any other act of violence perpetrated by one individual against another.[2]

The Convention merely aims to define and control the actions or measures which public authorities are permitted to take in breach of individuals' fundamental rights, for the good of society as a whole. From this standpoint, the Convention, like many international legal instruments, is a pledge of good conduct given by states that, at least in theory, have a monopoly on the lawful use of violence. The main difference from other international commitments to safeguard human rights entered into by the majority of states lies in the fact that the states of Europe have, subject to certain conditions, agreed to be bound by a mechanism for the judicial review of action or measures taken in breach of their obligations.

---

1. See, for example, the *McCann and others v. the United Kingdom* judgment of 27 September 1995, which concerned the killing by the British special forces of three alleged IRA terrorists suspected of preparing to carry out a car bomb attack in Gibraltar. The Court held (by 10 votes to 9) that there had been a violation of Article 2 on account of the authorities' negligence with regard to the organisation and control of the operation. For an opposite line of reasoning, see the *Andronicou and Constantinou v Cyprus* judgment of 9 October 1997, concerning action by special forces to release a young woman being held hostage by her partner, which led to the shooting of both young people. See also the Court's numerous judgments concerning the actions of Turkish security forces in south-east Turkey.

2. However, it should be noted that the Court's case-law has developed in recent years, placing an obligation on authorities to take practical measures to protect life, even when attacks against it come from a private individual: in this connection, see, for example, the judgment in *Osman v the United Kingdom* of 28 October 1998 (murder of a father by a teacher who had formed an obsessive attachment to his son) or, more recently, the judgments in *Keenan v the United Kingdom* of 3 April 2001 (suicide by a prisoner in custody) and *Calvelli and Giglio v Italy* of 17 January 2002 (death of a new-born baby in a private clinic as a result of medical negligence). All the judgments and decisions cited in this article may be consulted on the Court's web-site: www.echr.coe.int

Although, in the event of war or other public emergency threatening the life of the nation, Article 15 allows states to take measures derogating from their obligations under the Convention,[3] to the extent strictly required by the exigencies of the situation, no derogation with regard to the right to life is permitted, except in respect of deaths resulting from lawful acts of war. Nor is it possible to exclude the operation of the ban on torture, servitude or slavery, set out in Article 4, or the provisions of Article 7 prohibiting punishment without law (*nulla poena sine lege* – the principle that a person can be found guilty of an offence only recognised by law and that the penalty imposed must be prescribed by law).

The ban on taking measures derogating from Article 2 may, however, be undermined in respect of the death penalty, in that the requirement of a fair trial stipulated in Article 6 is not included on the list of hard-core guarantees. Would it be acceptable in time of war or other danger threatening the life of the nation for a court which was neither independent nor impartial, and which in no way respected the defendant's right to a fair hearing, to sentence someone to death? In our opinion, the answer must be no.[4] If such derogations were accepted, it would be of virtually no avail to protect the right to life, and this is what Article 15, paragraph 2, in fact seeks to avoid.

As we have seen, capital punishment, which is expressly provided for in Article 2 of the European Convention on Human Rights, is the only instance where intentional deprivation of life is permissible. Since this exception to the right to life is expressly provided for, there is only one judgment of the European Court of Human Rights on the imposition of the death penalty as such in a Council of Europe member state.

An application was lodged with the Court by Abdullah Öcalan, leader of the PKK, who was arrested in February 1999 and sentenced to death by the Turkish State Security Court in June 1999. In his application, Mr Öcalan claimed that the practice of the contracting states as a whole showed that the imposition (and/or execution) of the death penalty was interpreted

---

3. The Court has so far not been required to rule on the validity of derogations notified under Article 15 by the United Kingdom with regard to Northern Ireland (derogation withdrawn on 26 February 2001; however, another derogation to Article 5 was deposed by the United Kingdom on 18 December 2001 following the events of 11 September) and by Turkey with regard to the provinces of south-east Anatolia, where a state of emergency had been declared (derogation to Article 5, tabled in 1992 and withdrawn on 1 February 2002). It should be noted that, despite the situation in Chechnya since 1999, the Russian Federation has not tabled a derogation, and a state of emergency has never been officially proclaimed in this republic. Article 56 (2) of the 1993 Constitution states that a state of emergency may be imposed in the circumstances and under the procedures set out by the relevant constitutional law. In the absence of a majority in the State Duma over several years, this constitutional law was not promulgated until 2 February 2002.

4. See fn. 6, the Court's conclusions in the *Öcalan* judgment of 12 March 2003.

as a violation of the right to life guaranteed by Article 2 of the Convention. He also complained of a potential violation of Article 2 taken together with Article 14 (which forbids discrimination), in so far as his possible hanging would violate the government's consistent practice (since 1984) of no longer conducting executions.[5] In a chamber judgment of 12 March 2003,[6] the Court held that, with regard to the application of the death penalty, the allegations based on Articles 2, 3 and 14 should be rejected, since the death penalty had been abolished by Turkey and the applicant's death sentence had been commuted to life imprisonment.

With regard to the issue of whether the imposition of the death penalty was in itself likely to pose a problem in terms of Article 2 of the Convention, the Court preferred to examine the complaint from the perspective of Article 3, which forbids torture and inhuman and degrading treatment.

In the Court's view:

> To impose a death sentence on a person after an unfair trial is to subject that person wrongfully to the fear that he will be executed. The fear and uncertainty as to the future generated by a sentence of death, in circumstances where there exists a real possibility that the sentence will be enforced, must give rise to a significant degree of human anguish. Such anguish cannot be dissociated from the unfairness of the proceedings underlying the sentence which, given that human life is at stake, becomes unlawful under the Convention. Having regard to the rejection by the Contracting Parties of capital punishment, which is no longer seen as having any legitimate place in a democratic society, the imposition of a capital sentence in such circumstances must be considered, in itself, to amount to a form of inhuman treatment. (paragraph 207 of the judgment)

The Court drew attention to its conclusions regarding the applicant's complaints under Article 6 of the Convention: the applicant had not been tried by an independent and impartial tribunal, there had been a breach of the rights of the defence under Article 6, paragraph 1, taken together with paragraph 3(b) and (c), since he had not had access to a lawyer during police detention, he had been unable to communicate with his lawyers out of the hearing of officials, restrictions had been imposed on the number and length of his lawyers' visits to him, he was unable to consult the case-file until a late stage in the procedure, and his

---

5. See Application No. 46221/99, admissibility decision adopted by the Court (First Section) on 14 December 2000 following a hearing on 21 November 2000. It should be noted that the applicant submitted many other complaints concerning, *inter alia*, the conditions of his transfer from Kenya to Turkey, his detention conditions on the island of Imrali, the lack of a fair trial, etc.

6. This judgment is not final, since the case was transmitted to the Grand Chamber in July 2003 under Article 43 of the Convention.

lawyers did not have sufficient time to consult the file properly. The Court concluded that the death penalty had thus been imposed on the applicant following an unfair procedure which could not be considered compatible with the strict standards of fairness required in cases involving a capital sentence, and that imposition of the death sentence on the applicant following an unfair trial amounted to inhuman treatment in violation of Article 3.

Although a death sentence may be pronounced only in the instances provided by law, following a fair trial before an independent, impartial tribunal, as required under Article 6, it is still a homicide committed in cold blood for the greater public good. The fact that the death penalty might be considered morally right on the ground that crime must be punished or that society must be protected from those who break its rules does not make the slightest difference; nor does the never-ending debate on the value of capital punishment as a means of dissuasion.[7] To the best of our knowledge, no scientific study has so far provided the slightest element of proof that capital punishment in any way acts as a deterrent.

No judicial system can claim to be infallible, since justice is rendered by ordinary men and women who, even when acting in good faith, can make mistakes. This is why we cannot agree to "write off", for the sake of efficiency, the few innocent people who would be executed following miscarriages of justice. Life is priceless, and a society that takes the risk of killing an innocent person is not protecting itself, it is acting dishonourably.

Admittedly, the so-called civilised countries have long done away with the torments such as the wheel, quartering or the stake,[8] which used to be inflicted on offenders before they were put to death. Extracting confessions through torture is no longer used as a means of obtaining evidence of guilt, at least in law if not necessarily in fact, and there are

---

7. Article 2267 of the final version of the new catechism of the Roman Catholic Church, an 848-page document published in French on 13 October 1998 (see the issue of *Le Monde* of the same date), reads:
The Church's traditional teaching does not preclude capital punishment, where the offender's identity and liability have been fully ascertained and it is the only viable means of effectively safeguarding human life from undue assault. However, if non-violent means suffice to defend and protect individuals against assault, the authority should settle for such means... Nowadays, given the state's means of effectively punishing crime and rendering offenders incapable of doing further harm, without permanently depriving them of the possibility of repenting, instances where it is absolutely necessary to end an offender's life are rare, if not all but non-existent.
8. In contrast, there are regions of the world which still practise forms of torture, such as stoning for adultery imposed under Islamic law, which are considered in Europe as coming within the concept of inhuman and degrading treatment: on this subject, see the *Jabari v Turkey* judgment of 11 July 2000, regarding a decision by the Turkish authorities to expel a woman to Iran, where she risked stoning.

no more public executions. Similarly, developments in criminal law have increasingly limited the list of crimes punishable by the death penalty, and countries where it is still applicable reserve it for the most barbaric offences against the person. It was inevitable that this change in standards would raise the question of whether the death penalty itself should not simply be abolished, at least in peacetime.

Protocol No. 6 on abolition of the death penalty in peacetime

At European level, this will to abolish the death penalty led to the drafting of Protocol No. 6 to the Convention, which was opened for signature in April 1983 and came into force on 1 March 1985 after having been ratified by five states. This Protocol No. 6 was largely a result of the stubborn determination shown by Mr Christian Broda when he held office as Austria's Minister of Justice. In the preamble to the protocol, the signatory states noted that "the evolution that has occurred in several member states of the Council of Europe expresses a general tendency in favour of abolition of the death penalty".

Today, the death penalty is outlawed in practically every state on the European continent: of the Council of Europe's forty-five member states,[9] only the Russian Federation and Serbia and Montenegro have not yet ratified Protocol No. 6.[10] But the road towards this success has been long and difficult!

First ratifications

The first five states to ratify Protocol No. 6 in 1985, enabling it to come into force, were Austria, Denmark, Spain, Luxembourg and Sweden. There have been no executions in these countries since, respectively, 1967, 1950, 1975, 1949 and 1910 for Sweden.

France, which had abolished the death penalty in October 1981, did not ratify Protocol No. 6 until February 1986. A number of other countries, which had nonetheless long done away with the death penalty in their domestic law, were also slow to ratify the protocol: Switzerland, where use of the death penalty in peacetime had been abandoned as far back as 1942, ratified it only in October 1987; Portugal, where abolition had taken place in 1976, did so in October 1986. Belgium, which had signed the protocol as far back as 1983, ratified it only on 10 December 1998,

---

9. There are still two candidate countries for membership of the Council of Europe: Belarus, for which the application procedure has been frozen since 1998, and the Principality of Monaco, which abolished the death penalty in 1962 (the last execution dates back to 1847).

10. See the Council of Europe leaflet "Death is not justice" which provides country-by-country information on abolition of the death penalty.

although no civilian had been executed there since 1863, as a death sentence was automatically commuted to extended imprisonment through a royal pardon. Moreover, the death penalty had been abolished by a law of 10 July 1996.

Today, all forty-five Council of Europe member states have at least signed Protocol No. 6, the last signature to date being that of Turkey on 15 January 2003. Until 12 November 2003, when Protocol No. 6 was ratified, Turkey was the only state among the founder members of the Council of Europe not to have ratified the protocol, although it is de facto an abolitionist state. This can be seen not only from the fact that no one has been hanged in Turkey since 1984, but also from parliament's failure to confirm the enforcement of the approximately 300 death sentences passed since 1984.[11]

The Republic of Cyprus, which joined the Council of Europe in May 1961, ratified Protocol No. 6 only on 19 January 2000, although the death penalty had long been abolished in peacetime. Greece also ratified the protocol relatively recently, in September 1998.

The United Kingdom signed Protocol No. 6 in January 1999 and ratified it on 20 May 1999. Such delay is difficult to comprehend, given that the United Kingdom had not hanged anyone since the 1960s and, under an Act of 1965, the death penalty existed, until legislation in 1998, only for a limited number of crimes such as treason, piracy or committing adultery with the wife of the monarch's eldest son.

Ratifications by the new member states

Among the states which have become members of the Council of Europe since 1989, only the Russian Federation and Serbia and Montenegro have not yet ratified Protocol No. 6. Russia still maintains the death penalty on its statute book, although a de facto moratorium is applied, whereas Poland had already abolished capital punishment even before it ratified Protocol No. 6 on 30 October 2000.

Albania, which had applied a moratorium since June 1995 in view of its forthcoming membership of the Council of Europe, ratified the protocol on 21 September 2000. Bulgaria and Ukraine ratified Protocol No. 6 on 29 September 1999 and 4 April 2000 respectively. Georgia, which became the forty-first member state on 27 April 1999, ratified Protocol No. 6 on 13 April 2000.[12] "The former Yugoslav Republic of Macedonia"

---

11. As part of a constitutional revision in Turkey, the death penalty was abolished on 3 October 2001, except for terrorist crimes or criminal acts in wartime. A law of August 2002 abolished the exception for terrorist crimes, and all death sentences have been commuted to life imprisonment, including that of Abdullah Öcalan, leader of the PKK.
12. Georgia ratified the European Convention on Human Rights on 20 May 1999, almost immediately after its accession to the Council of Europe.

had ratified the Protocol on 10 April 1997; Moldova had done so on 12 September 1997 and Croatia on 5 November 1997. Estonia ratified the text on 17 April 1998, Latvia on 7 May 1999 and Lithuania on 8 July 1999.

To date, the most recent states to be admitted to the Council of Europe have been Armenia and Azerbaijan, in January 2001, followed by Bosnia and Herzegovina in April 2002 and Serbia and Montenegro in April 2003. For Armenia and Azerbaijan, whose membership applications had been examined respectively since March and July 1996, the Parliamentary Assembly issued[13] a favourable opinion. However, both Armenia and Azerbaijan undertook to ratify the Convention, and Protocol No. 6 in particular, within one year of their accession to the Council of Europe.

Armenia signed Protocol No. 6 on 25 January 2001 when it joined the Council, but had still not ratified it on 25 September 2002, in violation of the commitments made at the time of accession. Admittedly, Armenia is a de facto abolitionist country, since a moratorium on executions has been applied since 1991, but there is no moratorium on the imposition of the death sentence: consequently, the Armenian courts continue to pass death sentences, and there are currently about forty people sentenced to death in Armenia, whose sentences were recently commuted[14] to life imprisonment by President Kocharian, through a decree of 1 August 2003.

In its Resolution 1304 (2002) of September 2002, in which it evaluated the progress made since accession, the Assembly stated that it "cannot accept that Armenia has not honoured its commitment to ratify Protocol No. 6 to the European Convention on Human Rights, concerning the abolition of the death penalty, within a year of its accession".

The Assembly took note of the adoption, at first reading, of the new Criminal Code but declared itself shocked by the Armenian Parliament's decision to maintain the death penalty for people who have committed certain crimes, in violation of its commitment to abolish the death penalty within the year following its accession. Accordingly, it called on Armenia to amend its Criminal Code in this area.

The Criminal Code was indeed adopted at its second reading in December 2002, and finally at the third and final reading on 18 April 2003, when the death penalty was removed from the text of the Criminal Code. However, it should be noted that this was only a façade: the Armenian authorities actually used a legal subterfuge to maintain the death penalty in the country's criminal law.

---

13. See Parliamentary Assembly Docs. 8747 and 8748, reports by the Political Affairs Committee, dated 23 May 2000.
14. It would appear that almost half of those sentenced to death, some of whom have been in prison for almost ten years, are requesting immediate execution.

What happened was that, at the same time as it adopted the Criminal Code, the Armenian Parliament adopted a law on implementation of this Code. Article 3 (4) of this law stated that:

> the provisions of this Criminal Code with regard to the death penalty shall not apply to persons having committed, prior to the entry into force of the present Code, murder with aggravating circumstances, a terrorist act or the rape of an under-age girl.

It is evident that this provision was in total contradiction to the position of the Council of Europe and its Parliamentary Assembly, since it was equivalent to stating that, to date, Armenia continued not to honour its commitment to abolish capital punishment from its Criminal Code.

Through this law on implementation of the Criminal Code, Armenian courts will continue to have the option of imposing death sentences in certain cases. In particular, this concerns the perpetrators of the slaughter of October 1999, whose trial is still taking place. It will be recalled that five armed men invaded the parliamentary chamber on 27 October 1999 and shot on sight, killing eight prominent figures, including the Prime Minister and Speaker of Parliament, and wounding four others. This tragedy had a profound effect on the population, and continues to influence public opinion. It is mentioned by the Armenian authorities, especially parliamentarians, as the main obstacle to immediate abolition of the death penalty, since the public would not understand and would be opposed to abolition.

This was why, despite the pressure exerted by the Parliamentary Assembly, it was necessary to wait until after presidential elections in February 2003, and parliamentary elections in May 2003, before the Armenian Parliament would finally agree to consider this question seriously. This finally occurred on 29 September 2003, the date on which the Armenian Parliament ratified Protocol No. 6. The instrument of ratification was deposited with the Council of Europe on 29 September. This is an extremely positive development, even if the law on implementation of the Criminal Code has not yet been modified accordingly.

Azerbaijan, which had applied a moratorium since 1993, abolished the death penalty on 10 February 1998 and commuted the sentences of the 128 convicted prisoners who were awaiting execution. The European Convention on Human Rights and Protocol No. 6 were ratified on 15 April 2002.

The situation in Bosnia and Herzegovina, which became the forty-fourth member state of the Council of Europe in April 2002, is rather unusual. The 1995 Dayton Peace Agreement, which ended the war, imposed a new constitution on Bosnia and Herzegovina, a new state made up of two entities, the Federation of Bosnia and Herzegovina, and the

Republika Srpska, and integrated the Convention, including Protocol No. 6, into the domestic legal system.

Consequently, Protocol No. 6 was used as a source of law by a state that was not yet a member of the Council of Europe, and was therefore not a party to the Convention. The 1995 Dayton Peace Agreement also provided, in Appendix 6, for the establishment of a Commission on Human Rights, made up of an Ombudsman and a Human Rights Chamber for Bosnia and Herzegovina. Both the Ombudsman and the Human Rights Chamber would consider "alleged or apparent violations of human rights as provided in the European Convention for the Protection of Human Rights and Fundamental Freedoms and the Protocols thereto".[15]

As an example, the Human Rights Chamber for Bosnia and Herzegovina, which is based in Sarajevo, consequently declared admissible, in April 1997, an application submitted against the federation by a person sentenced to death in 1993 by a military court for the murder of three people, who had alleged a violation of Protocol No. 6 and Article 3 of the Convention.[16]

Bosnia and Herzegovina subsequently signed Protocol No. 6, on 24 April 2002 when it joined the Council of Europe, and ratified it on 12 July 2002.

Finally, Serbia and Montenegro, which became the Council of Europe's forty-fifth member state on 3 April 2003, signed Protocol No. 6 on accession; however, it has not yet been ratified.[17] Following the assassination of Prime Minister Zoran Djindjic on 12 March 2003, there was even talk of re-introducing the death penalty, and the Council of Europe's intervention was necessary before this plan was abandoned.

Abolition of the death penalty: an essential condition for becoming or remaining a member of the Council of Europe?

The general tendency towards abolition of the death penalty in Europe – whether de facto or de jure – has led the Parliamentary Assembly of the Council of Europe to require[18] states wishing to join the Organisation

---

15. See Article II, paragraph 2 of Appendix 6 to the Dayton Agreements.

16. See Application No. CH/96/30, *Damjanovic v the Federation of Bosnia and Herzegovina*, decision of 11 April 1997. Subsequently, in July 1997, the Chamber ruled that the application of the death penalty would be contrary to Protocol No. 6.

17. However, it should be noted that the Federal Republic of Serbia and Montenegro, where the Criminal Code still includes the death penalty for murder with aggravating circumstances, ratified the Second Optional Protocol to the International Covenant on Civil and Political Rights concerning abolition of the death penalty, in September 2001.

18. See Resolution 1044 (1994): an undertaking on the part of countries seeking membership to abolish the death penalty, ratify Protocol No. 6 and introduce a moratorium pending abolition became a prerequisite for admission as a Council of Europe member state.

to give a firm, solemn undertaking that they will apply a moratorium on executions until the death penalty is abolished in their states, which should take place within a variable time frame, usually three years.[19]

Ukraine, which became a member of the Council of Europe on 9 November 1995, was threatened with sanctions by the Assembly for failing to observe the moratorium: although executions were covered by official secrets legislation and there were therefore no reliable statistics or information on the number of executions, it would seem that a total of thirteen executions were performed as late as 1997.[20] Ratification of Protocol No. 6 finally took place on 4 April 2000, that is, with a delay of almost a year and a half, after the Ukrainian Constitutional Court had declared capital punishment to be unconstitutional in a judgment of 29 December 1999 and the parliament had abolished it on 22 February 2000.

The Russian Federation, a member of the Council of Europe since 28 February 1996, also undertook to abolish the death penalty within three years of accession and to ratify Protocol No. 6. The moratorium introduced on 2 August 1996 by President Yeltsin had admittedly been observed[21] and Russia signed Protocol No. 6 on 16 April 1997. To date, however, it has not yet ratified the protocol, a fact that the Assembly did not fail to criticise in its most recent report on the honouring of commitments and obligations by the Russian Federation.[22] The two co-rapporteurs have also expressed their shock at the vote held on 15 February 2002 in the State Duma, calling on President Putin to reinstate the death penalty.[23]

According to information released by the Ministry of Justice in October 1998, Russia has about 839 prisoners who have been sentenced to death. Since August 1996, there have been no further executions (with the exception

---

19. The Parliamentary Assembly had given Ukraine a 3-year deadline to ratify Protocol No. 6: see the Assembly's Opinion No. 190 (1995), paragraph 12.ii. on Ukraine's request for membership. The country's failure to meet the deadline was the subject of much criticism by the Parliamentary Assembly. On the other hand, in its Opinion No. 209 (1999) on Georgia's request for membership, presented on 14 July 1996, the Assembly set a deadline of only one year; however, the death penalty had been abolished in Georgia since autumn 1997, following the introduction of a moratorium in February 1995.
20. The last capital execution in Ukraine took place in March 1997.
21. Although the Assembly regretted four executions in 1997 in Chechnya (statement to the press on 17 November 1997 by Ms Renate Wohlwend, Rapporteur on the death penalty).
22. See the report by the Parliamentary Assembly' Monitoring Committee, dated 26 March 2002 (co-rapporteurs Mr Atkinson and Mr Bindig), Doc. 9396.
23. In this area, the Duma is subject to constant pressure from public opinion: according to surveys, 80% of the population is allegedly in favour of the death penalty. This was also the case in France, and proposals have repeatedly been tabled with the National Assembly calling for re-introduction of the death penalty, especially after particularly odious crimes against children or members of the police force.

of four in Chechnya in 1997). However, in a ruling of 2 February 1999, the Constitutional Court of the Russian Federation prohibited the imposition of the death penalty in cases not heard by a jury. The trial-by-jury system has so far been introduced in only nine of the Russian Federation's eighty-nine regions. For Amnesty International, this decision by the Constitutional Court amounted to a de facto abolition of the death penalty. In addition, the President has since 1999 systematically commuted death sentences to life imprisonment, on recommendations from the Pardons Commission.[24]

The Assembly's firm stance, albeit praiseworthy, can be justified only on the ground that it serves as a reminder to the states concerned of the importance of honouring their commitments: the Russian Federation and Ukraine both gave their word that they would apply a moratorium on executions and abolish the death penalty as soon as possible. The question whether, given the state of development of these countries which are making the transition to democracy and encountering huge economic and social problems, it was not premature and unrealistic to require them to abide by a rule which many other European countries had taken decades to adopt in domestic and European law, was apparently not raised, doubtless so as not to fuel criticism that these countries were being granted preferential treatment.

With what is, after all, a fairly abolitionist tendency in modern-day Europe, what contribution can the institutions of the European Convention on Human Rights make? Is there still scope for them to take a position on capital punishment?

Protocol No. 6 is worded in absolute terms, since Article 1 quite bluntly states "the death penalty shall be abolished" and continues "no one shall be condemned to such penalty or executed".

Article 2 then goes on to provide that this absolute ban on capital punishment shall not prevent states from making provision in their law for the death penalty to apply in respect of acts committed in time of war or of imminent threat of war.

It quite logically follows that a state which has, necessarily, already abolished the death penalty in its domestic law merely makes that abolition official by ratifying the protocol to the Convention. It also follows that, at least in respect of all acts previously punishable by death in time of peace, the Strasbourg institutions should no longer be asked to deal with applications alleging a violation of this protocol. As soon as it ratifies this instrument, a state commits itself not only to halt all executions, but also

---

24. However, it should be noted that the federal Pardons Commission was abolished in 2001 and replaced by regional committees.

no longer to sentence anyone to death. Indeed, in these circumstances handing down a death sentence would inevitably also constitute a breach of Article 7 of the Convention.[25]

Finally, it is worth pointing out that ratification of an international commitment such as Protocol No. 6 makes it more difficult for those national parliaments that may have vague tendencies in this direction to re-introduce the death penalty. When particularly odious crimes are committed, for example against children, it is common to hear certain parliaments demand reinstatement of the death penalty. However, any such re-introduction would, as a first step, require denunciation of Protocol No. 6, and especially of the Convention itself, of which it is an integral part.[26] Under the terms of Article 58 of the Convention as amended, this document may be denounced only after the expiry of five years from the date of its entry into force in the country concerned, and after six month's notice. Any undue haste is thus ruled out, not to mention the disastrous effect on public opinion of denunciation of the Convention.

Pressure applied to states having observer status with the Council of Europe

Under the terms of Resolution (93) 26 on observer status, any state wishing to acquire this status with the Council of Europe must be willing to accept the principles of democracy,[27] the rule of law and the enjoyment of all persons within its jurisdiction of human rights and fundamental freedoms. The Holy See has had observer status since 1970; Japan, the United States of America and Canada have had observer status with the Council of Europe since 1996 and Mexico since 1999.

On 25 June 2001, the Parliamentary Assembly adopted Resolution 1253 (2001), in which it noted that both Japan[28] and the United States[29] keep

---

25. Article 7 concerns the principle *nulla poena sine lege.*

26. See Article 7 of Protocol No. 6.

27. One might ask whether the Holy See, which has had observer status since 1970, fulfils this condition as it is usually understood (separation of powers, free elections, etc.); however, the Holy See has a very specific statute.

28. Japan applies the death penalty for murder with aggravating circumstances, and several hundred prisoners are awaiting execution. Since 1993, three to five people have been executed per year.

29. In the United States, thirty-eight out of fifty states currently have legislation allowing for the death penalty, which is also provided for in federal civil and military legislation, and there are more than 3 700 individuals awaiting execution. However, a moratorium has been imposed in certain states, such as Illinois in January 2000, especially following the revelation of several miscarriages of justice.

the death penalty on the statute books and carry out executions.[30] Viewing the application of the death penalty as a violation of the most fundamental human rights, such as the right to life and the right to protection against torture and inhuman and degrading treatment, the Assembly took the view that these two states were in breach of their obligations as observers, and required that they institute without delay a moratorium on executions and take the necessary steps to abolish the death penalty. It also required that they improve immediately the conditions on death row. Finally, it decided to call into question their observer status with the Organisation as a whole should no significant progress in the implementation of this resolution be made by 1 January 2003.

It is evident that such a call, by a political body such as the Council of Europe's Parliamentary Assembly, composed of parliamentarians from national parliaments in all the member states, is likely to bear fruit only if accompanied by a campaign to persuade and explain. Consequently, the Assembly has undertaken to encourage dialogue with parliamentarians from Japan and the United States (both at federal and state level) in all its forms, in order to support legislators in their efforts to institute a moratorium and abolish the death penalty, and to open a well-informed debate with the opponents of abolition. Such a debate is all the more necessary in that abolition of the death penalty is viewed in Europe as a sign of civilisation: the fundamental difference in values in this area between, on the one hand, the Council of Europe's member states and, on the other, Japan and the United States is the source of a gulf that is not merely cultural, and which is likely to lead to a mutual lack of understanding that could be detrimental to international relations.

By 1 September 2003, little progress had been made.[31] The Assembly has succeeded in establishing a dialogue with Japanese parliamentarians. In May 2002, the Assembly's Committee on Legal Affairs and Human Rights held a conference for this purpose in Tokyo, on Justice and Human Rights in Countries with Observer Status to the Council of Europe, which brought the abolition debate to the highest echelons of Japanese political circles. Unfortunately, while the dialogue with the Japanese parliamentarians has been fruitful and consistent, Japan has not yet abolished the death penalty and has carried out four executions

---

30. Canada abolished the death penalty for crimes committed in peacetime in 1976, and for those committed in wartime in 1998. Mexico is also an abolitionist state in peacetime, and there have been no executions since 1937. These two states will extradite individuals to the United States only when assurances have been given that they will not be sentenced to death.

31. See Parliamentary Assembly Resolution 1349 (2003), dated 1 October 2003 (Report by Mrs Wohlwend, Doc. 9908).

since June 2001. A draft law on abolition, which has nonetheless received increasing support, has not yet obtained the number of votes necessary for its adoption.

The situation is even more worrying in the United States, since the Assembly has on the whole failed in its attempt to promote a transatlantic dialogue at parliamentary level. A conference on Justice and Human Rights in the Countries with Observer Status with the Council of Europe, held in Springfield (Illinois) and Washington DC from 9 to 11 April 2003 by the Assembly's Committee on Legal Affairs and Human Rights, drew a few parliamentarians from the State of Illinois to the Springfield event, but failed to attract any senators or members of congress in Washington.

The number of abolitionist states, thirteen in all, remains low, while Illinois is still the only state to apply a moratorium on executions. Since June 2001, 137 executions have taken place in seventeen American states, including at federal level, which brings their total in the United States since the resumption of executions in 1977 to 858 (at 30 June 2003). Texas has the only legal system in the world known to have executed juvenile criminals in 2002 : three black juvenile criminals were put to death, namely Napoleon Beazley, T. J. Jones and Toronto Patterson. Oklahoma acted in a similar manner on 3 April 2003, when it executed Scott Hain for a crime committed when he was 17 years old. About eighty juvenile criminals are still on death row in the United States. The execution of juvenile criminals is not only a particularly odious practice ; it is also a clear violation of international law.

Since 1993, nineteen foreign citizens have been executed in the United States, and none of them were informed of their right to communicate with their consular representatives, in breach of international law ; more than 100 foreign citizens are on death row. Mexico, an observer state with the Council of Europe, asked in January 2003 for a ruling from the International Court of Justice to suspend the execution of more than fifty Mexican citizens, until such time as United States judges have ruled on their cases. In October 2002, the Inter-American Commission on Human Rights concluded, in the case of *Michael Domingues v the United States*, that the United States :

> has failed to respect the life, liberty and security of the person of Michael Domingues by sentencing him to death for crimes that he committed when he was 16 years of age, contrary to Article I of the American Declaration [...] and that the United States will be responsible for a further grave and irreparable violation of Mr. Domingues' right to life under Article I of the American Declaration if he is executed for crimes that he committed when he was 16 years of age.

Nonetheless, there have been positive signs since the re-introduction of the death penalty in the United States in 1977 : 108 prisoners who had been sentenced to death have been cleared in the country as a whole because their innocence has been proved, especially through the increasingly frequent use of DNA tests. It should also be noted that the US Supreme Court, in its judgment in *Atkins v Virginia* of 20 June 2002, prohibited the execution of mentally handicapped individuals, which is an important step forward.

In addition, on 11 January 2003, the outgoing Governor of Illinois, George Ryan, emptied death row in his state by commuting the sentences of 167 prisoners.[32] He stated: "Our capital system is haunted by the demon of error – error in determining guilt, and error in determining who among the guilty deserves to die". Governor Ryan had already suspended all executions in his state three years earlier, when the courts found that thirteen prisoners on death row in Illinois had been falsely convicted since the re-introduction of the death penalty in 1977, a period in which twelve other prisoners had been executed.

Abolition of the death penalty in all circumstances, including wartime: Protocol No. 13 to the Convention

Since 1994, the Assembly has also been calling for abolition of the death penalty in wartime,[33] but the Committee of Ministers considered at that time that the political priority was first of all to obtain and ensure observance of a moratorium on executions, which could subsequently be consolidated by the complete abolition of capital punishment. It was only on the occasion of the European Ministerial Conference on Human Rights, held in Rome in November 2000 to mark the 50th anniversary of the signing of the European Convention on Human Rights, that the ministers came out clearly in favour of abolition of the death penalty in time of war or of imminent threat of war.

In December 2000, the Swedish Government submitted a proposal for a draft additional protocol to the Convention, which was then studied by a committee of experts responsible for drawing up a draft protocol and an explanatory memorandum. This committee of experts completed its work in November 2001, and the draft protocol was then forwarded to the Parliamentary Assembly for opinion.[34]

---

32. In Maryland, Governor Parris Glendening announced that all executions in his state were to be suspended from 9 May 2002, pending publication and examination by the General Assembly of a study on racial discrimination. However, he failed to follow the example of Governor Ryan by commuting all death sentences, and his successor, Governor Ehrlich, lifted the moratorium in January 2003, a few days after taking office, when the study was published. In March 2003, a draft law on an "emergency moratorium" failed in the Senate by 23 votes to 24.
33. See Resolution 1246 (1994).
34. See the Report by the Committee on Legal Affairs and Human Rights, dated 15 January 2002 (rapporteur: Ms Wohlwend), Doc. 9316.

Protocol No. 13, as it is entitled, was opened for signature at the 110th session of the Committee of Ministers of the Council of Europe, held in Vilnius on 3 May 2002. It was signed by thirty-six states on that date, and ratified forthwith by three of them: Malta, Ireland and Switzerland. Protocol No. 13 entered into force after ten ratifications,[35] on 1 July 2003.

The states which have not yet signed (as of 1 February 2004) are Armenia, Azerbaijan, and the Russian Federation. It should be noted that, under Article 18 of the Vienna Convention on the Law of Treaties, of 23 May 1969, the very fact of signing a treaty obliges signatories "to refrain from acts which would defeat the object and purpose of a treaty".

Bulgaria, the Slovak Republic, Croatia and Azerbaijan are completely abolitionist states; that is, they have already abolished the death penalty for all crimes, both in peacetime and in time of war,[36] logically, ratification of the protocol should not pose any problems for them. Admittedly, Albania ratified Protocol No. 6 in October 2000, but it would appear that the legislation has still to be amended with regard to the death penalty in wartime.

At the time of writing (February 2004), the following states have still to ratify Protocol No. 13: Albania, Armenia, Azerbaijan, Czech Republic, Estonia, Finland, France, Germany, Greece, Iceland, Italy, Latvia, Luxembourg, Moldova, Netherlands, Norway, Poland, Serbia and Montenegro, the Slovak Republic, Spain, "the former Yugoslav Republic of Macedonia" and Turkey.

Article 3 of the Convention and extradition to a state which practises the death penalty

The right not to be expelled or extradited is not included per se among the fundamental rights recognised by the Convention. In fact, extradition and expulsion are mentioned only in Article 5 of the Convention, which specifically concerns deprivation of freedom pending extradition or expulsion.

The case-law of the Strasbourg institutions (that is to say the European Commission of Human Rights and the former European Court of Human Rights, which were operational until 1 November 1998, when they were replaced by a new single, permanent Court) has mainly come into being through active interpretation of the guarantees afforded by Article 3 of the Convention.

---

35. In total, seventeen states had ratified by 1 September 2003.
36. Abolition of the death penalty in the Slovak Republic in 1990; on 10 December 1998 in Bulgaria; and, under the constitution of the former Yugoslavia, in 1990 for Croatia. Protocol No. 6 entered into force in 1993 in the Slovak Republic, on 1 October 1999 in Bulgaria and on 1 December 1997 in Croatia.

Well before Protocol No. 6 was drafted and came into force, the question arose whether the death penalty, provided for in Article 2 of the Convention, might be regarded as "inhuman or degrading treatment or punishment" within the meaning of Article 3. No application ever questioned the method of execution used in capital punishment in those countries where capital punishment still existed (such as the garrotte in Spain or the guillotine in France) but the Commission had to deal with applications alleging a breach of Article 3 in the event of the applicants' expulsion or extradition to a third country, where they were liable to be executed on arrival, or to be subjected to torture or to inhuman or degrading treatment.

It took the view that, in exceptional circumstances, a problem might be posed under Article 3 of the Convention if the intention was to extradite a person to a country where "due to the very nature of the regime of that country or to a particular situation in that country, basic human rights … might be either grossly violated or entirely suppressed".[37] This approach was based on the reasoning that under Article 1 the member states undertook to secure the rights and freedoms guaranteed by the Convention to "everyone within their jurisdiction", which also applied to persons whom a state planned to extradite, deport or turn back, with the result that the protection afforded by Article 3 of the Convention extended to the obligation not to place such a person in an irremediable situation of objective danger, even outside a state's jurisdiction.[38]

This dynamic interpretation is very important, and it is no exaggeration to speak of the Convention's extra-territorial impact. Admittedly, it applies only to those states which have ratified it, but obliging the latter to observe it in their dealings with third party states is a major achievement.

One of the most sensitive cases examined by the Commission in the 1970s was that of *Amekrane v the United Kingdom* (Application No. 5961/72). This application was lodged by the widow and children of a Moroccan officer who, after a failed attempt at a coup in his country, had sought refuge in Gibraltar and whom the United Kingdom authorities had handed over to the Moroccan authorities the very next day. The officer was subsequently tried by a Moroccan court martial for his role in the attempted seizure of power, found guilty and shot. In 1974 a friendly settlement was reached, whereby the United Kingdom Government agreed to pay the widow and children a sum of £35 000 (approximately €51 000) as compensation.

---

37. See Application No. 1802/62, *X. v FRG,* Yearbook 6, pp. 463-481.
38. See, for an extradition to Turkey, which at the time had not yet recognised the right of individual appeal provided for in former Article 25 of the Convention, Application No. 10308/83, *Altun v FRG,* Decision of 3 May 1983, D.R. 36, p. 209.

This instance of extra-territorial application of the Convention was all the more unusual in that the Convention does not guarantee foreigners any right, as such, not to be extradited or expelled, and such an approach amounts to holding a state bound by the Convention liable for the fate inflicted on an individual by a state not party thereto. The state that expels or extradites the individual will be exculpated only if it can show that it obtained full assurances from the country of destination that no treatment contrary to Article 3 would actually be meted out.

Most of the cases examined by the Court have concerned allegations of a risk of torture or inhuman or degrading treatment in the country to which an individual was to be removed.[39] There are only a few cases which challenge extradition procedures.

Extradition to the United States of America

The best-known case brought before the European Court of Human Rights in the field of extradition is that of *Soering v the United Kingdom*.[40] Jens Soering, a German national who at the material time was 18 years old, was arrested in the United Kingdom in April 1986, along with his girlfriend, in connection with a routine case of cheque fraud. In August of the same year, the United States requested the couple's extradition under the terms of the extradition treaty of 1972 between the two countries. Mr Sœring was to face trial in the State of Virginia on charges of having murdered his girlfriend's parents (who were against their relationship) by repeated stabbing, a crime committed in March 1985, allegedly while the couple were prey to a *folie à deux*.

If he had been found guilty of capital murder after having been extradited, he would have been liable to be sentenced to death by electrocution, the punishment for that class of offence in Virginia, which had resumed executions in 1977 following a moratorium of several years.

In view of the wording of Article 2 of the Convention, it was not possible to contend that the death penalty per se breached Article 3.[41] The European Court of Human Rights therefore confirmed that the extradition of a person to a state where that person risked the death penalty did not in itself raise an issue under either Article 2 or Article 3, despite evolving standards in western Europe regarding the existence and use of capital punishment.

---

39. See, for example, the judgments for *Cruz Varas* (deportation to Chile, no violation), *Paez* (deportation to Peru, struck out following repeal of the measure), both *v Sweden*, and *Chahal v the United Kingdom* (deportation of a Sikh to India, violation). More recently, see also the judgment *K.K.C. v the Netherlands*, of 21 December 2001, concerning the deportation to Russia of a Chechen deserter.
40. Judgment of 7 July 1989, Series A No. 161.
41. Contrary to what the Parliamentary Assembly had stated, for example in Resolution 1187 (1999) and Resolution 1253 (2001).

The Court pointed out that, although de facto the death penalty no longer existed in the contracting states, they had chosen to amend the Convention by preparing a specific protocol on abolition, and it was therefore not possible to interpret Article 3 as generally prohibiting the death penalty as inhuman or degrading treatment.[42]

However, in the case under consideration, the applicant did not complain of a breach of Article 3 by reason of the almost certain imposition of the death penalty, but did so on the ground that, in his contention, his exposure to the "death row phenomenon" would result in inhuman and degrading treatment. Under US law, it is possible to lodge a number of appeals against enforcement of a death sentence, which may therefore be deferred several times. In paragraph 56 of its judgment, the Court noted that the average time between trial and execution in Virginia, calculated on the basis of the seven executions which had taken place since 1977, was six to eight years, and that the delays were primarily due to a strategy by convicted prisoners to prolong the appeal proceedings as much as possible.

The Court recalled that ill-treatment, including punishment, must attain a minimum level of severity to fall within the scope of Article 3, and that the assessment of this minimum was, in the nature of things, relative since it depended on all the circumstances of the case, such as the nature and context of the treatment or punishment, the manner and method of its execution, its duration, its physical or mental effects and, in some instances, the sex, age and state of health of the person concerned.

In Mr Soering's case the Court held that, despite the procedural guarantees offered to him in the United States, having regard to the very long period of time spent on death row, with the ever present and mounting anguish of awaiting execution of the death penalty, and to the personal circumstances of the applicant, especially his age and mental state at the time of the offence, his extradition to the United States would expose him to a real risk of treatment going beyond the threshold set by Article 3.

It should be noted that, since the United Kingdom had not ratified Protocol No. 6, the question whether extradition or deportation to a country applying the death penalty would, as with Article 3, render the extraditing or deporting state liable for having breached the protocol did not arise in the *Soering* proceedings.[43]

---

42. However, see on this subject the *Öcalan* judgment of 12 March 2003, cited above, and the consideration given by the Court to the question of the legal scope of contracting states' practice with regard to the death penalty in paragraphs 189 to 198 of this judgment.

43. The new Court, in place since 1 November 1998, has had only two opportunities to examine this issue : first in the case of *Aspichi Dehwari v the Netherlands,* in which the applicant alleged a violation of Protocol No. 6 (ratified by the Netherlands) in the event of deportation to Iran. However, the case was resolved by a friendly settlement, noted in a judgment of 27 April 2000. The question was also raised in the case of *Yang Chun Jin v Hungary,* concerning an extradition to China, which concluded with a striking out on 8 March 2001.

On the other hand, the Commission considered this issue in another case concerning extradition to the United States, brought against France, which had ratified the protocol.[44] After examining the firm assurances obtained by the French Government not only from the federal authorities, but also, and above all, from the prosecuting authorities of the State of Texas, who had promised not to seek the death penalty in the murder proceedings brought against the applicant, the Commission was of the opinion that those assurances were such as to eliminate the danger of the applicant's being sentenced to death and that extradition should therefore not expose her to a serious risk of treatment or punishment contrary to Article 3 or to Article 1 of Protocol No. 6.

From this point of view, the *Aylor-Davis* case differed considerably from the *Soering* case, where the United Kingdom Government had been able to obtain from the Virginia prosecuting authority only an undertaking to make a representation to the judge at the time of sentencing that it was the wish of the United Kingdom that the death penalty should not be imposed or carried out, an undertaking which the Court deemed insufficient to eliminate all risk of execution of the death penalty.

It cannot therefore be inferred that any measure extraditing someone to the United States would pose a problem under the Convention, whether owing to the existence of the "death row phenomenon" or because the country retains the death penalty. A cynic might even interpret the *Soering* judgment as meaning that provided a person condemned to death is executed promptly no problem is posed in respect of the Convention.

However, case-law evolves rapidly. The new Court has had occasion to rule on two recent cases of extradition from France to the United States: these were the *Nivette* and *Einhorn* cases, which were declared inadmissible by decisions dated respectively 3 July 2001 and 16 October 2001.[45] In the *Nivette* case, which concerned the extradition of an American citizen sought in the State of California for murder, the French court responsible for ruling on whether or not the extradition could take place had obtained an irrevocable undertaking from the Sacramento General Prosecutor not to call for the death penalty. The applicant then lodged an application with the Court, alleging that the risk of being sentenced to an incompressible life sentence was in breach of Article 3 of the Convention; in this instance, the application was clearly unfounded, since the undertaking by the Sacramento General Prosecutor also covered the hypothesis of imposition of a life sentence and the question of

---

44. Application No. 22742/93, *Joy Aylor-Davis v France*, Decision of 20 January 1994, D.R. 76-A, p. 164.
45. Application No. 44190/98, *Nivette v France* and No. 71555/01, *Einhorn v France*.

eligibility for release on parole. It can be inferred from this decision that the Court does not rule out that condemnation to an incompressible life sentence may pose a problem[46] from the standpoint of Article 3.

The *Einhorn* case is even more interesting : Ira Einhorn had been sentenced *in absentia* to life imprisonment in 1993 for the murder of his girlfriend, whose body had been discovered in 1979 in Pennsylvania, an American state which re-introduced the death penalty in 1978. The applicant had taken refuge in France, where he was arrested in 1997. The French authorities initially refused to extradite him on the grounds that the applicable legislation in Pennsylvania did not provide for re-opening of the case, and that it was contrary to French public policy to extradite a person who had been unable to benefit from the guarantees of a fair trial, in accordance with Article 6 of the Convention.

In January 1998, the relevant legislation was amended in Pennsylvania with retroactive effect in order to allow the re-opening of the trial, and the US Government accordingly repeated its request for extradition, undertaking at the same time not to call for the death penalty. The applicant, who had in the meantime attempted suicide, was eventually extradited on 19 July 2001, after the French Government had produced a medical certificate indicating that the applicant's state of health was compatible with transfer to the United States. From the perspective of Article 3, the application was found to be clearly ill-founded, for the same reasons as in the *Nivette* case : the Court considered that the guarantees provided by the US authorities concerning non-imposition of the death penalty and the possibility of parole in the event of a life sentence were sufficient.

In this case, the applicant also invoked a series of complaints under Article 6 of the Convention, alleging in particular that he would not receive a fair trial in the United States, especially as the 1998 law had been specially adopted to ensure his extradition, an unprecedented event. The Court held that it could not rule out the possibility of a problem arising under Article 6 of the Convention in the event of a flagrant miscarriage of justice in the country to which a person is expelled or extradited. However, it was for the applicant to prove that there were well-founded reasons to believe that he would not receive a fair trial. In this particular case, the Court considered that such evidence had not been submitted and rejected the application with regard to this point as well.

---

46. The question was also raised in the *Einhorn* case, and the Court referred to the ongoing work of the European Committee on Criminal Problems and to Committee of Ministers Resolution (1976) 2 on the treatment of long-term prisoners.

The *Einhorn* judgment is important, particularly in the context of the procedures for judicial co-operation in criminal matters between the United States and Europe following the attacks of 11 September 2001. Indeed, one might ask whether the Court would consider the procedures envisaged by the US authorities to judge the terrorists responsible for these attacks as a flagrant miscarriage of justice (special courts, restrictions on the rights of the defence, etc.).

Extradition to other states

Between 1998 and 2003, the only two other decisions handed down in the area of extradition were, first, the *Yang Chun Jin v Hungary* judgment[47] and, secondly, an inadmissibility decision in the case of *Ismaili*[48] *v Germany*. The *Yang Chun Jin* case concerned an extradition to China, and gave rise to a decision to strike out the case, as the applicant had eventually received permission to leave Hungary for Sierra Leone, whose nationality he also held. This case is interesting in that the applicant alleged a violation of Article 1 of Protocol No. 6, ratified by Hungary, and a potential violation of Article 3, and because he also submitted complaints concerning the lack of a fair trial (Article 6).

The *Ismaili v Germany* case concerned the extradition of a Moroccan to Morocco, where he had been sought for murder. The Court found the claim, based on alleged violation of Article 2 of the Convention, inadmissible on the grounds that the German authorities had received sufficient assurances that the death penalty was not imposed for the crime in question and that it would be neither called for nor executed.

Finally, for the sake of completeness, the *Mamatkulov and Abdurasulovic v Turkey* judgment[49] of 6 February 2003 should be noted. It concerns the extradition to Uzbekistan of two members of an Uzbek opposition party against whom an international arrest warrant had been issued, largely because they were suspected of involvement in terrorist acts and in the attempted assassination of the president of this republic. The Turkish authorities were of the opinion that the extradition request was not based on political crimes, and the applicants were accordingly extradited in March 1999,[50] despite a request addressed by the Court to the Turkish

---

47. See the *Yang Chun Jin v Hungary* judgment of 21 December 2001.
48. Application No. 58128/00, decision of 15 March 2001.
49. Applications No. 46827/99 and 46951/99, admissibility decision of 31 August 1999, judgment on the merits dated 6 February 2003. It should be noted that this judgment is not definitive, as the case has been sent to the Grand Chamber at the request of the Turkish Government, in line with Article 43 of the Convention.
50. More specifically, on 27 March 1999, although the applications were submitted by the two applicants only on 11 and 22 March respectively. On 28 June 1999, they were sentenced in Uzbekistan to twenty and eleven years' imprisonment respectively.

Government under Article 39 of the Rules of Court,[51] calling for non-implementation of the extradition ruling.

It was only after handing over the applicants to the Uzbek authorities that the Turkish Government informed the Court of the guarantees obtained regarding non-imposition of the death penalty and the under-taking not to torture the applicants.[52] Here too, the applicants referred both to Articles 2 and 3 of the Convention, and to Article 6. However, having regard to the circumstances of the case and the evidence brought before it, the Court considered that, notwithstanding the fact that the applicants' Turkish lawyers had been unable to maintain contact with their clients following extradition, the facts had not been sufficiently established to allow the conclusion that there had been violation of either Article 3 or Article 6.

On the other hand, the Court's judgment ruled on an important question, namely whether the fact that the Turkish Government had not complied with the instructions given by the Court under Article 39 of its Rules of Court was a breach of Article 34 of the Convention, which says that the states undertake not to hinder in any way the effective exercise of the right of individual application. The Court's option of indicating interim measures to governments, in other words of asking them not to carry out an expulsion or extradition measure pending a Court decision, is in fact provided for only in the Court's internal rules, and is not a stan-dard-setting rule in the actual text of the Convention, so that these interim measures are not binding in nature.

It should be noted that, at the beginning of the 1990s, the Court had already had to examine the question of whether, in the absence of an explicit clause in the Convention, its organs could find in Article 34 (previously 25), taken in isolation or jointly with Article 39 (previously 36) of the Rules of Court, or in other sources, the power to order interim measures (*Cruz Varas and others* judgment of 20 March 1991, concerning the deportation of Chileans to Chile), then again in the *Conka and others v Belgium* judgment,[53] which concerned the collective deportation of a

---

51. Article 39 of the Rules of Court concerns what are known as interim measures: the Chamber or its President may indicate to the parties any interim measure that it considers should be adopted in the interest of the parties or the good conduct of the proceedings. This article is mainly used to suspend the execution of a deportation or extradition order where there is an allegation of violation of Articles 2 and 3 of the Convention, until such time as the Court has reached a decision. As a general rule, the states comply with such requests. For an example of non-compliance, see the *Cruz-Varas v Sweden* judgment of 20 March 1991.

52. In particular, the Uzbek authorities had indicated that Uzbekistan was a party to the United Nations Convention against Torture, and that they intended to respect this treaty.

53. Application No. 51564/99, judgment of 13 March 2001.

group of Roma/Gypsies to the Slovak Republic. In these cases, it concluded that the power to order interim measures could not be inferred from either Article 34 *in fine* or from other sources, but that it was appropriate to consider that failure to comply with an indication given under Article 39 of the Rules as aggravating any subsequent breach of Article 3 found by the Court (the above-mentioned *Cruz Varas and others* judgment, pp. 36-7, paragraphs 102 and 103).

Should it be confirmed by the Grand Chamber, the *Mamatkulov and Abdurasulovic* judgment will establish a fundamentally important change in the case-law with regard to the protection of human rights in Europe, at least in terms of the responsibility of states which carry out expulsion or extradition measures without waiting for the Court's conclusions.

In fact, leaning on the practice of other international tribunals, such as the United Nations Committee on Human Rights, the United Nations Committee against Torture, the Inter-American Court of Human Rights or the International Court of Justice, the Court considered that any state party to the Convention has a duty to refrain from any act or omission that would prejudice the integrity and effectiveness of the final judgment, and held that the extradition of Mr Mamatkulov and Mr Abdurasulovic, carried out despite the indication given by the Court under Article 39, had cancelled out the applicants' right of appeal.

In this connection, the Court reiterated that the Convention's standards should be interpreted with due regard for the principle of good faith and for the treaty's purpose and objectives, as well as for the principle of effectiveness. This is also relevant with regard to the statutory provisions, which should be interpreted in the light of the Convention standards to which they are attached. Consequently, any state party to the Convention which receives a request for interim measures, recommended in order to avoid irreparable prejudice to the victim of the alleged violation, should respect these measures.

In certain other cases, which have not yet been judged by the new European Court of Human Rights, the Court will probably also be obliged to go beyond the principles laid down in the *Soering* judgment. For instance, two applications have been brought against Bulgaria,[54] concerning persons who were sentenced to death in 1989. The applicants allege a violation of Articles 2 and 3 of the Convention, arguing, among other things, that they were sentenced to death as the outcome of proceedings which did not satisfy the minimum guarantees of a fair trial; that, if they were to be executed, this would in itself amount to a violation of Article 3; and above all, that Article 3 is breached as a result

---

54. Application No. 40653/98, Iorgov and Application No. 42346/98, *Belchinov.*

of the prolonged uncertainty about their fate, which has lasted almost nine years. Their situation is exacerbated by the poor conditions in which they are being detained.

The issue of the poor detention conditions under which persons sentenced to death are imprisoned is also raised in a number of applications brought against Ukraine,[55] and both the Commission and the Court have already had occasion to travel to Ukraine in order to inspect the prison in which these prisoners are held.

Established precedents in many Council of Europe member states in fact go much further than the case-law of the European Court of Human Rights. At least in matters of extradition, where bilateral treaties permit the requested state to pose a number of conditions, certain national courts have established the principle that extradition must be refused not only in cases where there is a risk that the death penalty will be carried out, but also where the law of the state requesting extradition merely provides that a capital sentence may be imposed.

As far back as 1979, the Italian Constitutional Court refused to allow a person's extradition to France on the ground that the charges brought against the offender in France then carried the death penalty, which Italy had abolished under Article 27(4) of the 1948 Constitution. Similarly, in 1987, the French *Conseil d'Etat* overturned extradition orders against persons liable to be sentenced to death in, respectively, Turkey and Algeria, on the ground that handing them over to these countries would be contrary to French public policy.[56]

Many other examples could be cited. It is clear that there is a sort of moral consensus currently among the member states that any extradition request must be subjected to extremely close scrutiny to determine whether the available guarantees that the death sentence will not be enforced are sufficient. The best guarantee is still that the state requesting extradition should not issue any death sentence at all.[57]

---

55. See, for example, Application No. 38812/97, *Poltoratskiy v Ukraine*.

56. See the *Fidan* judgment of 27 February 1987, recueil *Lebon*, p. 81 and *Gacem* judgment of 14 December 1987, recueil *Lebon*, p. 733. It should, however, be noted that in these two judgments, as in the *Bamohammed* judgment of 1985, the French *Conseil d'Etat* referred again to the lack of sufficient assurances from the requesting states' authorities that the executions would not be carried out.

57. Thus, the United Kingdom Government, which was obliged to comply with the *Soering* judgment and could not retain the applicant indefinitely on its territory, decided to make his extradition to the United States conditional on an undertaking that Mr Soering would be prosecuted not for capital murder, but only for first degree murder, an offence which did not carry the death penalty; this condition was accepted by the United States authorities. See Resolution DH (90) 8, of 12 March 1990, by the Council of Europe Committee of Ministers, which is the body entrusted by the Convention with supervising execution of the Court's judgments. It may be noted that Mr Soering was eventually sentenced to ninety-nine years' imprisonment!

The death penalty and the fight against terrorism

This consensus also holds good with regard to the extradition or deportation of terrorists being sought in connection with the attacks of 11 September 2001. The Parliamentary Assembly adopted two resolutions[58] in January 2002 on the fight against terrorism, in which it recommended that the 1977 European Convention on Suppression of Terrorism be amended to provide that extradition may be refused where there are insufficient guarantees that the death penalty will not be called for against an accused person.

The guidelines in the fight against terrorism, drawn up by the Multidisciplinary Group on International action against Terrorism, a group set up by the Committee of Ministers after the events of 11 September, and which were adopted by the Committee of Ministers on 11 July 2002, state that the extradition of any person accused of acts of terrorism must be refused if he or she risks the death penalty, unless the requested state receives sufficient guarantees that the death penalty will either not be imposed or will not be carried out.

The protocol amending the 1977 European Convention on the Suppression of Terrorism was opened for signature of 15 June 2003. It will enter into force following ratification by all the parties to the Convention, something that is likely to take some time. However, it is encouraging to note that this protocol has been signed by almost all Council of Europe member states. Only ten states had still to sign as of 1 September 2003.

Although the Convention in itself does not directly govern the general issues involved in extradition (it deals with political offences only in so far as their perpetrators' extradition may be refused), the traditional non-discrimination clause (a necessary corollary to de-politicisation) has been extended to include a clause authorising the refusal to extradite a person to a country where s/he risks being sentenced to death, subjected to torture or sentenced to life imprisonment without the possibility of remission of sentence.

---

58. Resolutions 1271 (2002) and 1550 (2002).

The United Nation's work in the field of the death penalty[1]

Sir Nigel Rodley
Professor of law at the University of Essex and member of the UN human rights committee

The objective of abolition

There is a gradual, but firm movement internationally towards the abolition of the death penalty. As of November 2003, Amnesty International was able to list a majority of states as being abolitionist in law or in practice. While 83 states retained the penalty, 92 could be considered as having abolished it. In 76 states it had been abolished for all crimes and in another 16 for ordinary crimes. In addition, 20 states could be considered as abolitionist de facto, not having carried out any executions in the previous ten years. While the latter category must be treated with some caution, there seems to be a current general trend of about three states becoming abolitionist for ordinary crimes, or all crimes, annually.[2]

Nevertheless, while the trend seems inexorable,[3] the eighty-six countries that retain the death penalty cannot be ignored in assessing the status of the death penalty under general international law. They include two countries (China and the United States) whose positions in terms of world influence are considerable; they retain the penalty in law and practice.[4] This is so, even though successive UN studies have affirmed, in the words of the first of these, "that the deterrent effect of the death penalty is, to say the least, not demonstrated".[5] A later such report put it thus:

> With respect to the influence of the abolition of capital punishment upon the incidence of murder, all of the available data suggest that where the murder rate is increasing, abolition does not appear to hasten the increase; where the

---

1. This article is a partially updated rendering of the UN-related components of Chapter 7 of my *The treatment of prisoners under international law*, (2nd edn), Oxford University Press, Oxford, 1999.
2. See Amnesty International website: www.amnesty.org
3. Some fear it may be peaking: see Roger Hood, "Capital punishment – a global perspective", *Punishment and Society*, 2001, vol. 3, pp. 331-54, 339.
4. The Russian Federation is also formally retentionist, but since 1997 has been under a moratorium to which it was committed in the context of its admission to the Council of Europe and is probably on the way to abolition.
5. M. Ancel, *Capital punishment*, United Nations, New York, 1962.

rate is decreasing, abolition does not appear to interrupt the decrease; where the rate is stable, the presence or absence of capital punishment does not appear to affect it.[6]

Similarly, the latest such study to have examined the deterrence issue considered a number of statistical analyses based on experiences in the United States and concluded:

> Most of those who favour abolition (assuming that they are not opposed to execution under any circumstances) would demand proof that executions have a substantial marginal deterrent effect. Those retentionists who rely on their intuitive belief in deterrence would require substantial proof that there was no additional risk to the lives of citizens before sparing murderers from execution. The balance of evidence, looked at in this way, favours the abolitionist position.[7]

In the light of the number and importance of the retentionist countries, it is hardly surprising that general international law does not expressly require abolition of the death penalty.[8] On the other hand, given the spuriousness of the strongest argument the retentionists can muster – that by taking life the state aims to save other lives or prevent other offences of the type to which the death penalty applies – it is also not surprising that the public stance of the governments of the world, through both treaties and other instruments, has been that the abolition of the death penalty, while not an immediate requirement, is an ultimate goal in the field of human rights. Moreover, as will be seen below, some treaties do commit states parties to abolition.

The Universal Declaration of Human Rights is silent on the issue of the death penalty, although it was discussed in the context of consideration of the right to life. The many proposals that were discussed while the declaration was being drafted ranged from those that would have provided for the abolition of the death penalty, at least in peacetime, to those that would have maintained it without qualification as an explicit exception to the scope of the right to life.[9] The decision to leave a bare reference to the right to life in the declaration was partly a reflection of this diversity of view and partly the result of the decision that detailed provisions on the scope of the rights should be left to the planned convention that eventually became the International Covenant on Civil and Political Rights.[10]

---

6. N. Morris, *Capital punishment: developments 1961-1965*, United Nations, New York, 1967.

7. Roger Hood, *The death penalty – a worldwide perspective.* Report to the United Nations Committee on Crime Prevention and Control, Oxford University Press, Oxford, 1989, p. 148.

8. See, generally,W.A. Schabas, *The abolition of the death penalty in international law* (2nd edn), Cambridge University Press, Cambridge, 1997.

9. Landerer, "Capital punishment as a human rights issue before the United Nations", *Revue des droits de l'homme/Human Rights Journal,*1971, vol. 4, pp. 511, 513-18.

10. See fn. 9: Landerer, pp.517-18; and fn. 8: Schabas, Chapter 1.

The discussion below will deal essentially with norms relating to the protection of the right to life, since human rights treaties treat the death penalty as an explicit exception to that right. Had this not been the case, issues relating to the prohibition of torture or other cruel, inhuman, or degrading treatment or punishment could well have arisen. Indeed, the language of this prohibition is occasionally found in contexts concerning the death penalty: the preamble to General Assembly resolution 2393 (XXIII) of 26 November 1968, dealing with safeguards relating to the death penalty (see below), invoked Article 5 of the Universal Declaration of Human Rights (prohibiting torture and other ill-treatment), and a secretariat statement to the Sixth UN Congress on the Prevention of Crime and the Treatment of Offenders described the death penalty as "cruel, inhuman or degrading punishment".[11]

Nevertheless, it may one day be possible to argue that the death penalty is a violation of the prohibition on torture or cruel, inhuman, or degrading punishment. (This is already argued by the Parliamentary Assembly of the Council of Europe.)[12] Meanwhile, it is bizarre that corporal punishment may well fall foul of that prohibition,[13] while capital punishment apparently does not.

Consideration of the issue may begin with a review of the various UN instruments which suggest that abolition of the death penalty is a goal of international human rights law as well as of those that explicitly provide for abolition. The predominant approach in achieving this objective, however, has been the acceptance of certain categories of limitation on the lawfulness of the death penalty. Therefore, after the instruments envisaging abolition have been dealt with, the next three sections will examine these categories:

- limitations on the nature of the offences that may still attract the death penalty;

- procedural safeguards that are to be respected in the case of a capitally punishable offence;

- exemption of certain categories of potential death penalty victims.

This is followed by a consideration of remedial measures being undertaken by the UN to promote respect for the standards it has set.

---

11. UN document A/CONF.87/9, paragraph 98.
12. W.A. Schabas, *The death penalty: a cruel treatment and torture*, Northeastern University, Boston, USA, 1996.
13. See N. Rodley, *The treatment of prisoners under international law* (2nd edn), Oxford University Press, Oxford, 1999, Chapter 10.

International Covenant on Civil and Political Rights

One of the first, if implicit, statements of the goal of abolition is to be found in the International Covenant on Civil and Political Rights, adopted by the General Assembly of the United Nations in 1966.[14] It came into force on 23 March 1976 and 147 countries are now parties to it. Article 6 declares in its first paragraph: "Every human being has the inherent right to life. This right shall be protected by law. No one shall be arbitrarily deprived of his life".[15] This general statement cannot be construed as per se prohibiting the death penalty, since it is followed by a series of paragraphs stipulating restrictions on the use of the death penalty. The first of these, paragraph 2, which limits the nature of the offences for which the death penalty may be imposed, is introduced by the clause: "In countries which have not abolished the death penalty... ". The specific significance of the phrase will be considered below; here one may note only an implicit suggestion of approval for countries that have abolished the death penalty. The point is strengthened by paragraph 6 of the same article: after the various restrictions on the use of the death penalty have been listed in paragraphs 2 to 5, paragraph 6 states: "Nothing in this article shall be invoked to delay or to prevent the abolition of capital punishment by any State Party to the present Covenant."[16] This formulation in Article 6 led the Human Rights

---

14. General Assembly resolution. 2200 A (XXI), 16 December 1966. See, generally fn. 8: Schabas, Chapter 2.

15. Article 6:

   1. Every human being has the inherent right to life. This right shall be protected by law. No one shall be arbitrarily deprived of his life.

   2. In countries which have not abolished the death penalty, sentence of death may be imposed only for the most serious crimes in accordance with the law in force at the time of the commission of the crime and not contrary to the provisions of the present Covenant and to the Convention on the Prevention and Punishment of the Crime of Genocide. This penalty can only be carried out pursuant to a final judgement rendered by a competent court.

   3. When deprivation of life constitutes the crime of genocide, it is understood that nothing in this article shall authorize any State Party to the present Covenant to derogate in any way from any obligation assumed under the provisions of the Convention on the Prevention and Punishment of the Crime of Genocide.

   4. Anyone sentenced to death shall have the right to seek pardon or commutation of the sentence. Amnesty, pardon or commutation of the sentence of death may be granted in all cases.

   5. Sentence of death shall not be imposed for crimes committed by persons below eighteen years of age and shall not be carried out on pregnant women.

   6. Nothing in this article shall be invoked to delay or to prevent the abolition of capital punishment by any State Party to the present Covenant.

16. This language is an adaptation (GAOR, 12th Session, Annexes, Agenda item 33, A/3764 and Addendum 1(1957), paragraph. 106) of an Irish proposal aiming to compromise between those that wished at least "a provision requiring the progressive abolition of the death penalty" and those that did not. GAOR, 12th Session, Third Committee, Summary Records, A/C.3/SR.813, paragraph. 41 (1957); see fn. 8: Schabas, p. 70.

Committee (the eighteen individual experts elected by the states parties to the covenant to monitor the covenant's implementation) to observe:

> The article also refers generally to abolition in terms which strongly suggest (paras. 6(2) and (6)) that abolition is desirable. The Committee concludes that all measures of abolition should be considered as progress in the enjoyment of the right to life...[17]

Other United Nations' initiatives

Given that it comes from the body whose main function is to assess questions of compliance with the covenant, the statement of the Human Rights Committee quoted above is generally regarded as having persuasive authority. It is also in line with the political direction taken by the United Nations General Assembly and the Commission on Human Rights. After some twelve years of consideration of the topic by the Assembly, the Economic and Social Council (ECOSOC), and subordinate bodies of ECOSOC, including the Commission on Human Rights,[18] the Assembly, by resolution 2857 (XXVI) of 20 December 1971, affirmed that:

> in order fully to guarantee the right to life, provided for in Article 3 of the Universal Declaration of Human Rights, the main objective to be pursued is that of progressively restricting the number of offences for which capital punishment may be imposed, with a view to the desirability of abolishing this punishment in all countries.

When, in 1977, on the initiative of Sweden, the General Assembly considered the matter, it reaffirmed the goal it had set in 1971[19] and referred the question to the Sixth United Nations Congress on the Prevention of Crime and the Treatment of Offenders that would take place in 1980 (resolution 32/61 of 8 December 1977). Hope was thus placed in the congress to produce further normative proscription on the use of the death penalty. Indeed, at the opening of the congress the Secretary-General of the United Nations, in asking the congress to give serious consideration to the question of capital punishment, stated that:

> the taking of life of human beings violates respect for the dignity of every person and the right to life, as declared in the basic postulates of the United Nations.[20]

In addition, as noted above, the secretariat working paper on the topic stated that "the death penalty constitutes" cruel, inhuman or degrading

---

17. Report of the Human Rights Committee, GAOR, 37th Session, Supplement No. 40 (1982), Annex V, general comment 6(16), paragraph. 6.
18. See Amnesty International, *The death penalty* (1979), pp. 24-9.
19. With the omission of the words "in all countries".
20. Sixth United Nations Congress on the Prevention of Crime and the Treatment of Offenders-Report, A/CONF.87/114/Rev. 1 (1981).

punishment' which even in the light of the behaviour at which it is directed, should not be acceptable".[21]

In spite of these positive statements, the congress was unable to agree on a resolution on the death penalty. Austria and Sweden, subsequently joined by Ecuador and the Federal Republic of Germany, introduced a complicated draft resolution that would have declared that:

> capital punishment raises serious questions in relation to respect for the dignity of all human beings and for human rights, in particular the right to life, which is the most fundamental of all human rights, and the right not to be subjected to cruel, inhuman or degrading punishment.[22]

It would also have reiterated that "the ultimate objective is the total abolition of capital punishment throughout the world". In response to strong opposition, the sponsoring countries then introduced a revised draft in which several paragraphs of the original were weakened.[23] Under the new draft the congress would merely have declared that "further restriction in the application of capital punishment and its eventual abolition would be a significant contribution to the strengthening of human rights, in particular the right to life". While there was some strongly expressed opposition to the very concept of abolition, the doubts of many delegations focused on other aspects of the draft, especially on a proposal for a moratorium on executions (indefinite in the first draft, for five years in the revised one). In the end, "realising that there was inadequate time for the completion of work on the question, the sponsors withdrew the revised draft resolution".[24] This inconclusive result was followed by a further inconclusive, mainly procedural discussion at the 35th session of the General Assembly (1980). These developments represented a setback for the movement towards enhancing the UN normative proscription of the death penalty. Another attempt, this time initiated by Italy, at the Eighth UN Crime Congress, failed to achieve the necessary two-thirds majority.[25] By the draft resolution, the congress would have reaffirmed the General Assembly's line of the 1970s in favour of the progressive restriction of capitally punishable offences and asking states to consider imposing a moratorium on executions "at least on a three-year basis".[26]

---

21. UN document A/CONF.87/9, paragraph 98.
22. UN document A/CONF.87/C.I/L.1.
23. UN document A/CONF.87/C.I/L.1/Rev. 1; also reproduced in loc. cit. fn. 18, Chapter IV, Report of Committee I, Annex.
24. See fn. 20, paragraph 111.
25. There were 48 votes for, 29 against and 16 abstentions: Report of the Eighth United Nations Congress on the Prevention of Crime and the Treatment of Offenders. Havana, 27 Aug.-7 Sep. 1990, UN document A/CONF.144/28/Rev.1 (1991), paragraph 358.
26. *Ibid.*, paragraph 352.

However, Italy returned to the attack at the 49th session of the General Assembly in 1994. It proposed that the Assembly, among other things, invite non-abolitionist states "to consider the progressive restriction of the number of offences for which the death penalty may be imposed" (arguably a weakening of the language of the pre-1980 resolutions) and that it encourage the same states:

> to consider the opportunity of instituting a moratorium on pending executions with a view to ensuring that the principle that no State should dispose of the life of any human being be affirmed in every part of the world by the year 2000.[27]

After a procedurally complicated debate, the resolution failed by 44 votes to 36, with 74 abstentions.[28] This was because a substantial number of previously sponsoring states joined the ranks of the abstainers after an amendment proposed by Singapore was carried.[29] The same fate befell a similar 1999 initiative introduced at the 54th session of the General Assembly by Finland on behalf of the European Union.[30]

Meanwhile, Italy brought the matter to the 1997 session of the Commission on Human Rights. The language of the draft[31] was firmer than that proposed to the General Assembly and was adopted unchanged after the defeat of a number of amendments that would have weakened the text, including one modelled on the Singaporean amendment that had been successful at the 1994 General Assembly.[32] By the resulting resolution 1997/12 of 3 April 1997, the Commission "call[ed] upon" non-abolitionist states "progressively to restrict the number of offences for which the death penalty may be imposed... and to consider suspending executions, with a view to completely abolishing the death penalty".[33] That this was not a flash in the pan is evidenced by the adoption of further anti-death penalty resolutions in 1998, 1999, 2000 and 2001.[34]

---

27. UN document. A/C.3/49/L.32 (1994).
28. UN document. A/C.3/49/SR.61 (1994), paragraphs 55-6.
29. *Ibid.*, paragraphs 9-10. The Singapore text would have added a preambular paragraph "[a]ffirming the sovereign right of States to determine the legal measures and penalties which are appropriate in their societies to combat serious crimes effectively" (A/C.3/49/L.73 and Rev.1). It passed even after the Italian draft had already been amended by the ten sponsors in the direction of the draft Singapore amendment except that the determination had to be "in accordance with international law, including the Charter of the United Nations" (A/C.3/49/L.32/Rev.1). (1994).
30. See Roger Hood, fn. 3, p. 340.
31. UN document. E/CN.4/1997/L.20.
32. Resolution 1997/12, 3 Apr. 1997 (the vote was 27 for, 11 against and 14 abstentions): Commission on Human Rights, Report, 53rd Session, *ESCOR*, 1997, Supplement No. 3, Chapter II A. The draft amendments were contained in UN document. E/CN.4/1997/L.35.
33. Operative paragraphs 4 and 5.
34. Resolutions 1998/8, 1999/61, 2000/65 and 2001/68.

Effectively then, the issue has moved from the crime prevention organs to the principal human rights organ of the United Nations. The goal of abolition is reasserted, as is one road to it : progressive restriction of capitally punishable offences. The addition of requested action of a less long-term nature, in the form of a suspension of, or moratorium on, executions is a novelty that indicates a new momentum for the abolitionist cause at the universal level. This momentum could be enhanced if the General Assembly could muster the same political will as that found in the Commission on Human Rights. On the other hand, it was the General Assembly itself which, in 1989, was to adopt a ground-breaking instrument aimed outright at abolition of the death penalty. To this we now turn.

Optional Protocol to the International Covenant on Civil and Political Rights

At the same session of the General Assembly that had in 1980 received the inconclusive results of the Sixth UN Crime Congress debate on the death penalty, the governments of Austria, Costa Rica, Italy, the Federal Republic of Germany, Portugal, and Sweden introduced the text of a draft optional protocol to the International Covenant on Civil and Political Rights whereby the parties to such a protocol would commit themselves to abolition.[35] The General Assembly decided to consider "the idea" of such an optional protocol at its next session and sought governments' comments and observations.[36] It did the same at its next (36th) session.[37] By the time of the 37th session in 1982, the Assembly had received replies from only thirty-two governments, revealing no general policy line.[38] At that session it was decided to defer further consideration for two years while the matter (that is, the idea of elaborating an abolitionist optional protocol to the covenant) was studied by the Commission on Human Rights.[39] Although the issue was then raised at the 1983 session of the Commission on Human Rights,[40] no action was taken and it was not until 1984 that the commission decided to consult its Sub-Commission on Prevention of Discrimination and Protection of Minorities on how to deal with the proposal.[41]

---

35. Text in GAOR, 35th Session, Annexes, Agenda item 65, A/35/742, paragraph. 20. See generally, fn. 8 : Schabas, pp. 168-91.
36. General Assembly decision 35/437, 15 December 1980.
37. Resolution 36/59, 25 Nov. 1981.
38. UN documents. A/36/441 and Addenda. 1 and 2 (1981) ; A/37/407 and Addendum. I (1982).
39. Resolution 37/192, 18 December 1982.
40. UN documents. E/CN.4/1983/SR.17-20.
41. Resolution 1984/19, 6 Mach. 1984, Commission on Human Rights, Report, 40th Session, ESCOR, 1984, Supplement No. 4, Chapter II A.

The sub-commission entrusted its Belgian member, Marc Bossuyt, with the task of preparing the analysis.[42] His report was submitted in 1987 and contained a draft optional protocol to the covenant, somewhat revised from the version originally submitted to the General Assembly in 1980 by the governments that initiated the process.[43] In 1988, the sub-commission forwarded the text to the commission[44] which referred it, through ECOSOC, to the General Assembly. The General Assembly adopted the unamended text by resolution 44/128 on 15 December 1989.[45]

It is the first universal abolitionist treaty, entering into force on 11 July 1991 after receiving its tenth instrument of ratification. There are forty-six states parties as of November 2001. Article 1 contains the basic obligations. The first paragraph provides : "No one within the jurisdiction of a State Party to the present Protocol shall be executed." The focus here is on non-execution rather than on legislative abolition. The latter issue is addressed by the article's second paragraph : "Each State Party shall take all necessary measures to abolish the death penalty within its jurisdiction." It would appear from this language which envisages a process – in some states a complicated and protracted one – that the achievement of legislative abolition is not a condition of ratification. Arguably a state that was genuinely taking the prescribed measures could be a party without violating the protocol, as long as no one was being executed, even if courts had been imposing the death penalty under existing national law. In fact, adherence by a state that is non-abolitionist in law is unlikely.

The only reservations permitted under the protocol are those that would provide "for the application of the death penalty in time of war pursuant to a conviction for a most serious crime of a military nature committed during wartime" (Article 2(1)). This exception is narrower than that envisaged in the earlier abolitionist Protocol No. 6 to the European Convention on Human Rights, which also refers to the "imminent threat of war". It can be argued that the war in question must be a formally declared war between states, not a civil war.[46] Such interstate wars have

---

42. Sub-Commission resolution 1984/7, 28 August. 1984, UN document. E/CN.4/1985/3 ; E/C4/Sub.2/1984/43, Chapter XVIII A.
43. UN document. E/CN.4/Sub.2/1987/20.
44. Sub-Commission resolution 1988/22, 1 September. 1988, UN document E/CN.4/1989/3 ; E/CN.4/Sub.2/1988/45, Chapter II A.; Commission resolution 1989/25, 6 March 1989, Commission on Human Rights, Report, 45th Session, ESCOR, 1989, Supplement No. 2, Chapter II A.
45. The General Assembly adopted the text with 59 votes for and 26 against, with 48 abstentions. While those voting for were more than double those opposing, they were a minority of those present and voting. Many retentionist states were clearly unhappy with the initiative.
46. See Rodley, fn. 13, pp. 215-16.

in fact become obsolete; however, many states have left unabrogated laws that entered their statute books when such wars were prevalent. Formal abrogation could be politically sensitive, yet the states in question could still be considered abolitionist and should not be discouraged from adhering to the protocol. The further restriction, that the offence must be one of a military nature, would seem to suggest that only the "most serious" crimes committed by military personnel could be the targets of the permitted reservations. The reservation must include the relevant provisions of national legislation (Article 2(2)).

It is also worth noting that, unlike the first optional protocol providing for the right to individual petition, there is no provision in the second one for denunciation. If only on the basis of *a contrario* interpretation, this would seem to preclude any going back on the commitment.[47]

Of course, the protocol is binding only on the states that accept it. Nevertheless, it remains a standard that all states are urged to accept. The fact that this is so, no doubt explains the substantial opposition to its original adoption.[48] As such, it was an important step in the process of reversing the setback that the cause of abolition suffered at the 1980 Sixth UN Crime Congress.

Statutes of international criminal tribunals

Reference may also be made to the statutes of the tribunals set up by the UN Security Council to adjudicate crimes committed in the former Yugoslavia and in Rwanda, as well as to the statute of a permanent international criminal court. One notable absence from these texts is any provision for the death penalty. Despite the appalling nature of some of the crimes for which they aim to bring the perpetrators to justice – genocide, war crimes, crimes against humanity – the death penalty has been deemed to be incompatible with the values that international justice is meant to represent. This too, then, represents a step towards the abolitionist goal.[49]

---

47. The Human Rights Committee has made its view clear that the absence of a denunciation clause in the Covenant itself means that states parties cannot withdraw: see general comment 26(61), 29 October 1997, UN document. CCPR/C/21/Rev.1/Add.8/Rev./1997.
48. See fn. 45.
49. The same point was affirmed by the former UN Special Rapporteur on Extrajudicial, Summary or Arbitrary Executions, who himself considered the abolitionist trend as one that states should subscribe to: see, for example, UN document. E/CN.4/1997/60, paragraphs. 73-6. Similarly, the Commission on Human Rights has expressed itself as "[w]elcoming the exclusion of capital punishment from the penalties that the [international tribunals] are authorised to impose": resolution 1997/12, see fn. 32, preambular paragraph. 5.

Limits to capitally punishable offences

In this part, the general starting point for each topic is Article 6 of the International Covenant on Civil and Political Rights, as this may indicate, not only the law applicable to the states parties to it but also the position under general international law. This is because the right to life may, appropriately, be considered as a rule of general international law, if not of *jus cogens*. Accordingly, as the principal universal instrument on the topic, the covenant may be understood as reflecting the scope of that right. Certainly, as far as the death penalty is concerned, successive special rapporteurs on extrajudicial, summary or arbitrary executions have taken the view that Article 6, read with Articles 14 and 15, indeed states "customary international law".[50] It should also be noted that, by resolution 35/172 of 15 December 1980, the General Assembly urged states "to respect as a minimum standard the content of the provisions of Articles 6, 14 and 15 of the International Covenant on Civil and Political Rights", a call it has frequently reiterated.

However, this position cannot yet be taken as wholly applicable to all parts of Article 6, given that the Inter-American Court of Human Rights has interpreted the analogous non-derogable Article 4 of the American Convention on Human Rights as permitting reservations in respect of "certain aspects" of such a non-derogable right, as long as "the right as a whole" was not deprived of "its basic purpose".[51] The Human Rights Committee, it is true, has not been so tolerant, albeit its general comment on reservations has been challenged on various points by France, the United Kingdom and the United States.[52]

Lawful sanction

For particular capital offences to be compatible with Article 6 of the International Covenant on Civil and Political Rights, the death penalty must be prescribed by national law. This was the clear intention behind the provision that "no one shall be arbitrarily deprived of his life".[53] It follows that, unless a punitive killing by the authorities is provided for by national law, it will be an extra-legal execution.

---

50. UN document. E/CN.4/1992/30, paragraph 609; E/CN.4/1993/46, paragraph 678.
51. Inter-American Court of Human Rights: *Reservations to the death penalty (Arts. 4(2) and 6(4) American Convention on Human Rights),* Advisory Opinion OC-3/83, 8 Sep. 1983, Ser. A No. 3.
52. General comment 24 (52), Report of the Human Rights Committee, UN document. A/50/40 (1995), Annex V; for the comments of the USA and UK, see *ibid.,* Annex VI; for that of France, see *ibid.,* UN document. A/51/40 (1996), Annex VI.
53. GAOR, 10th Session, Annexes, Agenda item 28 (Part II), A/2929, Chapter VI, paragraph 3.

Only the "most serious crimes"

According to the International Covenant on Civil and Political Rights, "sentence of death may be imposed only for the most serious crimes" (Article 6(2)). Unfortunately, the term "the most serious crimes" remains undefined. The phrase was adopted in the covenant despite concerns expressed at the time that it lacked precision, since the concept of "serious crimes" differed from one country to another;[54] clearly the concept was expected to evolve. It is often thought that the death penalty is reserved for crimes involving loss of life, and it is therefore frequently justified on a principle, however retrograde, of retribution – an eye for an eye, a life for a life. In fact, the 1979 Amnesty International report *The death penalty*[55] shows that the penalty is often imposed for offences that not only involve no loss of life, but involve no use of violence at all. Therefore violence cannot necessarily be used as the sole measure of the crimes which states consider "serious" enough to warrant the death penalty. The Human Rights Committee's general comment on the phrase "the most serious crimes" gives little precision. The committee says that the expression "must be read restrictively to mean that the death penalty should be a quite exceptional measure."[56]

In the Safeguards guaranteeing protection of the rights of those facing the death penalty, adopted in 1984, ECOSOC expresses its understanding that the scope of the term "most serious crimes" "should not go beyond intentional crimes, with lethal or other extremely grave consequences"[57] The words "or other extremely grave" were added after a member of the Committee on Crime Prevention and Control (which drafted the safeguards) had argued that some acts (for example the provision of secret information to an enemy in wartime) could result in large-scale loss of life, even though the lethal results of the offence could not necessarily be proven.[58]

The Human Rights Committee has not had occasion to pronounce formally in an individual case whether a particular capitally punishable offence may or may not be a "most serious crime". However, in its review of states' periodic reports, the committee or, more frequently, its

---

54. *Ibid.*, paragraph 6.
55. See fn. 18.
56. See fn. 17, paragraph. 7.
57. ECOSOC resolution 1984/50, 25 May 1984, Annex, paragraph 1. It is worth noting that the General Assembly endorsed the ECOSOC Safeguards in resolution 39/118 of 14 December 1984, and asked the Secretary-General "to employ his best endeavours in cases 'where the safeguards ... are violated'" (operative paragraphs 2 and 5).
58. Recollection of the author, who attended the Eighth session of the Committee on Crime Prevention and Control (1984) on behalf of Amnesty International.

individual members, have been critical of resort to the death penalty for many crimes not resulting in death, notably political crimes, crimes against property and some drug offences.[59] The Special Rapporteur on Extrajudicial, Arbitrary or Summary Executions similarly considers that the death penalty "should be eliminated for crimes such as economic crimes and drug-related offences."[60] Similarly, the UN Commission on Human Rights has urged states to ensure that the death penalty "is not imposed for non-violent financial crimes or for non-violent religious practice or expression of conscience".[61]

No other human rights violations should be involved

By providing that "no one shall be arbitrarily deprived of his life", Article 6 of the covenant appears to have intended "arbitrarily" to mean both "illegally" and "unjustly".[62] The covenant addresses itself to unjust laws by its proviso that in any event the law providing for capitally punishable crimes must not be "contrary to the provisions of the present Covenant" (Article 6(2)). This stipulation would certainly preclude the use of the death penalty for some offences that, in some countries, currently attract it – for example, peaceful dissent or non-violent association and assembly.

It is clear, therefore, that where a particular act of government repression amounts to a violation of human rights as defined in the covenant then the use of the death penalty in furtherance of the repression is a violation of Article 6 of the covenant. This has more significance than merely that the government in question is violating international law twice. Many of the articles of the covenant may be suspended "in time of public emergency which threatens the life of the nation" (Article 4), but this is not true of Article 6. It may be argued on the basis of the Article 6 phrase "not contrary to the provisions of the present Covenant" that, even when in time of emergency an activity normally protected by a provision of the covenant (free speech, public assembly, and so on) becomes criminal, the right in question having been suspended, it may still not attract the death penalty.[63]

---

59. See fn. 8: Schabas, pp. 105-08
60. UN document. E/CN.4/1998/68, paragraph 94.
61. Commission on Human Rights resolution. 1999/61 (paragraph 3b), 2000/65 (paragraph 3b), 2001/68 (paragraph 4b).
62. UN document A/2929, see fn. 53, paragraph 3. See Nowak, U.N. Covenant on Civil and Political Rights - CCPR Commentary (1993), pp.110-11.
63. The point is further developed below in relation to fair trials; see fn. 93 and accompanying text.

Article 6(2) also provides that capitally punishable offences must "not be contrary to the Convention on the Prevention and Punishment of the Crime of Genocide". Nailing the point down even more firmly, paragraph 3 of the same article provides:

> When deprivation of life constitutes the crime of genocide, it is understood that nothing in this article shall authorise any State Party to the present Covenant to derogate in any way from any obligation assumed under the provisions of the Convention on the Prevention and Punishment of the Crime of Genocide.

The intention seems to have been to avoid any interpretation at all by which the covenant's admission of death sentences "might be abused to justify" executions punishable under the Genocide Convention.[64]

Non-retroactivity

A further restriction on crimes that may attract a death sentence is that such sentence may be imposed only "in accordance with the law in force *at the time of the commission of the crime"* (Article 6(2), emphasis added). This seems to be a shorthand way of stating the principle of non-retroactivity contained in Article 15 of the covenant[65] (another article which, like Article 6, may not be suspended). That is, that an offence must have been an offence at the time it was committed and that the penalty must have been laid down at that time: *nullum crimen, nulla poena sine lege.* Furthermore, Article 15 provides that, where the law is changed to provide a lighter penalty for the offence in question than that which existed at the time the offence was committed, the convicted person must benefit from the lighter penalty.

In recognition of the standards laid down in the covenant, the General Assembly, in a resolution on "Arbitrary or summary executions", urged UN member states to "respect as a minimum standard the content of the provisions of Articles 6, 14 and *15"* (emphasis added) of the covenant. This resolution (35/172 of 15 December 1980) was adopted without a vote in the context of discussions on the report of the Sixth Congress on the Prevention of Crime and the Treatment of Offenders mentioned above. While such a resolution has the status of a recommendation only, it tends to support the argument that the articles in question, in so far as they touch on the death penalty, may be held to apply to all UN member states, whether or not they are parties to the covenant. The General Assembly reiterated its position on numerous occasions.[66]

---

64. See fn. 9: Landerer, p. 525.
65. The provision that was to become Article 15 had not been adopted at the time this phrase was inserted; see Landerer, fn. 9.
66. See fn. 68.

Political offences

In one region, the Americas, another category of offence may not be made subject to the death penalty. Parties to the American Convention on Human Rights are bound by paragraph 4 of Article 4 which states: "In no case shall capital punishment be inflicted for political offences or related common crimes".

There is no similar treaty provision at the universal level. However, it is probable that many "political offences" of the sort covered by the American Convention on Human Rights would be "contrary to the provisions of the present Covenant" within the meaning of Article 6(2) of the covenant (see above).[67] Further, the UN General Assembly has expressed its concern "at the occurrence of executions which are widely regarded as being politically motivated",[68] and in 1981 the UN Sub-Commission on Prevention of Discrimination and Protection of Minorities called for the abolition of the death penalty for "political offences".[69] Once again, the definition of "political offences" is problematic. In particular, it would be difficult to gain acceptance for the restriction of capital punishment in respect of those politically motivated offences which, without the political motivation, would attract it (the "related common crimes" of the extradition treaties). Given this difference of definition and the limited likelihood of finding a definition that would meet with general international agreement, an internationally accepted restriction on the use of capital punishment for "political offences" is unlikely, at least in treaty form.

Non-re-introduction

Another approach to limiting the applicability of the death penalty is to prohibit its re-introduction once it has been abolished, or its extension to offences for which it is not already laid down. It will be recalled that Article 6(2) of the covenant begins: *"In countries which have not abolished the death penalty*, sentence of death may be imposed only for the most serious crimes..." (emphasis added). It has been argued above that the emphasised words imply the goal of abolishing the death penalty. The wording also implies that the rules that follow are extended only to countries that have not yet attained that goal. This would contain within it the further implication that abolitionist countries may not avail

---

67. See the generally critical approach of the Human Rights Committee, fn. 59 and accompanying text.
68. General Assembly resolutions 35/172, 15 December 1980; and 36/22, 9 November 1981.
69. Resolution 1 (XXXIV), 3 Sept. 1981, Report of the Sub-Commission on Prevention of Discrimination and Protection of Minorities, 34th Session (E/CN.4/1512; E/CN.4/Sub.2/-495), Chapter XX A.

themselves of the rule – that, therefore, they may not re-introduce the death penalty – and further that the principle on which this would be based (a "standstill" approach) would require that even in non-abolitionist countries the death penalty not be extended to cover offences for which it does not at present apply.[70] This view is, however, at odds with that taken by a Council of Europe expert committee.[71] The wording quoted above replaced an earlier phraseology ("in countries where capital punishment exists"),[72] leading one commentator to observe that the new language was "somewhat more emphatic, and possibly more restrictive".[73] The Human Rights Committee established under the covenant has not so far, in its general comment on Article 6, gone beyond the already quoted formulation that "all measures of abolition should be considered as progress in the enjoyment of the right to life... "[74] The non-re-introduction/non-extension approach was to be found in the abolitionist draft resolution submitted to, but then withdrawn from, the Sixth UN Crime Congress discussed earlier. Non-re-introduction is also implicit in the Second Optional Protocol to the Covenant.[75] In any event, regardless of what the legal significance of a General Assembly resolution may be, the clear political direction taken by the Assembly – "the main objective to be pursued is that of progressively restricting the number of offences for which capital punishment may be imposed" – seems to require the non-re-introduction/non-extension approach.

Mandatory death penalty

In one case, the Human Rights Committee found a violation of covenant Article 6, by virtue of the fact that the death penalty was mandatory for the crime of murder. The sparse reasoning of the committee fails convincingly to explain how it overcame the state party's argument that the death sentence "is only mandatory for murder, which is the most serious crime under the law", and that this in itself means that it is a proportionate sentence.[76] The UN's political and human rights bodies have not pronounced on the matter.

---

70. See fn.18. Amnesty International, *The death penalty*, p. 20.

71. Idem p. 32.

72. See fn. 16.

73. See fn. 9: Landerer, p.524; see also fn. 8: Schabas, pp. 101-03, who appears to see re-introduction as a retreat from the legally mandated goal of abolition and, thus, "incompatible with the Covenant".

74. See fn. 17. An opportunity for the issue to be tested in one case was missed, "since neither counsel nor the State party has made submissions in this respect": *Piandiong et al. v Phillipines* (869/1999), UN document. CCPR/C/70/D/869/1999 (2000), paragraph 7.4.

75. See fn. 45 and accompanying text.

76. *Thompson v Saint Vincent and the Grenadines* (806/1998), UN document. CCPR/C/70/D/806/1998 (2000), paragraph 8.2.

Procedural restrictions on the imposition of the death penalty

In addition to the substantive restrictions on the use of the death penalty described above (it may not be applied except for the most serious crimes, pursuant to law providing the penalty for the offending act, and not contrary to the other provisions of the covenant), the covenant also states certain fundamental procedural requirements that must be met in capital cases.

Fair trial

Article 6 of the covenant makes no direct reference to a requirement of "fair trial". The basic standards for a fair trial, including pre- and post-trial safeguards, are laid down in Article 14 of the covenant,[77] and under normal circumstances it would be unnecessary to make reference to them in Article 6. However, while, as noted earlier, Article 6 is one of those from which no derogation is permitted even in time of public emergency threatening the life of the nation, this is not so for Article 14. It may be argued that, despite this gap, an implied obligation not to execute convicted persons who have been denied the benefit of a fair trial must now be read into Article 6 by way of ensuring that the deprivation of life not be arbitrary.[78]

In 1968, nine years after it had first initiated a study of the death penalty, the UN General Assembly adopted its first substantive resolution on the topic. By resolution 2393 (XXIII) of 26 November 1968, the General Assembly invited member governments, among other things, to "ensure the most careful legal procedures and the greatest possible safeguards for the accused in capital cases".[79] By 1980, the General Assembly had become more explicit. Its resolution 35/172 of 15 December 1980 urged member states, among other things:

> to respect as a minimum standard the content of the provisions of Articles 6, 14 and 15 of the International Covenant on Civil and Political Rights and, where necessary, to review their legal rules and practices so as to guarantee the most careful legal procedures and the greatest possible safeguards for the accused in capital cases.

Here the General Assembly included reference to Article 14 as well as to the non-derogable Articles 6 and 15. The General Assembly was to reiterate this exhortation in 1981 and on subsequent occasions.[80]

---

77. Article 14: See the end of this chapter.

78. As Landerer (see fn. 9) puts it: "A proposal to tie the trial of capital offences explicitly to the obligations under the Covenant concerning a fair trial was not brought to the vote but it was pointed out that there was no need for such a cross-reference since the Covenant formed an integral whole".

79. This was a formulation first adopted by ECOSOC resolution. 934 (XXXV), 9 April 1963.

80. For example, General Assembly resolution. 36/22, 9 November. 1981; 38/96, 16 December 1983.

Resolution 36/22 of 9 November 1981 asked the Committee on Crime Prevention and Control to examine the problem. That examination culminated in the drafting of the safeguards that ECOSOC was to adopt in 1984.[81] The fifth of these reaffirmed the necessity of fair trials in capital cases, "including the right to adequate legal assistance at all stages of the proceedings".

Finally, and especially persuasively, the practice of the Human Rights Committee follows the same approach. In its general comment on Article 6 of the covenant it stated: "The procedural guarantees... prescribed [in Article 14] must be observed, including the right to a fair hearing by an independent tribunal, the presumption of innocence, the minimum guarantees for the defence, and the right to review by a higher tribunal".[82] A year after it formulated this approach, the committee had occasion to apply it in the *Mbenge* case.[83]

Daniel Monguya Mbenge, a former governor of the province of Shaba in Zaire was twice sentenced to death *in absentia*. While not precluding the possibility of a judgment *in absentia*, the Human Rights Committee considered that such a judgment "requires that, notwithstanding the absence of the accused, all due notification has been made to inform him of the date and place of his trial and to request his attendance". The committee seems to have accepted the uncontested claim by Mr Mbenge that he learned of the trials only through press reports after they had taken place, even though the judgment showed that the authorities were aware of his address in Belgium.

The Committee concluded that Zaire had not respected Mr Mbenge's rights under Article 14(3)(a), (b), (d), and (e) of the Covenant.[84] Referring to the requirement in Article 6(2) that death sentences must not be contrary to the provisions of the covenant, the committee further found that "the failure of the State party to respect the relevant requirements of Article 14(3) leads to the conclusion that the death sentences pronounced against the author of the communication were imposed contrary to the provisions of the Covenant and therefore in violation of Article 6(2)" (paragraph 17). Zaire was, accordingly, under an obligation to provide the victim with effective remedies, including compensation "for the violations he had suffered" (paragraph 22).

Since then, the Human Rights Committee has had occasion to read Article 14 together with Article 6 in a series of cases brought by persons

---

81. See fn. 57.
82. See fn. 17, paragraph. 7.
83. *Monguya Mbenge et al. v Zaire* (16/1977), Report of the Human Rights Committee, GAOR, 38th Session, Supplement No. 40, Annex X.
84. Paragraphs 14.1 and 14.2. Article 14 is reproduced in full at the end of this chapter.

on death row, mainly in Jamaica.[85] For instance, in one case the victim had been charged with manslaughter and pleaded guilty. The proceedings were then dropped and a murder charge was brought in respect of the same killing, to which he had already pleaded guilty. This was held to violate the Article 14(1) guarantee of a fair trial.[86] So, in another case, did the failure to inform the victim of an appeal hearing until after it had taken place.[87]

The Human Rights Committee has found numerous violations involving deficient or non-existent legal representation. The refusal of the court to postpone the trial of a person who had been able to consult his court-appointed lawyer only on the day of the trial involved a breach of Article 14(3)(b) (adequate time and facilities to prepare defence and communicate with counsel).[88] The same provision was violated in a case where there was only a brief meeting with court-appointed lawyers before a preliminary hearing, one 30-minute meeting one month before the trial and no consultation by the court-appointed lawyer before the appeal.[89] In a case from another Caribbean country, the right to legal assistance of choice (Article 14(3)(d)) was violated where an appeal went ahead with the original counsel at trial, despite the person's wish to be represented by new counsel.[90] Indeed, the absence of legal aid to file a constitutional motion to challenge irregularities at trial also involves violation of Article 14(3)(d), read with Article 6.[91] Also, a failure by a court-appointed lawyer

---

85. Jamaica denounced the optional protocol on 23 Oct. 1997.

86. *Richards v Jamaica* (535/1993), UN document CCPR/C/59/D/535/1993/Rev.1(1997), paragraphs 7.2, 7.5.

87. *Thomas v Jamaica* (272/1988), Report of the Human Rights Committee, UN document A/47/40 (1992), Annex IXG, paragraphs 11.5, 12 (unaccountably, Article 6 is overlooked in the Committee's final views).

88. *Reid v Jamaica* (No. 250/1987), Report of the Human Rights Committee, GAOR, 45th Session, Supp. No. 40, Vol. II (1990), Annex IX J, paragraphs. 11.3 and 11.5 and 4.

89. *Little v Jamaica* (No. 283/1988), loc. cit. see fn. 87, Annex IX J, paragraphs 8.4 and 3.2.

90. *Pinto v Trinidad and Tobago* (No. 232/1987), loc. cit. see fn. 87, Annex IX H, paragraphs 12.5-12.6. (Trinidad and Tobago, like Jamaica (see fn. 85), denounced the Optional Protocol on 26 May 1998; on the same day it re-ratified the protocol, but with a reservation excluding death sentence-related cases. Later, the committee found the reservation inapplicable in the case of *Kennedy v Trinidad and Tobago* (845/1999), UN document CCPR/C./67/D/845/1999 (1999). In the wake of this, Trinidad and Tobago denounced the protocol permanently, with effect from 27 June 2000. Guyana also denounced the Optional Protocol and re-ratified it, subject to a similar reservation, on 5 Jan 1999. Similarly, in *Reid*, see fn. 88, denial of self-representation and assignment of counsel who refuses to advance arguments on appeal violates the same provision: paragraph. 11.4; see also, on refusal by counsel to advance arguments: *Kelly v Jamaica* (No. 253/1987) Report of the Human Rights Committee, GAOR, 46th Session, Supp. No. 40 (1991), Annex XI D, paragraphs 5.10 and 5.14; *Price v Jamaica* (572/1994), UN document. CCPR/C/58/D/572/1994 (1996), paragraphs 9.2, 9.3; *Steadman v Jamaica*, (see fn. 93), paragraphs 10.3, 11.

91. *Taylor v Jamaica* (707/1996), UN document CCPR/C/60/D/707/1996 (1997), paragraphs 8.2, 9.

to call a suggested defence witness without explanation involved a violation of Article 14(3)(e) (right to call defence witnesses under same conditions as prosecution witnesses).[92] A long delay between a preliminary hearing and the trial, or between conviction and appeal, without adequate explanation, violates Article 14(3)(c) (trial without undue delay).[93]

In sum, it may safely be concluded that the covenant imposes on states parties to it a requirement in capital cases for a fair trial. Further, the recognition that a violation of Article 14 in capital cases entails violation of Article 6 suggests the conclusion that, in times of public emergency (when Article 14 might be suspended), the force of Article 6 (which may not be suspended) would be to prohibit the imposition of the death penalty in cases where the provisions of Article 14 had not been observed. This view is supported by the Human Rights Committee in its general comment No. 29 on states of emergency. Having affirmed that covenant Article 4 (providing for the possibility of derogations in certain circumstances) "may not be resorted to in a way that would result in derogation from non-derogable rights", the committee illustrates the point in relation to the rules for fair trial in the clearest terms:

> [A]s Article 6 of the Covenant is non-derogable in its entirety, any trial leading to the imposition of the death penalty during a state of emergency must conform to the provisions of the Covenant, including all the requirements of Article[..] 14 ....[94]

To the extent that Article 6 may reflect general international law and in the light of the repeated statements of the General Assembly and other UN bodies, it may well be that the right to a fair trial in capital cases is one that must be respected by all states. Moreover, in terms which support what has been said above regarding the inapplicability of the death penalty in circumstances where fair trial standards have been suspended, Article 3, common to the four Geneva conventions and relating to armed conflict not of an international character, prohibits, with respect to persons in the hands of a party to the conflict: at any time and in any place whatsoever... the passing of sentences and the carrying out of executions without previous judgment pronounced by a regularly

---

92. See fn. 89.
93. *Steadman v Jamaica* (528/1993), UN document CCPR/C/59/D/528/1993 (1997), paragraphs. 10.1, 11 (26 months between preliminary hearing and appeal); *Pratt and Morgan v Jamaica* (Nos. 210/1986 and 225 (1987), Report of the Human Rights Committee, GAOR, 44th Session, Supp. No. 40 (1989), paragraphs 13.4, 13.5, 14 (b) (45 months between conviction and appeal). *Johnson v Jamaica* (No. 588/1994), UN document CCPR/C/56/D/588/1994 (1996), paragraphs 8.8, 8.9 (51 months between conviction and appeal); *McLawrence v Jamaica* (702/1996), UN document CCPR/C/60/D/702/1996 (1997), paragraphs 5.11, 5.13 (31 months).
94. UN document CCPR/C/21/Rev.1/Add.11(2001), paragraph 15.

constituted court, affording all the judicial guarantees which are recognised as indispensable by civilized peoples".

A state of emergency not reaching the threshold of sustained armed conflict must require no less a standard.

Degree of proof

In 1984, the ECOSOC enunciated a new safeguard that is to be respected in capital cases. Specifically, it envisaged imposition of the death penalty "only when the guilt of the person charged is based upon clear and convincing evidence leaving no room for an alternative explanation of the facts".[95] This formulation may well be understood as a gloss on covenant Article 14 that stipulates "the right to be presumed innocent until proved guilty according to law". What it does is to establish the burden of proof of guilt, and it is a heavy burden. The effect of the safeguard could be to permit relevant international bodies, such as the Human Rights Committee and the Special Rapporteur on Extrajudicial, Summary or Arbitrary Executions (see below), to look beyond the substantive limitations discussed earlier and the procedural proprieties now under discussion. They can take cognizance of the facts of individual cases so as to ensure that the conviction and resultant death sentence could not have been erroneously arrived at on the basis of inadequate evidence.[96]

Appeals

Just as Article 6 of the covenant does not expressly require a fair trial, it also does not expressly require a right to appeal. It provides that the death penalty "can only be carried out pursuant to a final judgment rendered by a competent court", a formulation that is not defined and does not explicitly encompass an appeal. When the General Assembly adopted its resolution 2393 (XXIII) of 26 November 1968 mentioned above, which called for "the most careful legal procedures and the greatest possible safeguards for the accused in capital cases", it specifically said that these should be arrived at, among other things, "by providing that... a person condemned to death shall not be deprived of the right to appeal to a higher judicial authority or, as the case may be, to petition for pardon or reprieve". The wording of this formulation is imperfect, since it remains unclear whether a duty not to deprive of a right means that a right has to be afforded, even where such a right would not otherwise exist. Also the language could be taken to suggest that the right of appeal may be an alternative to the right to petition for pardon or reprieve.

---

95. See fn. 57, paragraph 4.
96. In practice, the Human Rights Committee, wishing to avoid being used as a further appellate court, will look to see that the trial court sought to apply the standard.

The attitude of the General Assembly was again clarified by its 15 December 1980 resolution 35/172 which, it will be recalled, urged member states "to respect as a minimum standard the content of the provisions of Article 6, 14 and 15" of the covenant. Since Article 14(5) of the Covenant provides for the right to have a conviction and sentence "reviewed by a higher tribunal according to law", this suggests a General Assembly position in favour of a right to appeal in death penalty cases. The ECOSOC resolution on safeguards in capital cases mentioned above provides: "Anyone sentenced to death shall have the right to appeal to a court of higher jurisdiction, and steps should be taken to ensure that such appeals shall become mandatory."[97]

Again, as with the right to a fair trial, the most authoritative statement is that of the Human Rights Committee that the "procedural guarantees prescribed [by Article 6] must be observed, including... the right to review by a higher tribunal."[98] Indeed, in insisting on this right as well as on those relating to a fair hearing mentioned above, the committee states: "These rights are applicable in addition to the particular right to seek a pardon or commutation of the sentence." Thus the same argument applies with the right to appeal as with the right to a fair trial; where the right to appeal has not been afforded, by virtue of suspension of the right in time of public emergency, the death penalty may not, it is submitted, be imposed.

Moreover, the appellate procedure needs to be effective. Thus, failure even by an appellate court to provide a written judgment when that is a condition for a further appeal to a higher instance, in this case, the Judicial Committee of the Privy Council in the United Kingdom, entailed a violation of Articles 6 and 14(5). Similarly, a protracted delay in making the judgment available will violate the same provisions.[99]

Clemency

Whatever imprecisions there may be regarding the rights to a fair trial and to appeal, there are none regarding the right to petition for clemency (amnesty, pardon or commutation). Article 6 of the covenant, from

---

97. See fn. 57, paragraph. 6. This is the first instrument to contain an obligation to make the appeal procedure operate independently of the action of the convicted person. States had been urged "to examine the possibility of making automatic the appeal procedure" by General Assembly resolution 35/172, 15 December 1980.

98. See fn. 17, paragraph 7.

99. *Kelly v Jamaica* (No. 253/1987), Report of the Human Rights Committee, GAOR, 4th Session, Supp. No. 40 (1991), Annex XI D, paragraphs 5.12 and 5.14 (a five-year wait); *Johnson v Jamaica* (No. 588/1994), UN document CCPR/56/D/588/1994 (1996), paragraphs. 8.8 and 3.3 (over four years); *Pratt and Morgan v Jamaica* (Nos. 210/1986 and 225 (1987), Report of the Human Rights Committee, GAOR, 44th Session, Supp. No. 40 (1989), paragraphs 13.5, 14 (b) and 15.

which no derogation is permitted, provides unambiguously in its fourth paragraph:

> Anyone sentenced to death shall have the right to seek pardon or commutation of the sentence. Amnesty, pardon or commutation of the sentence of death may be granted in all cases.

Non-execution pending appeal and clemency procedures

For any right to have meaning there must be opportunity for its enjoyment. Thus, it may well be implicit in the covenant that the right to appeal in Article 6, read together with Article 14, and the express right to seek pardon or commutation of sentence in Article 6 includes also an obligation on governments not to carry out a death sentence pending appeal or petition. Again the General Assembly addressed this matter in its resolution 2393 (XXIII) of 26 November 1968: "A death sentence shall not be carried out until the procedures of appeal or, as the case may be, of petition for pardon or reprieve have been terminated".

In addition, at its last three sessions, the Commission on Human Rights has urged retentionist states "[n]ot to execute any person as long as any related legal procedure, at international or national level, is pending".[100] This language clearly covers non-execution pending the exhaustion of judicial appeals at the national level, as well as legal proceedings before courts such as the International Court of Justice (ICJ) and regional human rights courts. It will be recalled that two states of the United States of America have executed people while proceedings were pending before the ICJ, in violation of provisional measures indicated by the ICJ under Article 41 of its statute.[101] Proceedings before regional human rights courts or other treaty bodies, such as the Human Rights Committee should also be understood as a related legal procedure.[102] In so far as covenant Article 6 contains a legal right to seek pardon or commutation of sentence, it would appear to follow that execution before this remedy has been exhausted, would fall foul of the commission's exhortation.

---

100. Commission on Human Rights res. 1999/61 (paragraph 3f), 2000/65 (paragraph 3f) and 2001/68 (paragraph 4f).

101. Vienna Convention on Consular Relations *(Paraguay v. United States of America)*, text of Order of 9 April 1998 available on the court's website: www.icj-cij.org (see also Order of 10 November 1998, whereby the court accepted Paraguay's withdrawal of the case from the court's list, the execution having been carried out as scheduled five days after the provisional measures were ordered *(ibid))*; *La Grand (Germany v United States of America)*, text of judgment of 27 June 2001, available on the court's website).

102. However, the Human Rights Committee, which found a violation of the Optional Protocol when the Philippines executed three persons whose cases were before the committee, failed to find a violation of Article 6; the record does not disclose whether the lawyers raised this issue: *Piandiong et al. v Philippines*, see fn. 74, paragraphs 5.1-5.4

Humane treatment

For many, including the present writer, if international treaties did not permit the death penalty as an exception to the right to life, it would be obvious that it would violate the prohibition of cruel, inhuman or degrading punishment, such as found in covenant Article 7.[103] Indeed, that view would be irresistible in view of the apparent prohibition by such provisions of corporal punishment. The exception of the death penalty requires us to consider the distasteful notion of whether there can be attendant circumstances which, above and beyond the cruelty and inhumanity inherent in the death penalty, condemns an execution as legally cruel and inhuman. There is now unassailable authority for the proposition.

The leading case is a regional one, *Soering v United Kingdom*,[104] in which the European Court of Human Rights held unanimously that, in the absence of satisfactory assurances that the death penalty would not be carried out, the circumstances of the case indicated that extradition "would expose him to a real risk of treatment going beyond the threshold set by Article 3".[105] The circumstances were:

1. a predicted period of six to eight years spent on death row;

2. stringent, austere conditions on death row;

3. the young age of the applicant (18 years old) at the time of the offence;

4. his mental state (he was allegedly under the dominating influence of his co-accused girl-friend who was 20 at the time, engaged in the syndrome known as *folie à deux*); and

5. the fact that he could be tried in abolitionist Germany.[106]

The European Court of Human Rights did not single out any one of these circumstances as sufficient in itself. The accent was on their combination. Whether all of them were equally necessary to the finding is also unaddressed.

---

103. See, generally, fn. 8: Schabas. The Human Rights Committee has also taken the same view: *Ng v Canada* (No. 469/1991), Report of the Human Rights Committee, Vol. II, GAOR, 49th Session, Supp. No. 40 (1994), Annex IX CC, paragraph 16.2; reproduced in *Human Rights Law Journal* (1994), vol. 15, pp. 149, 157.
104. European Court of Human Rights, Series A No. 161; reproduced in *Human Rights Law Journal* (1990), vol. 11, p. 335.
105. *Ibid.*, paragraph 111. The Court considered that an assurance from the local county attorney that the UK's wish that the death penalty not be carried out would be conveyed to the judge at the time of sentencing was not sufficient to eliminate the risk of the death penalty being imposed: (paragraph 98). The UK had accepted that the US was constitutionally debarred from promising more. After the case, the US Department of State did give a satisfactory assurance, on the basis of which Mr Soering was extradited to Virginia.
106. See fn. 104, paragraphs 106-11 and 121.

The principle enshrined in *Soering* applies also at the universal level. The Human Rights Committee has affirmed that the death penalty "must be carried out in such a way as to cause the least possible physical and mental suffering".[107] Similarly, the ECOSOC Safeguards require the penalty to be "carried out so as to inflict the minimum possible suffering" (paragraph 9). Applying the principle in practice the committee has been cautious. In a series of cases, the committee has refused to consider the time element as a factor bringing the case within Article 7.[108] It articulated its position at length in *Johnson v Jamaica*. Starting from the premise that the covenant encourages avoidance of the use of the death penalty, it took the view that to impose a time limit, explicitly or implicitly, would indicate to a state that the penalty should be carried out before the limit expires, thus discouraging initiatives such as moratoria or simply executive reluctance to order executions when abolition (or, presumably, commutation) is not politically feasible and thereby, possibly encouraging use of executions.[109] It is hard not to sympathise with this "while there's life, there's hope" argument, especially as it makes clear that it is addressing only the relevance of the time factor per se, not "other circumstances connected with detention on death row [that] may... turn that detention into cruel, inhuman and degrading treatment or punishment".[110] In fact, in the actual case, it found a 51-month delay between conviction and appeal to constitute a violation of Articles 14(3)(c) and 14(5), together with Article 6.[111]

In one case, the Human Rights Committee found that poor conditions on death row violated Article 10(1) (the right to be treated with humanity and respect for human dignity), the implication of which is not clear, as

---

107. General comment 20 (44), Report of the Human Rights Committee, UN document A/47/40 (1992), Annex VI A, paragraph 6.

108. For example, *Cox v Canada* (No. 539/1993), UN document CCPR/C/57) WP.1 (1996), *X M* and cases listed therein at paragraph 17.2, footnote 34, reproduced in *Human Rights Law Journal*, vol. 15, pp. 410, 417, footnote 7 (1994).

109. *Johnson v Jamaica* (No. 558/1994), UN document CCPR/C/56/D/588/1994 (1996), paragraphs 8.2-8.4. Six members disagreed with the majority view, insisting that the facts of individual cases should be taken into account: Ms Chanet (France), Mr Bhagwati (India), Mr Bruni Celli (Venezuela), Mr Pocar (Italy), Mr Prado Vallejo (Ecuador), Mr Aguilar Urbina (Costa Rica). Also cf. *Pratt and Morgan* in the Judicial Committee of the Privy Council, see fn. 113.

110. *Ibid.*, paragraph 8.5.

111. *Ibid.*, paragraphs 8.8-8.9. In two cases the victims spent 16 and 18 years respectively on death row, leading to a common dissent by five committee members challenging the majority's "lack of flexibility": *Bickaroo v Trinidad and Tobago* (555/1993) (UN document CCPR/61/D/555/1993 (1998), Appendix; *La Vende v Trinidad and Tobago* (554/1993), UN document CCPR/61/D/554/1993 (1998), Appendix. The dissenters were Mr Pocar (Italy), Mr Bhagwati (India), Ms Chanet (France), Mr Prado Vallejo (Ecuador) and Mr Yalden (Canada).

it also found a violation of various other articles, including 14(3)(c) and (d) and (5), with Article 6.[112] It also found a particularly gratuitous cruelty involving a delay of close to 20 hours, that is, waiting until 45 minutes before scheduled execution before communicating a reprieve to the accused, that violated Article 7. This required, in the view of the committee, commutation of the sentence.[113] However, here too there were violations of Articles 14(3)(c) and (5).

The method of execution was decisive in one case. In *Ng v Canada*, it found that Canada, by having extradited Charles Ng to California to face charges "on 19 criminal counts, including kidnapping and 12 murders", had violated covenant Article 7, because "execution by gas asphyxiation may cause prolonged suffering and agony and does not result in death as swiftly as possible, as asphyxiation by cyanide gas may take over 10 minutes."[114] The case can be compared with the Committee's decision in *Kindler v Canada* that no violation was involved in extraditing to Pennsylvania a person already convicted of first-degree murder, who escaped to Canada before sentencing but after the jury recommended the death penalty, which is by lethal injection in that state[115] It is hard to know what other methods of execution would fall foul of Article 7. One type was signalled by two members who dissented from this finding: a "method of execution such as death by stoning, which is intended to and actually inflicts prolonged pain and suffering".[116] The key point here would seem to lie in the intention.

The observer may be forgiven the suspicion that the Human Rights Committee might have preferred to avoid treading the path of choosing between different methods of achieving what they themselves agree is already cruel, inhuman and degrading, but legally permitted by Article 6.[117] But they had already decided *Kindler* in favour of Canada. There, they apparently followed *Soering*, but distinguised on the facts.[118] Five dissenters

---

112. *Kelly v Jamaica* (No. 253/1987), Report of the Human Rights Committee, GAOR, 46th Session, Supp. No. 40 (1991), Annex XI D, paragraphs 3.8, 5.7, 6.
113. *Pratt and Morgan v Jamaica* (No. 210/1986 and 225/1987), Report of the Human Rights Committee, GAOR, 44th Session, Supp. No. 40 (1989), Annex IX F, paragraphs 13.7, 15. The case also involved non-production of an appeal judgment preventing appeal to the Judicial Committee of the Privy Council. Eventually such an appeal was made, the panel holding, effectively, that a five-year period between sentence and execution would probably be inhuman and degrading: *Pratt and another v Attorney General for Jamaica* [1993] 4 All E.R. 769; reproduced in *Human Rights Law Journal*, (1993) vol. 14,.pp. 338, 346.
114. See fn. 103, paragraphs 2.1, 16.4.
115. *Kindler v Canada* (No. 470/1991), Report of the Human Rights Committee, UN document A/48/40 (Part II) (1993), Annex XII J; reproduced in *Human Rights Law Journal* (1993), vol. 14, p. 307.
116. *Ibid.*, Appendix A: Herndl (Austria); Sadi (Jordan).
117. *Ng v Canada*, see fn. 103.
118. See fn. 115, paragraph 15.3.

argued cogently that Canada, an abolitionist state (except for certain military offences), could not avail itself of an exception which could only be invoked by non-abolitionist states and indeed it was violating the mandated goal of restriction by exposing the person to the death sentence.[119] Having been unable to persuade the majority of this view, presumably it was only the issue of method on which a majority could be forged.

Persons who may not be executed

The foregoing has dealt with restrictions on capitally punishable offences and procedural safeguards that must be respected in such cases. The death penalty is further restricted in that certain categories of individual may not be executed in any circumstances.

Persons below 18 years of age

Under the covenant, the death sentence may not be imposed "for crimes committed by persons below eighteen years of age" (Article 6(5)). Also, according to Article 37 of the Convention on the Rights of the Child, "[n]either capital punishment nor life imprisonment shall be imposed for offences committed by persons below 18 years of age."[120] This wording evidently refers to the age of the person at the time the crime was committed rather than at the time of trial or sentence: a crime committed by someone who is 18 years or over at the time of coming to trial, but was under 18 at the time of the offence, would be "a crime committed by [a] person below eighteen years of age". This is corroborated by the fact that during the process of drafting Article 6, a proposal that would have fixed the age of an offender at the time of trial, and thus merely prohibited the passing of a death sentence on one under 18 years old, was rejected.[121]

The rule is reaffirmed by the ECOSOC Safeguards and reflects overwhelmingly state practice. Nevertheless, a number of states parties have not always adapted their laws to comply with the rule, although there is rarely any evidence of an intention to execute persons under 18.[122]

Of the seven countries that are known to have executed persons below the age of 18 since 1990, four are non-reserving parties to the

---

119. *Ibid.*, Appendix B: Mr Wennergren (Sweden); Appendix C: Mr Lallah (Mauritius); Appendix D: Mr Pocar (Italy); Appendix E: Ms Chanet (France); Appendix F: Mr Aguilar Urbina (Costa Rica).

120. General Assembly resolution 44/25, 20 November 1989.

121. See fn. 9: Landerer, p. 526, citing UN document A/C.3/SR.820.

122. See fn. 8: Schabas, pp. 124-5.

covenant.[123] The United States has entered a controversial reservation to the covenant effectively preserving the punishment for anyone (except a pregnant woman) "including such punishment for crimes committed by persons below eighteen years of age".[124] The Human Rights Committee, in its final comments on the first United States periodic report, considered the reservation to be "incompatible with the object and purpose of the Covenant"[125], called for its withdrawal,[126] and "exhort[ed] the authorities to take appropriate steps to ensure that persons are not sentenced to death for crimes committed before they were 18".[127] The UN Sub-Commission on the Promotion and Protection of Human Rights adopted a strongly worded condemnation of the imposition and execution of the death penalty on persons under 18 at the time of the offence, declaring this to be a violation of international law.[128]

Pregnant women and "new mothers"

The covenant also prohibits the carrying out of death sentences on pregnant women (Article 6(5)). The difference in wording between the language relating to persons under 18 years of age ("shall not be imposed") and that relating to pregnant women ("shall not be carried out") suggests the distasteful conclusion that once the pregnant woman has given birth, she may be executed. The ECOSOC Safeguards in capital cases would also forbid the carrying out of executions on "new mothers."[129]

---

123. The seven countries are Congo (Democratic Republic), Iran, Nigeria, Pakistan, Saudi Arabia, USA and Yemen. The four non-reserving states parties are Congo (Democratic Republic), Iran, Nigeria and Yemen. The USA, responsible for 15 of the 29 executions of offenders aged under 18 sentenced since 1990 (the largest total), is also a state party, but has made a reservation to Article 6, as to which see below: Amnesty International, website against the death penalty: facts and figures on the Death Penalty (www.web.amnesty.org). The other three (Bangladesh, Pakistan and Saudi Arabia) are parties to the Convention on the Rights of the Child, Article 37a of which prohibits execution of persons under 18; but Pakistan and Saudi Arabia have submitted sweeping reservations subjecting their obligations to the dictates of Islamic law. On 13 December 2001, the President of Pakistan commuted the death sentences of "around 100 young offenders": AI Index ASA/33/029/2001.

124. 31 ILM 653 (1992). See fn. 8: Schabas, pp. 83-90; Stewart, "U.S. ratification of the Covenant on Civil and Political Rights: the significance of the reservations, understandings and declarations", *Human Rights Law Journal* (1993), vol. 14, p. 77. See, on the customary international law, nature of the rule and its relevance to courts in the US, Hartman, "'Unusual' punishment: the domestic effects of international norms restricting the application of the death penalty", *University of Cincinnati Law Review* (1983), vol. 52, p. 655.

125. Report of the Human Rights Committee, UN document A/50/40 (1995), paragraph 279. The view is shared by the Special Rapporteur on Extrajudicial, Summary or Arbitrary Executions: UN document E/CN.4/1998/68, Addendum 3, paragraph 140.

126. *Ibid.*, paragraph 292.

127. *Ibid.*, paragraph 296.

128. Resolution 2000/17, 17 August 2000.

129. See fn. 57, paragraph. 3.

Persons with mental disabilities

Under many, if not most legal systems, insanity is a ground to vitiate criminal responsibility and even to prevent trial in the first place. It is also possible for people to become insane after conviction. In 1984, ECOSOC addressed itself to the issue for the first time and concluded in its safeguards that the death sentence is not to be carried out "on persons who have become insane".[130] In its resolution on implementation of the safeguards, ECOSOC proposes non-execution of "persons suffering from mental retardation or extremely limited mental comptence".[131] From 1999, the Commission on Human Rights has been urging retentionist states neither to impose the death penalty on, nor execute, "a person suffering from any form of mental disorder".[132] The resolutions are not per se legally binding.

International remedies

Although the Sixth UN Crime Congress in 1980 and the General Assembly of the same year both failed to strengthen the declared objective of abolition, the General Assembly took the first steps towards an attempt to enforce the standards that had already been agreed.

Secretary-General's "best endeavours" and action by the High Commissioner for Human Rights

In its resolution 35/172 of 15 December 1980, whose first paragraph, urging member states to "respect as a minimum standard the content of the provision of articles 6, 14 and 15 of the International Covenant on Civil and Political Rights", has already been frequently cited here, the General Assembly also requested the Secretary-General "to use his best endeavours in cases where the minimum standard of legal safeguards referred to in paragraph 1 above appears not to be respected". This mandate was reiterated in several General Assembly resolutions. It is understood that the Secretary-General has taken this mandate seriously when apprised of impending executions that may not conform to the safeguards. Accordingly, individuals or organisations having knowledge of such impending executions are known to have invoked these resolutions and presented their information to the Secretary-General, with a view to seeking his intercession.[133]

---

130. *Ibid.*
131. ECOSOC resolution 1989/64, 24 May 1989, paragraph 1(d). As Schabas points out (see fn. 8, pp. 166-68) this addressed practice in the United States.
132. Resolutions 1999/61 (paragraph 3e), 2000/65 (paragraph 3e) and 2001/68 (paragraph 4e).
133. While the Secretary-General's appeals will normally be confidential, he is free to make his concerns public. For example, the Secretary-General is reported as having appealed, albeit in vain, for the life of James Terry Roach, who was executed in the United States (South Carolina) for murder committed when he was 17. The appeal was because of the "age issue": *The New York Times,* 11 January 1986, p. 7.

Since the establishment of the office of High Commissioner for Human Rights, it may be expected that most high-level representations will be made by the incumbent. For example, in June 2000, the High Commissioner wrote to Texas Governor George W. Bush appealing for a stay of execution in the case of Gary Graham, who had been under 18 at the time of the murder for which he was convicted. When the execution went ahead, the High Commissioner issued a press release expressing deep regret.[134]

Special Rapporteur on Extrajudicial, Summary or Arbitrary Executions

ECOSOC, at its spring session of 1982, approved a resolution drafted by the Commission on Human Rights at its 1982 (38th) session whereby the chairman of the Commission was authorised to appoint a special rapporteur on summary or arbitrary executions.[135] The special rapporteur was mandated to submit to the commission at its 1983 session "a comprehensive report... on the occurrence and extent of the practice of such executions together with his conclusions and recommendations." This mandate has been consistently renewed, most recently in 2001 for a three-year period.[136] The mandate deals with extra-legal executions as well as with death penalties imposed without safeguards described above.

Of especial importance here is the technique developed by the special rapporteur of sending "urgent messages" to governments in the case of imminent or threatened executions falling within his mandate.[137] The urgent appeals technique is particularly useful in cases where the death penalty is formally pronounced and announced. This was recognised by ECOSOC which at the suggestion of the commission, when renewing the special rapporteur's mandate in 1984, requested him "to pay special attention to cases in which summary or arbitrary execution is imminent or threatened" and "to respond effectively to information that comes before him".[138] Later that year the General Assembly added its authority to a similar request.[139]

While the original commission mandate directed the special rapporteur to seek and receive information from various official sources and non-governmental organisations in consultative status with ECOSOC, this

---

134. UN Human Rights website: Press release, 23 June 2000.
135. ECOSOC resolution 1982/35, 7 May 1982.
136. Commission on Human Rights resolution 2001/45, 23 April 2001, (paragraph 23). The mandate is now described as covering "extrajudicial, arbitrary or summary executions".
137. UN document E/CN.4/1984/29, paragraph 33.
138. ECOSOC resolution 1984/35, 24 May 1984.
139. General Assembly resolution 39/110, 14 December 1984.

specification has not been reproduced in more recent resolutions renewing the mandate[140] and the twelfth report lists main non-official sources as "non-governmental organizations", without qualification, and indeed "individuals".[141] The latter are particularly important given that lawyers and even persons on death row themselves may be valuable sources of information.

Most of the special rapporteur's country visits have focused mainly on problems of extra-legal executions. One, however, has dealt predominantly with the death penalty. This was the 1997 visit of the second special rapporteur to the United States. In the report of that visit, he expressed concern about many facets of the application of the death penalty in that country, the imposition of which is "marked by arbitrariness. Race, ethnic origin and economic status appear to be key determinants of who will, and who will not, receive a sentence of death".[142] He made special note of the execution of juveniles, which "violates international law", as well as of the re-introduction or extension of the scope of the death penalty, and expressed concern "about the execution of mentally retarded and insane persons".[143] One hopes that his scathing observations on the "non-existent" knowledge at state level of the country's international legal obligations did not represent the measure of the report's impact.[144]

The creation and continuation of the post of special rapporteur is evidence that the UN has embarked on a serious, and potentially effective, approach which seeks in specific cases to hold governments to the standards they have proclaimed for themselves and attempts to prevent violations that may be about to occur. Indeed, a sophisticated combined use of both the Secretary-General's "best endeavours" and the special rapporteur's urgent appeals could prove helpful.[145]

Summary

The adoption of the Second Optional Protocol to the International Covenant on Civil and Political Rights (paralleling analogous European and Inter-American regional initiatives), with the explicit aim of abolishing the death penalty in states party to them, has made the contention

---

140. For example, see fn. 136.
141. UN document E/CN.4/1994/7, paragraph 17.
142. UN document E/CN.4/1998/68/Add.3, paragraph 148.
143. *Ibid.*, paragraph 145.
144. *Ibid.*, paragraph 142.
145. For instance, the Special Rapporteur issued a press release in the case of Gary Graham on the same day as did the High Commissioner for Human Rights, see fn. 134 and accompanying text.

that the death penalty is not a human rights issue but merely a penal policy matter, unsustainable. General international law does not yet prohibit the death penalty, but it does envisage the goal of abolition. The death penalty is not a sanction available to international penal tribunals established within the framework of the United Nations. It may be that the covenant contains an implicit obligation not to re-introduce the death penalty after it has been abolished, nor to extend it to cover crimes for which it does not at present apply. States are, in any event, expected to restrict the number of offences for which the death penalty may be applied. Further, whatever the circumstances, certain offences (non-serious or incompatible with other human rights standards) may not be made capitally punishable and certain safeguards (including the right to a fair trial, to appeal, and to petition for clemency) are to be respected if executions are not automatically to amount to arbitrary deprivation of life. Moreover, the circumstances of the death penalty must not be more inhumane than necessarily attendant on an intrinsically inhumane process. Most of these guarantees are contained in Article 6 of the International Covenant on Civil and Political Rights (especially when read together with the ECOSOC Safeguards), which deals with the right to life and must generally be seen as stating a rule of general international law, binding on all states whether or not they are parties to the covenant. In particular, no derogation from the right is permitted, even in time of grave emergency. Although the right to a fair trial and the right to appeal are not included expressly in Article 6, they should be understood as being implicitly included. Certain categories of people may not be executed in any circumstances: those 18 years of age or under when they committed a capitally punishable offence and pregnant women. ECOSOC resolutions have extended this protection to "new mothers" and "persons who have become insane" and the mentally retarded. The Commission on Human Rights adds "persons suffering from mental disorder". The UN Commission on Human Rights Special Rapporteur reports on the incidence of arbitrary and summary executions (which include death penalties carried out without proper safeguards), and can intercede to seek to prevent them. This power could well be used effectively in combination with the "best endeavours" that the General Assembly has asked the Secretary-General to deploy.

Text from Article 14 as referred to in footnote 77:
"Article 14:

1. All persons shall be equal before the courts and tribunals. In the determination of any criminal charge against him, or of his rights and obligations in a suit at law, everyone shall be entitled to a fair and public hearing by a competent, independent and impartial tribunal established by law. The press and the public may be

excluded from all or part of a trial for reasons of morals, public order (ordre public) or national security in a democratic society, or when the interest of the private lives of the parties so requires, or to the extent strictly necessary in the opinion of the court in special circumstances where publicity would prejudice the interests of justice ; but any judgement rendered in a criminal case or in a suit at law shall be made public except where the interest of juvenile persons otherwise requires or the proceedings concern matrimonial disputes or the guardianship of children.

2. Everyone charged with a criminal offence shall have the right to be presumed innocent until proved guilty according to law.

3. In the determination of any criminal charge against him, everyone shall be entitled to the following minimum guarantees, in full equality :

   (a) To be informed promptly and in detail in a language which he understands of the nature and cause of the charge against him ;

   (b) To have adequate time and facilities for the preparation of his defence and to communicate with counsel of his own choosing ;

   (c) To be tried without undue delay ;

   (d) To be tried in his presence, and to defend himself in person or through legal assistance of his own choosing ; to be informed, if he does not have legal assistance, of this right ; and to have legal assistance assigned to him, in any case where the interests of justice so require, and without payment by him in any such case if he does not have sufficient means to pay for it ;

   (e) To examine, or have examined, the witnesses against him and to obtain the attendance and examination of witnesses on his behalf under the same conditions as witnesses against him ;

   (f) To have the free assistance of an interpreter if he cannot understand or speak the language used in court ;

   (g) Not to be compelled to testify against himself or to confess guilt.

4. In the case of juvenile persons, the procedure shall be such as will take account of their age and the desirability of promoting their rehabilitation.

5. Everyone convicted of a crime shall have the right to his conviction and sentence being reviewed by a higher tribunal according to law.

6. When a person has by a final decision been convicted of a criminal offence and when subsequently his conviction has been reversed or he has been pardoned on the ground that a new or newly discovered fact shows conclusively that there has been a miscarriage of justice, the person who has suffered punishment as a result of such conviction shall be compensated according to law, unless it is proved that the non-disclosure of the unknown fact in time is wholly or partly attributable to him.

7. No one shall be liable to be tried or punished again for an offence for which he has already been finally convicted or acquitted in accordance with the law and penal procedure of each country."

Alternatives to the death penalty – The United Kingdom experience

Peter Hodgkinson[1]
Director, Centre for Capital Punishment Studies, School of Law, University of Westminster

By charting the origins and subsequent changes and developments of the penalty that replaced capital punishment in the United Kingdom in 1965 I hope to identify those practices that have made a positive contribution to this debate and those which, in my opinion, have hindered the establishment of what could have been a humane, effective and proportionate punishment. Because this article is written with the intention of informing those engaged in devising and implementing penal policy it is necessarily detailed in its content in order that problems and pitfalls can be flagged. Though the temptation to substitute draconian prison terms or whole of life imprisonment in the belief that this is necessary to "buy" the support of a public generally opposed to abolishing the death penalty may be understandable politically, it has to be avoided. This is the moment when rational penal policy should prevail over expediency and compromise. The UK experience illustrates how easily, though perhaps inadvertently, how the best of intentions at the time of abolition can saddle nations with long-term problems. In February 2003 there were over 5 500 prisoners serving life imprisonment in England & Wales, 569 in Scotland (February 2001) and 85 in Northern Ireland (February 2002).

The term "life imprisonment" is itself a source of much confusion and, judging by the responses to the enquiries we have been making of Council of Europe member states, this confusion is widespread.[2] From the evidence so far received most states have a form of life imprisonment as the alternative though few anticipate that those sentenced will in fact remain in prison for the whole of their lives. The process of selecting the alternative penalty appears not to have been the subject of much discus-

---

1. I am very grateful to Ms Seema Kandelia and Ms Seetal Purohit, Researchers with the Centre for Capital Punishment Studies for their invaluable contribution to this article.
2. Ongoing research being conducted by the Centre for Capital Punishment Studies concerning the replacement penalties for capital punishment amongst member states of the Council of Europe.

sion other than, we suspect, the decision to choose a harsh alternative as the only acceptable measure to a public hostile to abolition. The decision about alternatives highlights the need to exercise scrutiny of the process to ensure that no "net-widening" occurs especially in those states where a number of offences, in addition to murder, formerly attracted capital punishment. One thing is clear and that is there is no consistency across states as to what constitutes the most serious offence(s) attracting the alternative to the death penalty, thus potentially breaching the ECOSOC[3] Safeguards that outline the basic guarantees to be respected in criminal justice proceedings to ensure the rights of offenders charged with a capital offence. The EU has similar guidelines.[4] Our information thus far indicates that there is also a wide variation of procedures relating to periods of imprisonment to be served before release into the community is considered. In Austria 22 years is the average term served; 20 to 40 years in Croatia; maximum of 20 years in Denmark; in Estonia a minimum of 30 years of a life sentence; in Finland an average of between 10 and 15 years is served and release is in the gift of the President of the Republic; Hungary has no special alternative but on average between 20 and 30 years of a life sentence is served; Latvia has a mandatory life sentence and sentences served are between 6 months and a maximum of 15 years, though occasionally for especially serious crimes a maximum of 20 years is the norm; Germany is one of few countries that has a mandatory life sentence but in fact 15 years is the maximum term served prior to consideration for release; Luxembourg has life imprisonment with a minimum of 15 years to be served before parole is considered; in Poland there is a life sentence of which a minimum of 25 years is to be served prior to consideration for release. From the data so far available, Sweden and Bulgaria appear to be the only countries that have whole of life imprisonment – in Sweden it is possible to petition the parliament for a pardon as it is in Bulgaria to petition the president. Ukraine has whole of life imprisonment but provides an opportunity at 15 years to petition the president – no information has been made available to us about the grounds for such an appeal or the outcome. The strategy in Georgia, we have been informed, was to provide a whole of life sentence at the time of abolition to satisfy the public but it was always the intention to revise this to a reviewable sentence after a few years, once the heat had gone out of the debate.

---

3. "Safeguards guaranteeing protection of the rights of those facing the death penalty," ECOSOC resolution 1984/50 Annex, 25/05/1984, UN document E/1984/150; "Implementation of the safeguards guaranteeing protection of the right of those facing the death penalty', ECOSOC resolution 1989/64, 24/05/1989; Reports of the Secretary-General on these ECOSOC resolutions UN document E/1995/78 (08/06/1995) and UN document. E/CN.15/2001/10 (29/03/2001).
4. "Guidelines to European Union policy towards third countries on the death penalty", Part 111, www.eurunion.org/legislat/DeathPenalty/Guidelines.htm

One of the few nations that does set out to incarcerate its citizens for their natural lives is the United States of America, achieving this through a combination of determinate sentences of epic dimensions, whole of life sentences as an option for capital crimes and as part of the "three strikes and you are out" policy. Dirk van Zyl Smit elaborates on this:

> There is no general restriction on the length of prison sentences that can be imposed, either for a single offence or cumulatively, with the result that effective life sentences may be imposed indirectly by imposing a term that is far beyond the normal life expectancy of the offender. Although civil confinement of the sane, merely on the grounds of the danger they present to the public, is not allowed, there is the further possibility that forms of indefinite further detention may be ordered after a determinate sentence has been completed by a "dangerous" offender, thus ensuring that the offender is effectively subjected to a life sentence in this way. Finally it should be noted that life sentences, including life without the prospect of parole, may be, and are, imposed on very young juveniles.[5]

Figures based on US Bureau of Justice Statistics for 1992 revealed that thirty states and the Federal Bureau of Prisons had a specific sentence of life without parole (LWOP) accounting for some 13 937 prisoners.[6] In 2003, thirty-five of the thirty-eight states with capital punishment (together with the federal and military statutes) offered LWOP, the exceptions being Kansas, New Mexico and Texas, and of the twelve states without the death penalty all except Alaska have LWOP. Death penalty activists in the latter states consider this to be vital to the campaigns repelling calls for the restoration of capital punishment.[7] In 1999, figures based on the data from forty-eight reporting agencies and the federal system show that 25 554 prisoners were serving LWOP, in addition there were 80 142 prisoners serving life sentences and a further 178 363 serving sentences of over twenty years comprising in total 26.2% of the total prison population. This has contributed to an imprisonment industry that houses some two million citizens, the largest prison population in the world accounting for 25% of the world prison population (686 per 100 000 of the national population) whilst representing a mere 4% of the peoples of the world.

Commentators in the United States see no end to the year on year growth of the LWOP with all the demands that this ageing population will

---

5. Dirk van Zyl Smit, *Taking life imprisonment seriously in national and international law*, Kluwer Law International, Aspen Publishers, New York, 2002. This volume provides an excellent analysis of the principles and development of life imprisonment with specific reference to the experiences of the USA, England & Wales and Germany and I refer frequently to its findings – with thanks.

6. US Department of Justice: Bureau of Statistics, @Sourcebook of Criminal Justice Statistics 1992, Washington DC. Table 6.81,633.

7. Death Penalty Information Centre, Washington, DC. www.deathpenaltyinfo.org (10/05/2003).

161

make on the exchequers of the states concerned let alone the questionable evidence on which such a penal philosophy is based. In fact what evidence there is points in the opposite direction as Marquart[8] and more recently Cunningham in the United States have demonstrated; that is, just how difficult it is to predict future "dangerousness" on the basis of a past murder.[9] A key piece of research on this issue in the UK was carried out by Hood and Shute[10] and included a detailed examination of the decision-making processes of the parole board and whether the balance between the need to reintegrate prisoners back into society and public protection was correct. Further valuable research into the decision-making processes of the discretionary lifer panels has been carried out by Padfield, Liebling and Arnold.[11]

I will dwell no further on the excesses of the United States, as the purpose of this article is to focus on strategies that have something constructive to contribute in the areas of effectiveness, proportionality and humanity in sentencing, none of which are either sought or achieved in that country. Thus the debate about alternatives joins the general debate about the administration of capital punishment in the United States which I believe has little relevance to the wider world other than to continue to provide compelling evidence of all that is flawed about capital punishment. The US experience of the implementation of whole of life imprisonment should serve as a warning to abolitionists worldwide that it is irresponsible not to engage in the discussion about alternative penalties and that the acceptance of a whole of life alternative is a compromise too far.

The final steps to abolition

The Royal Commission on Capital Punishment 1949-53

> To consider and report whether liability under the criminal law in Great Britain to suffer capital punishment for murder should be limited or modified, and if so, to what extent and by what means, for how long and under what conditions persons who would otherwise have been liable to suffer capital punishment should be detained, and what changes in the existing law and the prison system would be required; and to enquire into and take account of the position in those countries whose experience and practice may throw light on these questions.[12]

---

8. James Marquart and Jonathan Sorensen, "A national study of the Furman-commuted inmates: assessing the threat to society from capital offenders," in H.A.Bedau, *The death penalty in America – current controversies,* Oxford University Press, Oxford, 1997.
9. Mark Cunningham, et al., "Integrating base rate data in violent risk assessments at capital sentencing," *Behavioural Sciences and the Law,* 1988, vol. 16, pp. 71, 85.
10. Roger Hood and Stephen Shute with Aidan Wilcox, "The parole system at work: a study of risk based decision making", Home Office Research Study 202, 2000.
11. Nicola Padfield, Alison Liebling with Helen Arnold, "An exploration of decision-making at discretionary lifer panels," Home Office Research Study 213, 2000.
12. The terms of reference of the Royal Commission on Capital Punishment, 1949-53.

The Gower Report (so named after its chairman) made a number of observations that touched on the issue of alternatives to capital punishment including the view that judges should not be given the discretion to select between hanging or life imprisonment, but they did suggest that juries – after convicting a defendant – should have the additional responsibility of deciding whether a sentence other than death should be imposed. As to the "other" sentence, they were clear that this should always be life imprisonment. Their observations on the existing life sentence were that they knew of no occasion where anyone had been sentenced to prison for the whole of their life and furthermore had, "received no evidence that the public regards as inadequate the periods at present served by life sentence prisoners...which were on the whole longer than those served for any other crimes". Professor van Zyl Smit quoting from Nigel Walker notes that "between 1950 and 1960 almost three-quarters of released lifers (all except four who were reprieved murderers) were released after eight, nine or ten years."[13] Length of sentence served and consideration for release were entirely in the gift of the Home Secretary who in his submission to the Gower Report commented that:

> The punishment must be sufficient to deter others and to be accepted by public opinion as an adequate vindication of the law: it ought not to suggest that the crime of murder is regarded lightly by the state or can be put on the same level with other crimes. It is therefore desirable to grade the terms as far as possible according to the degree of culpability in each case. Account must also be taken of the length of sentences imposed by the courts for other offences.[14]

Their research on terms served before release revealed that in 1866 a minimum of twenty years had been the tariff; by the late 1890s this was effectively the maximum and then prisoners were being routinely released at fifteen years. By 1939 between ten and thirteen years were terms commonly served prior to eventual release on licence. The 1940s witnessed further reductions to terms served between six and ten years.[15] The home secretary's powers to determine the term to be served were not problematic for Gower and his colleagues, in fact the process and the principle of the release under supervision of life sentence prisoners was in the commission's opinion accepted by the public.

The 1957 Homicide Act

The Homicide Act 1957, hastily introduced in conjunction with the Abolition of the Death Penalty bill tabled by Sidney Silverman MP in 1956, was – many believed – an attempt to thwart the progress of that

---

13. Nigel Walker, *Crime and punishment in Britain.* University of Edinburgh Press, Edinburgh, 1965.
14. The Royal Commission on Capital Punishment, p. 226.
15. From *Taking life imprisonment seriously,* Dirk van Zyl Smit, see fn. 5.

bill and any future abolitionist attempts.Therefore it is ironic that the act unwittingly provided succour to the abolition movement, because it was ill-conceived, poorly drafted and contained manifestly unjust anomalies leading to both perverse jury decisions and hostile judicial direction. In essence, what it set out to achieve was to limit the scope of capital punishment by making distinctions between different sorts of murder, those thought to be susceptible to deterrence attracted the death penalty and for the rest the penalty was to be mandatory life imprisonment. These were measures specifically advised against by the Gower Commission whose principal recommendations had already been rejected.[16] In Van Zyl Smit's opinion: "In the history of life imprisonment this was a key development, for there was now for the first time a category of crime, non-capital murder, for which life imprisonment was a mandatory sentence."[17] Additionally, as a means of further reducing murders, and therefore capital murders, two special defences were introduced in the act, which if successful would have the effect of reducing murder to manslaughter.[18] Between 1958 when the provisions of this act were enacted and the publishing of the abolition bill in December 1964, 43 people had been convicted of capital murder (30 for theft followed by murder, 11 for murder by shooting and 2 for theft followed by shooting) and of this number 26 had been executed.[19]

The Abolition of the Death Penalty bill

After decades when abolition was advanced by the House of Commons (the elected chamber of the Houses of Parliament) and invariably rejected by the largely hereditary House of Lords invariably with the support of the Anglican bishops,[20] the likelihood of an incoming Labour government provided sufficient sustenance for the abolitionists in Parliament and elsewhere to prepare for what they optimistically hoped would be success in abolishing the death penalty. Their optimism was nearly misplaced as in October 1964 when the Labour party scraped home with "a majority of 15 over the Conservatives and an overall majority of just four seats."[21] Whilst the Labour party manifesto published in September 1964 made no mention of capital punishment the leader of the party, Harold Wilson, indicated that the issue would be

16. "The Royal Commission on capital punishment, 1949-1953". Report (Cmnd. 8932), London, HMSO, 1953.
17. From *Taking life imprisonment seriously*, Dirk van Zyl Smit, see fn. 5.
18. Diminished responsibility (Section 2) and Provocation (Section 3) of the Homicide Act 1957.
19. Hansard, vol. 703, 146, 7 December 1964.
20. Harry Potter, *Hanging in judgment – from the bloody code to abolition*, SCM Press, Oxford, 1993.
21. Brian P Block and John Hostettler, *Hanging in the balance – a history of the abolition of capital punishment in Britain*, Waterside Press, Winchester, 1997.

dealt with through a free vote in Parliament and that government time would be found for this,[22] a promise confirmed when it appeared in the Queen's Speech. Prior to any draft legislation being introduced, the issue of the alternative penalty was being raised in many quarters and in response to a question on this topic from a Conservative MP, Sir Frank Soskice, the Labour Home Secretary, replied that he was "reluctant to make it higher than nine or ten years because that was the maximum period a prisoner could undergo before his personality deteriorated, but if it was in the interests of society he could be kept inside longer".[23] In addition to the discussion about alternative sanctions there was of course the general challenge to the whole notion of abolition, with those opposed to it at any price and those who wanted to exempt murderers of police and prison officers from any such legislation, though the resistance was noticeably less enthusiastic than on previous occasions.

When Sidney Silverman eventually presented his bill[24] to Parliament the debate intensified with recommendations that sentences of twenty to twenty-five years would more accurately reflect the seriousness of the crime and provide reassurance to the families of murder victims. Note that no mention was made of life imprisonment or sentence length, though it was assumed by all that life imprisonment would be the favoured alternative, to which Edward Gardner commented: "Life imprisonment was a vague and indeterminate sentence and was unlikely to frighten anyone but the potential victim".[25] In welcoming the bill, Hugh Klare, secretary of the Howard League for Penal Reform, said that "life imprisonment should be an indeterminate sentence the length of which should be decided by the Home Secretary on the basis of an assessment programme."[26]

On the matter of the sanction to replace the death sentence, Sidney Silverman's views were expressed thus:

> I suggest to the Committee that on consideration it will be felt that there ought to be retained, first the principle that murder is an exceptional crime and that there ought to be an automatic life sentence for it. There is no reason why we should depart from that principle, and certainly no reason why retentionists should want to depart from it. Secondly, a life sentence should not now begin to be regarded as literally a life sentence since it has never been so

---

22. *The Times*, 21 April 1964, p.10.
23. Hansard, p.5, 25 November 1964.
24. "A Bill to abolish capital punishment in the case of persons convicted in Great Britain of murder or a corresponding offence by court martial, in connection therewith, to make further provision for the punishment of persons who are convicted. Further provision will be a proposal to allow judges to prescribe long sentences." *Hansard*, p.10, 3 December 1964.
25. *The Times*, p.5, 8 December 1964.
26. See fn. 5: Dirk van Zyl Smit: p. 235, *Hanging in the balance*.

regarded. Thirdly, there are two factors in determining the date on which a man might be released on licence, one of them capable of being determined by the trial judge – namely, the inherent wickedness of the crime – and the other not capable of being determined by the trial judge because it would depend on what happened to the man in the course of years.
(*Hansard*, 5 May 1965, col. 1293)

And he continued:

[I]n this question of how long a life prisoner should be detained we must consider three elements: one, the gravity of the offence; two, the safety of the public; and three the danger of destroying by degrees over long, long years a life which we have refrained from destroying at the beginning. All these factors have to be taken into consideration, and the Home Secretary has the right, has the duty, has the responsibility and has the means, if we keep the life sentence, of taking them into consideration.
(*Ibidem*, col. 888)[27]

The Home Secretary put on record his understanding of the replacement sentence:

[He] ...recognised that in the case of extreme necessity, lifelong detention might be necessary. But, he recognised that this would occur only in the context of a need to protect society from an extremely dangerous offender.

But he clearly stated:

Even with the worst type of prisoner, I would always be loathe...wholly to extinguish any hope in the mind of any human being that he would ever be allowed to walk outside the prison walls.
(*Hansard*, 21 December 1964, col. 928)

Later he stated:

It would be terrible if anything said during this debate led any prisoner, any human being who is in custody... to say to himself, "I have no hope of ever regaining my future". It would be dreadful to say that.
(*Hansard*, 31March 1965, col. 1579)

He did not reject the judicial determination of tariffs on the ground that the sentence already ordered lifelong detention on punitive grounds. On the contrary, he considered that the judiciary were not well placed to take account of "far the most important consideration after a long period of imprisonment", namely "the condition, character and reaction of the individual to his confinement." (*Hansard*, 28 October 1965, col. 379-80).

Further, he stated on 21 December 1964:

It may well be... that in cases hereafter, if there were no commutation because of mitigating circumstances, the death penalty having gone, it would seem

---

27. Extracted from the brief (counsel for the appellant) in *Regina v Secretary of State for the Home Department, (respondent) ex parte Anthony Anderson (appellant)*. In the House of Lords on appeal from the Court of Appeal [England], In the matter of an application for Judicial Review. Edward Fitzgerald QC, Sally Hatfield, Phillippa Kaufman, pp.16-17. Referred to from now as the as *Doughty Street/Anderson* case.

proper, having regard to the nature of the crime and the character of the individual, that the sentence should be longer than nine years. I would be reluctant to make it much longer…because, generally speaking, experience shows that nine years, ten years, or thereabouts is the maximum period of confinement that normal human beings can undergo without their personality decaying, their will going and their becoming progressively less able to re-enter society and to look after themselves and become useful citizens. That is the position.[28]
(*Hansard*, 21 December 1964, cols 929-30)

A few weeks before the second reading of the bill, opposition took the form of those who wanted the death penalty retained for the murder of police or prison officers and another group that wanted the discretion on sentence to be served to remain the prerogative of the courts and yet another group of thirty Conservative MPs signed a motion tabled by Thomas Iremonger seeking to reject the bill altogether as no "deterrent of comparable gravity" to the death penalty had been proposed.[29] Sir Edward Gardner tabled an amendment requiring that the penalty for murder should be for life unless the court decided otherwise.[30] *The Times*,[31] which had been thoughtfully commenting on the passage of the bill, finally declared its support for the replacement of the death penalty but in so doing suggested that judges should be responsible for setting the sentences as for other offences and that more consideration should be given to the process through which prisoners were to be released. A further suggestion advanced by David Walter MP was that he preferred to allow the courts to have discretion as to whether someone should be sentenced to life or receive some other term of imprisonment,[32] whereas Sir Thomas Moore offered a rather unique justification for the retention of capital punishment through his observation that "watching people rot away in prison was too horrible to contemplate so the death penalty should be the punishment for all types of murder"[33] – an unusual alternative to imprisonment!

Whilst not directly related to the issue of alternatives I cannot resist sharing a flavour of the passion that this debate provoked. During the second reading Brigadier Terence Clarke MP launched a personal attack on Sidney Silverman and the Home Secretary Sir Frank Soskice by suggesting that all murderers should hang and that Silverman and Soskice should hang too! As Block and Hostettler record it:

> He [Clarke] believed that British juries never made mistakes, or if they did, the odd man executed in error was well worthwhile in the cause of saving

---

28. *Doughty Street/Anderson case*, pp.17-18, see fn. 27.
29. *Hansard*, p.12, 12 December 1964.
30. *The Times*, p.6, 16 December 1964.
31. *Ibidem*, 18 December 1964.
32. *Hansard*, p.7, 19 December 1964.
33. *Hansard*, p.7, 21 December 1964.

innocent children. More children were going to be killed and it was all Mr. Silverman's fault. When Silverman pointed out that child murder had not been a capital crime since 1958, Clarke retorted that lawyers could prove anything.

The second reading was carried with a surprisingly large majority of 185 votes, which included eighty Conservatives. At the committee stage a number of new amendments were tabled including one that sought to reserve the death penalty for murder committed by anyone who had previously been sentenced to life imprisonment for murder (this amendment was tabled again at the second committee stage and defeated),[34] and Sir Edward Gardner's revised amendment sought to impose a minimum sentence of twenty-five years before consideration for release. Henry Brooke, a former Conservative Home Secretary tabled an amendment which would in effect suspend the death penalty for a period of five years before which time the act would need to be affirmed by both Houses of Parliament.

The third reading debate provided the last opportunity for those opposed to abolition to marshal their arguments, many of which focused on the issue that the alternative sentence being proposed neither reflected the seriousness of the offence, the feelings of the victims' families nor provided sufficient deterrent to the crime of murder. Nearly forty years on these remain the concerns of those opposing abolition. From the opposition benches Sir John Hobson was convinced that abolition would lead to an increase in murder and armed robbery, others were just opposed without any obvious considered position to support their opposition other than perhaps that Conservatives support the status quo. On the question of the appropriateness of the life sentence alternative, Sir Henry Brooke believed that it would be a deterrent and suggested that such prisoners should remain in prison for a maximum of fifteen years unless there were mitigating circumstances to reduce the term. The third reading was carried by 200 votes to 98 – voting with the majority were twenty-three Conservatives including nine former ministers.[35]

The bill then moved to the House of Lords, which had become the graveyard of many previous attempts to abolish the death penalty and Silverman was by no means confident that the inbuilt hereditary Conservative party membership was yet persuaded of the arguments for abolition. This was the arena for concession and compromise, which very quickly became apparent when Baroness Wootton introduced the bill as providing an automatic life sentence for murder or detention during Her Majesty's Pleasure (i.e. indeterminate sentence nominally as long as the Queen sees fit, although in practice it is the Parole Board who

---

34. *Hansard*, cols.1571-1620, 31 March 1965.
35. *The Times*, p.8, 14 July 1965.

reviews the length of the sentence) for those convicted of murder before their eighteenth birthday. Additionally the act, if passed, would remain in operation for only five years unless affirmed by both Houses of Parliament.[36] The Lord Chief Justice Lord Parker, whilst generally supportive of the bill was concerned that under the proposed life sentence, terms of nine and ten years were insufficient and should be longer but served in humane conditions. As a judge he was especially conscious of what he thought were the "absurdities" of the existing provisions of the Homicide Act, which he needed assuring would not be repeated under the proposed legislation. Some of the arguments opposing abolition were based on rejecting the utilitarian claims of deterrence and rehabilitation believing that the retributive goals of capital punishment should not be discarded or discounted – if there were flaws in the 1957 Homicide Act then Parliament should be concentrating on correcting them not on drafting new legislation. On this occasion, and quite exceptionally on this topic, the House of Lords voted for a second reading by a majority of 100. Important to note that what made this exceptional was the coalition of the Government, the Lord Chancellor, the Lord Chief Justice and judges and the Archbishop of Canterbury and the bishops – this last group historically had provided a stumbling block to previous abolition bills. The position of this archbishop is in stark contrast with that adopted by Archbishop Geoffrey Fisher in his evidence to the Royal Commission on Capital Punishment. Quoting from Block and Hostettler:

> Of the death sentence, he said in words that have since passed into history, " it was intolerable that this solemn and significant procedure should be enacted when in almost half the cases the consequences would not follow." He added, "speaking as a churchman, so long as this awful punishment...is retained it should be delivered from every circumstance which may make it anything less than it is...." It was only his flowery turn of phrase that delayed for a moment or two the stark meaning of his words: hang the lot! He considered that unpremeditated and provoked killings were both murder and the meaning should be the same. "Occasionally" there might be extenuating circumstances, but he would not remove mercy killing from the category of murder.

Furthermore he added he was not here as an advocate of the death penalty nor did he "commit himself to any view on the ethical side"![37]

At the report stage of the bill the Lord Chief Justice tabled an amendment carried by 80 votes to 78 (supported by 10 of the 11 judges) the effect of which would be to abolish mandatory life imprisonment leaving the sentence to the discretion of judges. Later Lord Parker conceded to the government's request to drop this amendment and in its stead agreed to the amendments that judges would be able to recommend a minimum

---

36. *Hansard*, (268) 456, 19 July 1965.
37. See fn. 20: Harry Potter *Hanging in judgment*, p.131.

term to be served and that the Home Secretary would be required to consult the Lord Chief Justice and the trial judge, if available, before a lifer was released.[38] The force of this coalition was sufficient to persuade the opposition not to divide the House and the bill was passed with but two amendments added to those from the committee stages: the first related to placing a five year limit on the life of the provisions and the second enabled the trial judge to recommend to the Home Secretary the minimum period to be served prior to being released on life licence. The bill received the Royal Assent on the 8 November 1965 and passed into law as the Murder (Abolition of the Death Penalty) Act 1965.

So much for the death throes of capital punishment (for ordinary offences in peacetime) and despite the occasionally arcane parliamentary procedures that guided or thwarted its passage one issue shines through the deliberations about the alternative sentence and that is the near consensus that only in the rarest circumstances would anyone be confined to imprisonment for the whole of their life and that the minimum sentences set by the judiciary would be proportionate, reviewable and served in humane conditions followed by supervision in the community.

Disagreements about the role of the judiciary and the executive and of their combined effects on the rights of those sentenced to life imprisonment were voiced from the outset and have consumed the energies of many since abolition – the ensuing sections paraphrase some of the legal challenges and enquiries that have addressed these perceived problems and should help the reader identify potential pitfalls in replacement strategies.

Activities since abolition

Miscellaneous enquiries into the life sentence

The earliest review following abolition on the issue of mandatory sentences was carried out in 1973 by the Criminal Law Revision Committee (CLRC): it came to an interim conclusion that the advantages of the mandatory sentence far outweighed any disadvantages.[39] In rejecting the proposal that the mandatory nature of the sentence denied judicial discretion they felt that:

> ...the release procedure which had operated since 1967 gave the judiciary an increased role in this procedure both because they were consulted and because they were involved in the parole process.

---

38. Section 1(2) Murder (Abolition of the Death Penalty) Act 1965.
39. Criminal Law Revision Committee, Twelfth report: Penalty for murder (Cmnd. 5184), HMSO, London, 1973.

Particularly revealing was the 1970 annual report of the Parole Board,[40] which the committee quoted with explicit approval. In it the Parole Board claimed that with indeterminate sentences such as life imprisonment its function assumed a sentencing character.[41] The Butler Committee in 1975 believed that many in the "legal and related professions" wanted the mandatory sentence repealed but this view was unlikely to prevail, as it would fall foul of public opinion. Given the committee's remit to examine the policy on mentally abnormal offenders their views on this matter have particular authority when they highlight what is in effect a serious anomaly that forbids judges' discretion for those convicted of murder yet permits them the discretion to impose any sentence, including life imprisonment, on a category of life taker convicted of the lesser offence of manslaughter, as arguably this group present a greater danger to the public because of their "diminished responsibility."[42]

The Advisory Council on the Penal System (1978) in arguing for the abolition of the mandatory life sentence for murder also took issue with a number of the findings of the 1973 CLRC report.[43] In 1980 the CLRC[44] revisited its interim conclusion reached in 1973 and whilst there were indications that the committee was evenly split over the issue of mandatory life sentences they came to no conclusion on the issue, merely rehearsing the pros and cons of the debate. In Dirk van Zyl Smit's opinion this was the last occasion when an "expert" view supported the retention of the mandatory life sentence for murder.

The next concerted effort challenging the mandatory sentence was mounted by the senior judges on the issues of the definition of murder and the mandatory sentence it attracted; the preference of most judges was that life imprisonment should be a maximum not a mandatory sentence for murder. The House of Lords' select committee[45] refuted the proposition that unique offences such as murder required unique sanctions arguing that there was nothing unique about murder in that:

> its definition was so wide that it encompassed crimes where the offender may have intended to wound rather than kill (and) moreover, the life sentence was not unique to murder.[46]

---

40. Annual Report of the Parole Board, HMSO, London, 1970.

41. See fn. 5: Dirk van Zyl Smit, *Taking life imprisonment seriously*, p.99.

42. Report of the Committee on Mentally Abnormal Offenders, (Cmnd. 6244), HMSO, London, 1975, p. 245.

43. Advisory Council on the Penal System, *Sentences of imprisonment: a review of maximum penalties,* HMSO, London, 1978.

44. Criminal Law Revision Committee, Fourteenth report: Offences against the person.

45. "Report of the Select Committee of the House of Lords on murder and life imprisonment" (HL paper, 78), HMSO, London, 1989.

46. See fn. 5, Dirk van Zyl Smit, *Taking life imprisonment seriously,* p. 101.

The select committee also recommended that the trial judge should state in open court the length of imprisonment to be served to fulfil the requirements of deterrence and retribution (the tariff), that this term be subject to appeal and the release of the prisoner on licence should be determined by a judicial tribunal. Evidence produced by the Home Office in its submission revealed that during a six-month period in 1988 the Home Secretary had set a higher tariff than that recommended by the trial judge in 63 of 106 mandatory life sentence cases.

In arguing that the sentence should be left to the discretion of the judges they went on to say:

> After the introduction of a discretionary sentence for murder, the Committee anticipate that the average length of time served under a life sentence will be considerably longer than it is now. The Committee expect that their proposals will lead to very lengthy penal sanctions being set in the most grave cases. In some cases, this may result in imprisonment for the rest of the prisoner's life.

The National Council for Civil Liberties (Liberty) in its submission to the select committee rejected the principle of life imprisonment believing it was "contrary to the basic tenets of English criminal justice whereby citizens should be punished for what they do, not for what they might do".[47]

Several of the select committee's recommendations appeared as amendments to the 1991 Criminal Justice bill where they were passed only to be rejected when the bill returned to the House of Commons, among these was the amendment that "No court shall be required to sentence a person convicted of murder to imprisonment for life". The progressive and rational principles on which elements of the 1991 Criminal Justice Act were based soon suffered a setback as the climate of public and political opinion were to change radically to a punitive position, also adopted by the Labour party opposition who opportunistically hitched itself to the populist bandwagon of the right-wing law and order movement. This new punitive climate did not augur well for a number of attempts to address the mandatory life sentence including the Penalty for Murder bill introduced in the House of Lords (1993);[48] the Penal Reform Trust[49] enquiry into the penalty for murder chaired by the former Lord Chief Justice Lord Lane (1993) and the Justice Report of 1996.[50] Contemporaneous to the Justice Report the All-Party Home Affairs

---

47. Select Committee, vol. 2, p.327.
48. Lord Windlesham, *Responses to crime,* Clarendon Press, Oxford, 1996.
49. "Report of an independent inquiry into the mandatory life sentence for murder," Prison Reform Trust, 1993.
50. "Sentenced for life: reform of the law and procedure for those sentenced to life imprisonment", *Justice,* 1996.

Select Committee,[51] with an in-built Conservative party majority, recommended that tariff and release decisions for lifers should be removed from the Home Secretary and that "both prosecution and defence should be able to appeal against length of tariff (which should be decided by the trial judge) to the Court of Appeal."[52] The arrival of the first "socialist" government for nearly two decades with a landslide victory in 1997 soon proved to be a disappointment in this arena as policies and principles expressed in opposition were jettisoned; one such was the statement of unequivocal opposition to replacing the mandatory life sentence for murder made in the House of Commons by the Home Secretary Jack Straw,[53] contrary to the views expressed in 1991 when the Labour party was in opposition.[54]

Executive changes and the battles in the courts

Since the abolition of the death penalty, a range of issues relating to the mandatory sentence of life imprisonment has been brought before the domestic courts and the European Court of Human Rights challenging the mandatory nature of the sentence, the process by which lifers have their tariffs set and conditional release determined and the powers of the executive to influence all aspects of this sentence. In this section I will review in brief some of the landmark cases that have brought important changes to the process.

At the time of abolition it was agreed that the Home Secretary would have to consult with the Lord Chief Justice and the trial judge before establishing a timetable for and authorising release on licence, although no procedure was agreed as to the timing of this decision. In effect what used to happen was that the Home Secretary would take on average some three to four years before deciding on a timetable and only then consult the Lord Chief Justice and trial judge (known as the Joint Consultative Committee) after which the Parole Board[55] was involved in more detailed assessment about the time to be served prior to active consideration for release. As someone who was intimately involved in this process from a probation service perspective I can remember well that between five and seven years on average could elapse before a timeline

51. Home Affairs Select Committee, (Session 95-96), 1st report: "Murder: the mandatory life sentence" (HC 111); 2nd report: "Murder: the mandatory life sentence (supplementary report) (HC 412).
52. See Justice Intervention in *R v Secretary of State for the Home Department, ex parte Anderson and Taylor.*
53. *Hansard,* vol. 346, col. 28, 13 March 2000.
54. *Hansard,* vol. 193, cols 868-74, 25 June 1991.
55. The Parole Board was created by Section 61(1) of the 1967 Criminal Justice Act, putting the process for the early release of prisoners on a statutory footing. It became an independent executive non-departmental public body on the enactment of the Criminal Justice and Public Order Act 1994.

was known, bringing significant anxiety not just to the prisoner but to all those professionally engaged in working with him/her. In effect these became wasted years delaying the crucial work during what has now become to be known as the sentence-planning phase.

The term "tariff" formally entered the vocabulary of the life sentence process in 1983 when the Home Secretary Leon Brittan announced it at a Conservative party conference as one of a number of changes, another being the introduction of a minimum tariff of twenty years for certain types of murder. These "executive" changes brought considerable turmoil to the prison system and the lifers because some who were already being actively considered for release on licence were effectively returned to the early parts of the process rather like the random experience of landing on a long snake in Snakes and Ladders [board game]! A challenge to this policy at the time was unsuccessful.[56] The tariff was the period of detention to be served by lifers, after consultation with the Lord Chief Justice and trial judge, to satisfy the needs of deterrence and retribution after which a recommendation to release on licence would be the responsibility of the Parole Board, confirmed or not by the Home Secretary who had the power of veto though only in the direction of yes to no – signalling a punitive phase and a risk phase. Important to note that this seismic change to the procedures that life-sentenced prisoners were subjected was put in place not by the courts or parliament but entirely on the authority of a individual politician – an indication of just how much unfettered discretion the Home Secretary had.

Following the policy change to the process introduced by Leon Brittan, the first legal challenge on these issues was mounted in 1987 by *Handscomb and others*[57] sentenced to discretionary life imprisonment. The petitioners argued that it was unreasonable to subject them to such a delay and the court agreed that the delay was unreasonable and that in future judges were to be consulted immediately after the trial and a tariff set.

> Although the judgment applied only to discretionary life sentence prisoners, the Home Secretary, Douglas Hurd, announced in his statement of 23 July 1987 (Hansard, cols. 347-9) that, in the future, the judicial recommendation on tariff would be obtained as soon as practicable after sentence. This practice was to be adopted for mandatory life sentence prisoners as well as discretionary lifers. This change further assimilated the procedure of fixing a tariff to a sentencing exercise and was prompted by a recognition that this was, in fact, the nature of the exercise.[58]

---

56. *Findlay* (1985) AC 318.
57. *R v Secretary of State for the Home Department, ex parte Handscomb and others,* (1987) 86 Cr. App. R 59.
58. See fn. 27:*Doughty Street/Anderson case.*

These welcome changes were soon to be consolidated by yet a further challenge this time in the European Court of Human Rights on behalf of three discretionary lifers *Thynne, Wilson and Gunnell* in 1991.[59] The Court referred to its findings in *Weeks,*[60] a 1988 case, when it had decided that the direction in which the practice had developed for discretionary lifers underlined the fact that the tariff and risk phases could be clearly identified and that the issue of risk was one that should be decided through judicial not executive procedures. Neither the protections of judicial review nor the Parole Board procedures met the standards required by Article 5, paragraph 4[61] of the European Convention on Human Rights. The required changes were implemented during the passage of the 1991 Criminal Justice Act when "Parliament duly adopted a provision that provided explicitly not only that the tariff part of the sentence would have to be announced in court but also that, once the tariff period was over, release would have to be considered by a specially constituted Discretionary Lifer Panel of the Parole Board. These panels would have to follow court-like procedures. Importantly, once the Parole Board, as represented by the panels, had decided on release, the state, as represented by the Home Secretary, would be compelled to carry out the decision".[62] During the passage of this bill, the Home Office Minister Mrs Rumbold justified the government's decision to continue to treat mandatory lifers (including the sentence of Her Majesty's Pleasure for juveniles) thus:

> The presumption is, therefore, that the offender should remain in custody until and unless the Home Secretary concludes that the public interest would be better served by the prisoner's release than by his continued detention.[63]

In *Doody,*[64] Lord Mustill stated that the traditional theory of the life sentence (as a sentence ordering lifelong punitive detention subject only to the merciful grant of the privilege of "early release") had been replaced by a "wholly new explanation of the life sentence" and could "hardly be sustained any longer [even] as theory" and that "lifelong punitive detention was neither the usual nor the intended effect of a sentence of life imprisonment". Furthermore he based his approach to the rights of mandatory lifers on the

---

59. *Thynne, Wilson and Gunnell v the United Kingdom,* judgment of 25 October 1990, Series A No. 190-A.

60. *Weeks v the United Kingdom* (Article 50), judgment of 5 October 1988, Series A No. 145-A.

61. Article 5, paragraph 4 of the ECHR: "Everyone who is deprived of his liberty by arrest or detention shall be entitled to take proceedings by which the lawfulness of his detention shall be decided speedily by a court and his release ordered if the detention is not lawful".

62. See fn. 5: Dirk van Zyl Smit, *Taking life imprisonment seriously,* p.116.

63. *Hansard,* col. 301, 16 July 1991.

64. *R v Home Secretary, ex parte Doody* (1994) 1 AC 531.

reality of the system and not on the discredited Rumbold theory; in other words the ratio of the decision was based on the similarity of the exercise of fixing a tariff to a sentencing exercise. The rights to which mandatory lifers were held to be entitled as a result were declared as follows:

- to be afforded an opportunity to submit in writing representations as to the appropriate tariff;

- to be informed, before making such representations, of the judicial recommendation on tariff and any other opinion expressed by the judiciary bearing upon tariff;

- to be given reasons for any departure by the Secretary of State for the Home Department from the judicial recommendation.

However he:

> nonetheless rejected the argument that the mandatory and discretionary life sentences now fell to be administered in the same way and that the judicial view as to tariff should be determinative in the case of mandatory lifers.

Following the judgment in *Doody* the Home Secretary Michael Howard agreed to introduce changes in that he would "consider not only, (a) whether the period served by the prisoner is adequate to satisfy the requirements of retribution and deterrence and, (b) whether it is safe to release the prisoner, but also (c) *the public acceptability of early release* (Author's emphasis). This means that I will only exercise my discretion to release if I am satisfied that to do so will not threaten the maintenance of public confidence in the system of criminal justice"[65] – effectively at the whim of politicians and public opinion. Building on this in 1995, Michael Howard announced that once the tariff had been fixed and the prisoner had been informed the information would be made available publicly.[66]

Section 1(5) of the Murder (Abolition of Death Penalty) Act 1965 provides that a person convicted of murder committed when s/he was under 18 years of age will be detained during Her Majesty's Pleasure, and "if so sentenced he shall be liable to be detained in such place and under such conditions as the Secretary of State may direct". Thus the juvenile equivalent of the mandatory life sentence did not benefit from the changes brought about through *Thynne, Wilson and Gunnell* in the 1991 Criminal Justice Act. It was not until 1996 that this anomalous position was challenged in the European Court of Human Rights in the cases of *Hussain* and *Singh*[67] where the Court held that the appellants'

---

65. *Hansard,* cols 861-64, 27 July 1993.
66. *Hansard,* col.1353, 17 July 1995.
67. *Hussain v the United Kingdom,* judgment of 21 February 1996, *Reports of Judgments and Decisions* 1996-I and *Singh v the United Kingdom,* judgment of 21 February 1996, *Reports of Judgments and Decisions* 1996-I.

Article 5, paragraph 4 rights had been infringed; meaning that he and other prisoners held at Her Majesty's Pleasure (HMP) should be subject to the same procedures that applied to discretionary lifers – the required changes were given effect by Section 28 of the Crime (Sentences) Act 1997.

Masters Thompson and Venables were 10 and a half years old when they killed 2-year-old James Bulger and perhaps uniquely in western Europe were tried in the adult court, duly convicted of murder, sentenced to HMP and then "in the public interest" had their identities disclosed. Following the established procedures the trial judge set their tariff at eight years adjusted by the Lord Chief Justice to ten years then raised by the Home Secretary Michael Howard to fifteen years, because, as he explained, he had been influenced by the state of public opinion – it was a particularly gruesome incident. The House of Lords,[68] in deciding that he was wrong to exercise what was in fact a sentencing function to reflect public opinion and furthermore that he was not able to judge juveniles on the same principles as adults, struck down the tariff asking him to reconsider. The European Court of Human Rights in 2000[69] found that the trial, the sentence and the actions of the Home Secretary had violated Articles 6 and 5, paragraph 4 of the European Convention on Human Rights and perhaps as an indication of the direction of the jurisprudence of the Court, seven of the seventeen members of the Court held that Article 3 of the Convention had been violated because children so young had been sentenced to life imprisonment. This case was heard some two and a half years after the House of Lords hearing and still no new tariff had been set by the Home Secretary. The Lord Chief Justice was required to review the tariffs of all juveniles affected by the judgment and set new ones.[70] The Parole Board ordered the release of Thompson and Venables on the 22 June 2001.

In 1994 the Home Secretary announced that several mandatory lifers would remain in prison for the whole of their life by virtue of his discretion not to confirm any recommendations for their release that the Parole Board may make, and by 2000 there were some twenty-three prisoners with this status. Myra Hindley was one of those by virtue of the fact that she had achieved iconic status as a hate figure for the crimes she and Ian Brady had committed in the mid-1960s when, but for the abolition of the death penalty, they would certainly have been sentenced to death. Having served in excess of thirty years and having received on a number of occasions the approval from the Parole Board to progress towards release, she sought application to challenge the Home

---

68. *R v Secretary of State for the Home Department, ex parte Venables and Thompson* (1998) AC 407 (HL).
69. *V. v the United Kingdom* [GC], no. 24888/94, ECHR 1999-IX and *T. v the United Kingdom* [GC], No. 24724/94, 16 December 1999.
70. *Re Thompson and another* (tariff recommendations) (2001) 1 All ER 737 (CA).

Secretary's part in rejecting the Parole Board's recommendation. The House of Lords unanimously refused the application as they decreed that it was acceptable for the Home Secretary to set, in effect, a whole of life punitive phase.[71] From my understanding of this decision it does not close the door on the whole of life issue being re-visited and their lordships did extract a reassurance from the Home Secretary that such whole of life prisoners would continue to be regularly reviewed, although I am not entirely clear – given the unambiguous nature of the judgment – what the purpose of such reviews would be.

Having established that for HMPs, discretionary and automatic lifers there is a punitive phase and a risk phase, the next step was to develop the jurisprudence in the same direction for mandatory lifers. There was initially a setback to this agenda as in *Wynne v United Kingdom* (1995)[72] the European Court of Human Rights found that Article 5, paragraph 4 did not apply to the post-tariff phase of the mandatory life sentence, believing it to be wholly punitive punishment, but when a further challenge on this issue was made in the case of *Stafford*[73]

> The Court found that its decision in *Wynne* could no longer be sustained and that the mandatory life sentence had wrongly been characterised in that case as a sentence ordering lifelong detention on punitive grounds. In *Stafford* the Court held that the sentence is an indeterminate sentence comprising a punitive and thereafter, a preventative component. As such it is a sentence, which attracts the guarantees of Article 5(4) once the preventative phase is entered. It was an essential part of the Court's reasoning that the tariff fixing exercise is a sentencing exercise according to which the quantum of punishment merited by the individual circumstances of the offence and offender is ascertained. As such it necessarily follows that Article 6(1)[74] applies to the tariff fixing exercise.[75]

The effect of *Stafford* was to remove the Home Secretary's power to veto a recommendation of the Parole Board to release a mandatory lifer, bringing this category of prisoner into line with HMPs, discretionary and automatic lifers. *Stafford* was followed in 2002 by a landmark decision in the UK courts. The House of Lords held in *Anderson*[76] that the Home Secretary:

> should not play any part in fixing the tariff of a convicted murderer, even if he did no more than confirm what the judges had recommended. The fixing of

---

71. *R v Secretary of State for the Home Department, ex parte Hindley* (2000) 2 All ER 385 (HL).
72. (1995) 19 EHRR 333.
73. *Stafford v the United Kingdom* [GC], No. 46295/99, ECHR 2002-IV.
74. Article 6, paragraph 1 of the ECHR: "In the determination of his civil rights and obligations or of any criminal charge against him, everyone is entitled to a fair and public hearing within a reasonable time by an independent and impartial tribunal established by law".
75. *Doughty Street/Anderson* case, see fn. 27.
76. See fn. 27: *R v Secretary of State for the Home Department, ex parte Anderson* (2002) UKHL 46.

such a tariff was a sentencing exercise involving an assessment of the quantum of punishment that the convicted murderer should undergo. The Secretary of State's role was objectionable because he was not independent of the executive.

This finally removed all the powers of the Home Secretary to in any way alter the tariff, set whole life tariffs or veto recommendations of the Parole Board for the range of indeterminate sentences.

Facts about life imprisonment

The numbers

The *World Prison Population List* places the United Kingdom at just above the halfway point with a rate of 139 per 100 000 (England & Wales: 72 669; Scotland: 6 417; Northern Ireland: 1 058 – figures for October 2002) the highest in the European Union.[77] An accomplishment due in great part to Michael Howard the last Conservative Home Secretary, compounded by a continuing flirtation with his populist though wholly discredited "prison works" policy by the two Labour Home Secretaries Jack Straw (1997-2001) and David Blunkett (2001 to present) since New Labour came to power in May 1997.

The figure in February 2003 for the life-sentenced population in England & Wales was 5 352 of which 3 811 (71%) were mandatory and 1 541 (29%) were discretionary life sentences.[78] Of this population 97% are male, 162 are young offenders and 856 (16%) are from ethnic minorities who comprise approximately 9% of the general population. An additional component in this calculation is the growing number (estimated to be 298 in May 2001) of automatic lifers following the legislation in 1997,[79] which provided for this "new" indeterminate category. The figures for Northern Ireland (February 2002) were 85 lifers and 3 detained at the Secretary of State's Pleasure – since 1981, 457 lifers have

---

77. Roy Walmsley, UK Home Office Research, Development and Statistics Directorate, Findings 188, *World prison population list* (4th edn), 2003.
78. See the report of the Advisory Council on the Penal System, "Sentences of imprisonment: a review of maximum penalties,": HMSO, London, 1978 which identified fifty statutory offences and fifteen common law offences for which either no maximum was fixed or the maximum was life imprisonment. See also *R v Hodgson* [1968] 52 Cr App 113 in which the Court of Appeal placed restrictions on the use of life imprisonment.
79. Section 2 of the Crime Sentences Act 1997 provides for an automatic life sentence for a second serious violent or sexual offence. Provision incorporated in Section 109 of the Powers of the Criminal Courts (Sentencing) Act 2000. A product of the "tough on crime" populist agenda which believed that judges were not acting "tough" enough on such offenders. This legislation virtually removes judicial discretion in sentencing of such offenders. See *R v Offen* (2001) 1 WLR 253. For an excellent review and analysis of this issue, see Nicola Padfield, *Beyond the tariff – human rights and the release of life sentence prisoners*, Willan Publishing, Devon, 2002.

been released on licence.[80] The figure for Scotland in 2001 was 569, which included adult mandatory life imprisonment and those sentenced under Section 205 of the Criminal Procedure (Scotland) Act 1995 (Discretionary Life)[81] – a total for the UK of 6 307. According to the 2001 figures for the Council of Europe some 6 224 life-sentenced prisoners were held in the rest of the member states combined – the size of the problem for the UK is plain to see. The country with the next largest lifer population was Turkey with 2 349.[82]

Of the 126 mandatory lifers released in England & Wales to supervision in the community during 2001 the mean time served was 13 years and for discretionary lifers the mean time served was 9 years. The figures for Scotland relate to the 491 prisoners released from mandatory life sentence between 1965 and 1996 – the mean time served was 11 years and 1 month as compared to discretionary lifers, which was 15 years and 8 months. The Scottish figures reveal that over the years the mean time served has increased from, for example, 10 years and 4 months in 1986 to 13 years and 2 months in 1996 – a trend also identified in England & Wales where the mean time served in 1987 was 11 years and 2 months rising to 14 years and 2 months in 1998.

Forty-six percent of the victims in the Scottish sample of mandatory lifers were persons with whom the prisoner was acquainted, a further 14% had killed their spouse or partner and 6% had killed a blood relative. Thus 66% had killed someone they knew and 33% killed strangers – these are comparable to the figures for England & Wales and Northern Ireland. The profile of the victims of discretionary lifers is the reverse of this with nearly two-thirds (56%) being strangers.

Managing the life sentenced prisoner – reception to release

The prison and probation services in the United Kingdom have accumulated a wealth of experience in the management and treatment of prisoners sentenced to indeterminate imprisonment, an experience garnered even before the mandatory life sentence was introduced in the 1957 Homicide Act and even before the establishment of a formal Parole Board in 1967. Partnership between the services is supplemented by a requirement to establish sound relationships with broader society whose support is crucial to the success of any community-based initiative and in this respect "success does breed success" as the incremental rise of

80. www.niprisonservice.gov.uk/lifers1.htm

81. www.scotland.gov.uk/stats/bulletins/00194-01.asp and www.scotland.gov.uk/cru/doc/life-sent-02.htm

82. Annual statistics for the Council of Europe (Space 1), 2001 Enquiry, European Committee on Crime Problems, PC-CP (2002) 1 Rev.

those considered for and granted release on licence since 1967 demonstrates. A major conference was staged in April 2000 to address the issue of a "seamless sentence for lifers". Speaking at the Conference on the Prison and Probation, Minister for Home Affairs Paul Boateng, emphasised that "at a time when the number of lifers has increased by 88% in the last decade, this has become a critical issue for the prison and probation services." Whilst the thrust of the minister's presentation was couched in terms of efficiency and cost-effectiveness he rightly acknowledged the quality of the partnership between prison and probation and the effectiveness of their professionalism, one indicator of which was the continuing low re-conviction rates for lifers. The conference was staged in the aftermath of the 1999 joint thematic review on lifers published by the Chief Inspectors of Prisons and Probation, which made twenty-five recommendations and fifty associated action points.[83]

The lesson to be learnt from the working practices with lifers is that planning for release at a future date, potentially on expiry of the tariff period, starts on the first day of the sentence. Detailed evaluations are made from materials already available (trial transcripts, probation and psychiatric reports) together with the information gleaned from the series of assessments made during the sentence-planning phase of the life sentence. The UN guidelines referred to in footnote 96 set out best practice, which I believe is achieved by the professionals in the England & Wales prison and probation services despite the continuous interference of politicians obsessed by costs, targets and populism.

It has been my experience in all my country work that when alternative sentences to death are being discussed there is a universal assumption that this "new" population of prisoners needs to be housed in purpose-built prisons totally segregated from the general prison population on the assumption that there is something so different (dangerous) about this group that requires separate facilities. The Council of Europe draft recommendations referred to later expressly recommend that "life sentence and other long-term prisoners should not be segregated solely because of their sentence (non-segregation principle)" and that "individual planning for the management of the prisoner's life or long-term sentence should aim at securing progressive movement through the prison system (progression principle)."

The practice in the United Kingdom reflects these principles and in my experience many prison managers would go so far as to claim that a certain level of integration between life sentence prisoners and the "normal" prison population has beneficial effects for both groups: lifers exert a

---

83. Lifers – a joint thematic review by Her Majesty's Inspectorates of Prisons and Probation 1999. http://www.homeoffice.gov.uk/docs/lifers1.html

calming influence. One cannot help thinking occasionally that prison managers seize on this as an opportunity for empire building and I have heard some managers, while acknowledging the benefits of the integration model, consider this too good an opportunity to miss for a general improvement in the prison estate and a means to reduce overcrowding. They go on to say that following the implementation of these improvements they would then introduce an integration policy.

The United Kingdom on the whole enjoys the benefits of a healthy economy and is able therefore to afford the investment in the services necessary for a professional response to the management of the lifer both in and out of prison and it would be unrealistic to expect a similar level of resources being available, in the short term, to countries with less well developed economies and more pressing priorities. However, during the early stages of transition appropriate resources could be provided by faith communities, NGOs and other voluntary agencies; afterall the probation service in England & Wales started life in the late nineteenth and early twentieth centuries modestly but successfully as Police Court Missionaries, a Christian foundation. Those engaged in this "missionary" work offered services in the courts, the prisons and through community supervision and support of offenders. Lack of financial resources should not inhibit the creation of the necessary responses especially when the experiences of other countries can be drawn on, and in my opinion it is the responsibility of those promoting change to provide the necessary support for these initiatives.

Effectiveness

Reconviction rates are traditionally used as the measure of the effectiveness of sentences even though it is considered rather limited as it fails to reflect other positive changes in the behaviour of offenders, which might have been brought about through the experience of the sentence whose effectiveness it claims to measure. Nonetheless this measure of effectiveness does provide one with some sort of comparison between sentences and the influence they have on future offending. Figures for England & Wales reveal that:

- In 1996, 57% of all prisoners discharged from determinate sentences were reconvicted of a "standard list"[84] offence within two years of their release. Of these 53% were adult males; 76% male young offenders and 47% females.

---

84. The standard list of offences covers all indictable offences, including triable either way offences, and a number of the more serious summary offences.

- Between 1975 and 2000 9% of life licensees were reconvicted of a "standard list" offence within two years. 1998 is quoted as a particularly "good" year with only 3% of those discharged being re-convicted for a standard list offence.[85]

- Of the 19 female lifers released between 1972 and 1980, 5 [26%] had been reconvicted by the end of 1995. Of the 52 female lifers released since 1981 none had been convicted of a "standard list" offence – this compares with 46% of determinate sentenced females in 1994.[86]

- Only 1% of life licensees released between 1972 and 1995 were reconvicted of a "grave list" offence.[87]

- Reconviction for "standard" offences for mandatory lifers is 3% as compared to 26% for discretionary lifers.[88]

It is clear from the England & Wales data that the likelihood of a life sentence prisoner re-offending after release is minimal and that is as it should be to ensure public safety and confidence. An explanation for this low re-offending rate is offered in part by the rigorousness of the preparation for release, assessment of future risk coupled with rigorous supervision and support after release. One of the conditions of release to which all lifers are subject is the liability to be recalled to prison at any time during the rest of their life if they commit another offence or violate any of their licence conditions – to this extent life imprisonment in the United Kingdom can be seen as a whole of life sentence.

Conclusions

In 1998 the United Kingdom finally removed capital punishment from all its statutes for all crimes in all circumstances (civil and military) in legislation confirmed by ratification of all the protocols in domestic (Protocol No. 6 to the European Convention on Human Rights) and international law (Second Optional Protocol to the International Covenant on Civil and Political Rights) in stages between 1999 and 2003. Interestingly, those offences for which we still reserved the death

---

85. Figures provided in a personal communication by the Home Office Research Development Statistics, 16 April 2003.

86. Data from the Home Office "Joint thematic review of Her Majesty's Inspectorates of Prisons and Probation", 1999.

87. A "grave" offence is one which can attract a maximum sentence of life imprisonment – mainly homicide, serious wounding, rape, buggery, robbery, aggravated burglary and arson endangering life. *Home Office Statistical Bulletin*, Issue 19/99, "Reconvictions of offenders sentenced or discharged from prison in 1995, England and Wales".

88. Nicola Padfield, Alison Liebling with Helen Arnold, "An exploration of decision-making at discretionary lifer panels," Home Office Research Study 213, 2000.

penalty after abolition in 1965 were replaced by a maximum sentence of discretionary life imprisonment not, as in the case of murder, mandatory life. So finally after over half a century the United Kingdom subscribes to the same position as the other nine member states that founded the Council of Europe in 1948. Better late than never!

What I hope has emerged from this catalogue of the deliberations in the UK – though more accurately in England & Wales – is evidence of the pitfalls to be avoided and of the strengths of the correctional policies developed under the professionals who have directed prison and probation practice in this area for the past forty years, and even where there have been criticisms of some of these policies the "blame" for these can invariably be placed at the door of politicians.

I had hoped to be able to complete this review of the British experience on a relatively optimistic note but unfortunately the UK Home Secretary David Blunkett has managed to tarnish that optimism with one of his most retrograde proposals to date (see below). This is motivated more by his very public "serial frustration" with the judiciary, – whose judgments have often found his policies wanting – than a rational evidence-based analysis of penal policy with respect to sentencing for murder. In this particular regard the promised reaction is to the implications of the *Stafford* and *Anderson* cases in the House of Lords, which removed the powers of the Home Secretary to fix the minimum term and to veto recommendations of the Parole Board, and to the Lord Chief Justice's practice guidelines to the judges recommending that fourteen years was the appropriate entry point when setting the tariff for murder.[89]

He proposes three levels that judges would be required to adhere to when sentencing for murder:

- level one would be whole of life sentences for "multiple murderers that show a high degree of premeditation involving the abduction of the victim prior to the killing or are sexual or sadistic; murder of a child as above; terrorist murder and when the offender has been previously convicted of murder;"

- level two would attract a starting point of thirty years for those who "murder police and prison officers during the course of duty and murder involving the use of a firearm or explosive; killing done for gain; killing intended to defeat ends of justice (for example, killing a witness); killing

---

89. Practice Statement as to Life Sentences, 31 May 2002. Life Sentences, Lord Chief Justice's Court: 31 May 2002 Kennedy LJ, sitting in the Court of the Lord Chief Justice, handed down the practice statement on behalf of Lord Woolf, Lord Chief Justice, replacing the Practice Statement (Juveniles: Murder Tariff) ([2000] 1 WLR 1655) handed down on 27 July 2000.

motivated by race/religion/sexual orientation; single sadistic or sexual murder of an adult and multiple murders (excluding those above);

- Any other murders will have a fifteen-year starting point on which judges can build as necessary to ensure the appropriate sentence."

Those aged 17 years or less will be subject to the fifteen-year starting point only, though those aged 18 years but less than 21 years will be eligible for both the fifteen- and thirty-year starting points. The proposed changes and "principles" to the sentencing of murderers he announced on the 6 May 2003,[90] if accepted, will mark a return to a retributive climate not witnessed for generations in the United Kingdom or continental Europe. They will however find resonance in the United States. These proposals are indefensible and there would appear to be no evidence that either the wealth of research available worldwide or the effects of the debacle that was the 1957 Homicide Act have been taken into consideration.

However, returning to cautious optimism, let us consider some constructive suggestions relating to infrastructure changes and the necessity of transitional strategies. Encouraging western European penal policies and practice with regard to capital punishment has to be accompanied by patience and tangible evidence that adequate support, including resources, will be offered. The enormity of the changes that accompany abolition can be quite daunting and it is understandable in such circumstances that the status quo is sometimes a more attractive option.

The potential for challenges to the whole of life sentence placing limits on extradition treaties has to be taken seriously. Evidence for this is provided by Mexico which will not extradite suspects to the United States without securing an undertaking both that the death penalty will not be imposed and more recently that undertakings are given that whole of life sentences will not be imposed.[91] Another recent example is provided by Uruguay which attached conditions to its recent decision to extradite Mohammed Ali Hassan Mukhlis, a suspected Al Qaeda follower for his part in the 1997 attack at a temple, which led to the deaths of fifty-eight foreign tourists in Egypt. Uruguay had agreed to extradite Mukhlis only after receiving guarantees from Egypt that he would not receive the death penalty or a life sentence. Uruguay had also sought guarantees that he would not be tried in a military court and that his lawyer would be allowed to attend.[92]

---

90. "Home Secretary announces tougher sentences for murder," UK Home Office Press Release, Ref: 126/2003 –7 May 2003.
91. *Chicago Tribune*, 14 June 2002.
92. Reuters, 12 July 2003.

In Europe, ongoing negotiations with the US Attorney General's office begun in September 2002 reveal that the European Union is also considering extending its restrictions to extradition to include undertakings not to impose sentences of life imprisonment without benefit of parole.[93] The basis for this Reuters report remains obscure, though a partial explanation is that it may refer to concerns raised under Article 3 of the European Convention on Human Rights following the case of *Einhorn v France* (16 October 2001) when the European Court of Human Rights held (at paragraph 27) that it "does not rule out the possibility that the imposition of an irreducible life sentence may raise an issue under Article 3 of the Convention" and continued "...it is not to be excluded that the extradition of an individual to a State in which he runs the risk of being sentenced to life imprisonment without the possibility of early release may raise an issue under Article 3 of the Convention." The other possibility is that the statement arises from the fact that, unlike the United Kingdom, many European Union states will not extradite their own nationals. The European Court of Human Rights has as yet not ruled on whether whole of life sentences would violate the prohibition on inhuman and degrading treatment or punishment as expressed in Article 3 of the European Convention on Human Rights.

In the European context, the Council of Europe produced in April 2003 a first draft by the Committee of Ministers to member states on the management by prison administrations of life-sentence and other long-term prisoners[94] and given its draft nature it is not possible for me to discuss in any detail its principles and recommendations other than to mention that the document builds on a range of previous recommendations relating to imprisonment policies published by the Council of Europe, the European Union and the United Nations. They represent a mixture of measures reflecting a proper balance between the needs of society and its responsibilities to prisoners and the staff that care for them in a framework of what can be described as positive, proportionate, humane and effective measures for management in prison and upon release. There is a single concession to the possibility of whole of life imprisonment even though this is restricted to underlining the need to be especially responsive to the needs of such prisoners. One hopes that the phrase "Special management care and attention should be given to the particular problems posed *by prisoners who are likely to spend their natural life in prison*" (Author's emphasis) does not concede either the inevitability or acceptability of the whole of life sentence but simply relates to the remote possibility that because of the high-profile risk someone poses

---

93. Reuters, 5 September 2002.
94. Draft recommendation as revised by the Secretariat following the 5th meeting of the PC-LT, Council of Europe, April 2003.

they may need to be detained for the whole of their life. An EU memorandum of 2001 notes that all long-term and life sentences should be susceptible to some sort of review and did not envisage the need to make provision for whole of life sentences.[95]

Guidance internationally is contained in the UN recommendations on life imprisonment,[96] which make no concessions to the possibility that any prisoner will remain in prison for the whole of their life.

I referred earlier to the UK Parole Board's role in this process and stress here the crucial contribution that a genuinely independent board makes to the justice and transparency of the review of prisoners' applications. On many occasions since 1967 the integrity and the credibility of the board has been jeopardised because of the periodic changes announced by various home secretaries. The fact that a home secretary announces, as Michael Howard did in 1993 and 1994, that certain "types" of lifer would not be released before twenty years or ever can act as a powerful disincentive to the thoughtful evaluations being conducted by the Parole Board and the prison and probation services, let alone the impact this has on the prisoner's motivation to adhere to his/her sentence plans.

As mentioned earlier, it is crucial to engage with the prison department at the earliest possible opportunity to harness their experience in prison management and to solicit their support for proportionate and reviewable prison sentences as the alternative to the death penalty. In my experience many prison managers who have already begun to contemplate the prospect of working with prisoners who have had their death sentences commuted and have understandable concerns about their future management. In the absence of the "ultimate" penalty they are concerned about the most effective strategies to adopt for working with people who have been sentenced to whole of life imprisonment – how to provide a regime that is constructive to the prisoners and the staff yet still ensures the safety of both groups. With no prospect of release, what incentives are available to ensure the co-operation and compliance of prisoners who have neither hope nor anything to lose? There has to be light at the end of the tunnel. Every minister of justice and prison manager I have had the benefit of meeting starts from the position that separate prisons have to be built to house those previously sentenced to death, overlooking in many instances that they have been adequately managing death-sentenced prisoners in buildings within existing general prisons. The important lesson to be taken from the British experience is

---

95. EU Memorandum on the Death Penalty – Part 3 – 18/09/2001 www.eurunion.org/legislat/DeathPenalty/eumemorandum.htm
96. United Nations (1996) *The life sentence*, Report of the Criminal Justice Branch of United Nations Office at Vienna, UN Publications, Geneva.

that, subject to the need to make some special provisions for life sentenced prisoners at all stages of their sentence, integration with the determinate prison population has benefits for all prisoners and staff, in whose experience life sentence prisoners provide a calming influence. This is certainly true of those subject to reviewable life imprisonment as they have demonstrable goals to be achieved before they can be considered for release on licence into the community.

Invariably the transition from death to life is going to take time and require considerable resources and it is the duty of organisations such as the Council of Europe and the European Union who promote these ideas to support the development of the necessary infrastructure changes. In impoverished, fragile, emerging democracies priorities, understandably, would not normally include the provision of such a corrections service and I have heard several administrations referring to the resource implications as a significant obstacle to abolishing the death penalty.

Frequently, rather than address the issues that such an impasse produces, an alternative to abolition is mooted in the shape of the compromise "solution" of a moratorium, which in itself raises fundamental questions, such as what precisely is the purpose of the moratorium? What activities specifically are being suspended during this moratorium? For my part the only justification for a moratorium is to provide breathing space to prepare for total removal of capital punishment and this "space" should be one free of the total apparatus of the death penalty – no prosecutions, no sentences and no executions. The period of this suspension is one that should be agreed at the outset, as should the agenda and timetable for action and this underlines just how crucial is the support of the "promoters" of abolition. The Council of Europe model of requiring suspension of executions immediately on accession followed by an agreed timetable to the signing and ratification of the Protocol No. 6 to the European Convention on Human Rights comes closest to this model. However, it falls short in not requiring a suspension of the total apparatus of capital punishment or providing sufficient support (technical and financial) for the necessary infrastructure changes such as activities on prisons, probation, victims, alternatives and public awareness and public reassurance (all influential agencies should be included in this last activity).

The debate about alternatives – more correctly its absence – is all too characteristic of mainstream traditional abolitionists, which in my view represents a fundamental omission equalled only by their failure to explicitly address the issue of crime victims. Pre-eminent among abolitionist organisations is Amnesty International (AI) which takes no active position on either victims or alternatives, and as recently as 2002 AI sections rejected the recommendations of its own review of work against the death penalty. To quote:

> The classic AI position has been that the organisation does not advocate any specific alternative penalty but that any such alternative must not constitute cruel, inhuman or degrading punishment. Amnesty's unwillingness to recommend [or oppose] specific substitute punishments may undermine the credibility of its overall argument for abolition.

Later on under the same heading of "Enhancing credibility" it went on to say that "AI materials may not always sufficiently recognise the impact of capital crimes on the victims' families". One of two recommendations under this section concerned the issue of alternatives:

> 4.1: AI should initiate a thorough and inclusive policy discussion on alternatives to the death penalty, based on a discussion paper setting out arguments pro and con and developing a set of policy options for later decision making.

The authors of this review noted that of all their recommendations only this one was contentious and "The recommendation has therefore been amended to call for a discussion paper with policy options, rather than proposing any specific policy direction".

No specific recommendation was made about the issue of homicide victims' families.[97] I believe the authors were absolutely correct in their expressed view that AI's continuing failure to grasp the nettle on this issue undermines its credibility and I hope that the proposed discussion paper will result in a policy change that is long overdue.

It has not been possible due to space constraints to do proper justice to a topic that has been overlooked for far too long but I hope that I have been able to provide sufficient information to encourage further enquiry into the vexed problems that long-term imprisonment raises. One of the issues raised by Dirk van Zyl Smit in his unique text, *Taking life imprisonment seriously in national and international law* is that of questioning the life sentence not just in terms of its implementation but also against first principles of the very purpose and limits to punishment as we move through the twenty-first century. Progress has been made in recognising that life imprisonment is a judicial sentence and that both the "punitive" phase and the "risk" phase should be left entirely to judges or at least to tribunals governed by judicial not political imperatives. The system in England & Wales has finally achieved this as a result of *Stafford* and *Anderson*, a position already reached by its neighbours. The Life Sentence (Northern Ireland) Order 2001 and the Convention Rights Compliance (Scotland) Act 2001, which came into force in October 2001

---

97. Amnesty International, " Review of AI work against the death penalty – original discussion paper" (ACT 51/003/2002) and Full Draft Report (ACT 50.008/2002).

had the effect in both countries of removing the power of veto from the executive. In both countries judges now set the tariff and parole boards determine the time of release. The mandatory nature of life imprisonment and the whole of life possibility are challenges still be faced and if the UK's current Home Secretary gets his way then I anticipate a further series of protracted battles in the courts. However, if our politicians turn to the evidence rather than the tabloid newspapers for their advice then such a future can be avoided.

Abolition in France

Anne Ferrazzini and Michel Forst
Members of Amnesty International, French section

Up to the end of the eighteenth century, those who questioned the legitimacy of the death penalty, anywhere in the world, were few and far between. But the publication in Libourne in 1764 of a treatise *Des délits et des peines* (Crimes and punishments) by Cesare Beccaria, a young man of 26, sparked a gradual change in mentalities, opening up a new era and firing debate. It was the first awakening of an early abolitionist movement in Europe.

"If I prove that this punishment is neither useful nor necessary, I will have won a victory for humanity", wrote Beccaria. In much of Europe, and elsewhere in the world, Beccaria's work proved a stunning success and for two centuries the debate on the death penalty never fell completely silent.

In France, the argument raged between those for and those against but, in 1791, when a new criminal code was adopted by the Constituent Assembly, Article 3 was quite clear on the matter: "All convicted persons shall be decapitated". And the Convention sent the king and his family to the guillotine, despite the best efforts of the philosopher Condorcet, who unsuccessfully tabled a motion in favour of abolition on the day after their sentencing.

Nevertheless, the idea of abolition made headway in France. In a law of 4 Brumaire, year IV, the Convention abolished the death penalty, but with a proviso that proved fatal: "dating from the promulgation of general peace". The Napoleonic Civil Code would put an end to this provisional abolition in 1810! Abolition does not come with half-hearted gestures: it must be total and without reservation.

The debate in France over the legitimacy of capital punishment took off again in the nineteenth century when Victor Hugo published *Le dernier jour d'un condamné* (the last day of a condemned man). Eminent academics, law specialists and literary and political figures argued the case. The death penalty was criticised as a barbarian and needless practice upheld in the name of social order, based on the claim that "if a state abolishes the death penalty, it runs the risk of a massive influx of criminals from neighbouring states".

On 17 March 1838, Lamartine pleaded the case for abolition before the Chamber of Deputies, arguing that the death penalty had become detrimental within a developed society. But ten years were to pass before some small progress was achieved: in a decree of 1848, confirmed by the Second Empire on 15 June 1853, the provisional government of the Second Republic abolished the death penalty for political crimes. "Political crimes" remained to be defined...

In the face of strong opposition, the abolitionist movement born of Beccaria's work progressed. In Europe, Grand Duke Leopold of Tuscany promulgated a criminal code in 1786 that completely did away with the death penalty. In the United States in 1794, the Quakers of Pennsylvania brought their abolitionist ideals to bear. In 1846, the American territory of Michigan, later to become a state, was the first jurisdiction in the world to abolish the death penalty for a deliberate act of homicide. In 1863, Venezuela became the first country to definitively abolish it for all crimes. Other countries followed this lead. In Europe the small Republic of San Marino abolished the death penalty for all crimes in 1865, having first abolished it for crimes in ordinary law in 1848 and, in any case, never having executed a single person since its independence in 1468! In several European countries, the death penalty fell into disuse. The last execution to take place in Monaco dates back to 1847, in Liechtenstein to 1785 and in Portugal to 1849. In Africa, the Cap Verde islands have never applied the death penalty since their independence.

In France, in January 1906, Armand Fallières, a convinced abolitionist, was elected President of the Republic. His predecessor, Emile Loubet, had already made extensive use of presidential clemency and expressed his abhorrence of the death penalty. The budget committee of the Chamber of Deputies voted to do away with funding for the maintenance of the guillotine and the executioner's wages.

Aristide Briand, Minister of Justice in the Clemenceau government, submitted a bill to abolish the death penalty, making a fervent speech to the Chamber. Although it was tabled in 1906, the bill was not debated by the French Assembly until 1908. In the meantime a little girl had been murdered. The trial of the accused opened on 23 July 1907 and the press fanned the flames of popular indignation. When the death penalty was pronounced, Armand Fallières, true to his convictions, commuted the capital penalty to deportation, provoking outcry in the press, which followed public opinion and disowned the decision.

At the end of September, *Le Petit Parisien* daily newspaper launched what it called a referendum featuring free gifts, then re-launched it in October to draw a larger response. The results were published on 5 November: nearly 77% of respondents were in favour of the death penalty.

When the Assembly voted on 8 December, 333 members were in favour of maintaining capital punishment, with 201 against. Legislation retaining the death penalty was adopted. After a three-year pause, executions resumed: 223 people were executed between 1906 and 1929, and 89 between 1934 and 1938.

In 1939 just before the second world war a public execution that went horribly wrong might have tipped the balance of public opinion. In Versailles near Paris on 16 June, the guillotine was badly installed and the neck-restraint and blade were faulty. The execution was particularly horrific and once again a massive draw for spectators. Numerous photographs appeared in the press. Following certain incidents of this nature, the government held an extraordinary cabinet meeting and, by decree of 25 June, banned the publicity surrounding executions, which were no longer public after that date.

The guillotine and special courts were a feature of the German occupation from 1940 to 1944. In the throes of war, Europe saw an increase in sentences and executions. In France, Marshall Pétain used his constitutional powers to break with a tradition some fifty years old and send five women to the guillotine. President Auriol took up from here by refusing, in 1947 and 1949, to commute the sentences of two women convicted of murdering their husbands.

The abolitionists' pleas now fell on deaf ears. There was still a long way to go from the guillotine to the abolition of capital punishment. Elsewhere in Europe abolition of the death penalty for ordinary capital offences continued to gain ground but in France executions continued at the rate of between one and four a year.

However, in 1957 Albert Camus and Arthur Koestler published a plea against the death penalty: *Réflexions sur la peine capitale.* A few courageous politicians tirelessly tabled bills to abolish the death penalty, on behalf of parliamentarians from all parties. They were never debated.

The election of Georges Pompidou as President of the Republic raised a few abolitionist hopes. On 15 June 1969 he commuted the sentences of six people condemned to death since the beginning of his term in office. The opinion polls backed his decision: in May 39% of the French people had been in favour of the death penalty and 58% against, with 9% uncommitted. A fresh poll in October gave 33% for, 50% against and 11% don't-knows.

But public opinion is fickle and the National Assembly was not ready: abolitionist bills continued to be rejected and the opinion surveys soon swung the other way.

On 21 September 1971, in one of France's toughest prisons, two inmates took a nurse and a warden hostage. One of the men had already been sentenced to life imprisonment for murder, while the other was serving twenty years for aggravated theft and assault. There were tense negotiations between the hostage-takers and the prison authorities, which refused their demands. The building was stormed, and the two hostages were found with their throats cut.

Prison staff reacted angrily. Wardens attempted to overturn the vehicle transporting the prisoners to the Paris region, and several trade unions organised a national day of protest. Statements came thick and fast, and public opinion was roused. The mob surrounding the van carrying the prisoners bayed for blood.

When the trial opened, some of the newspapers, radio stations and television channels covering the proceedings had already made up their minds. The subsequent death sentences were greeted by many with satisfaction: "Cut-throat killers Buffet and Bontems sentenced to death", said the front page of *Le Parisien Libéré* on 30 June 1972.

This verdict, from the Court of Assizes, came on the day when the US Supreme Court declared the death penalty "unconstitutional".

Once again, public opinion had shifted: in September 53% were in favour of capital punishment, 39% against, with 8% uncommitted. President Pompidou refused presidential clemency, and justice took its course with Buffet and Bontems being executed on 29 November 1972, although Roger Bontems had not killed anyone.

"Once again, the prison authorities have gone over the heads of the courts," wrote the sociologist, Michel Foucault. "They have set themselves up as a power and the head of state has just signalled his acceptance." In the same year, Mohamed Libdiri, convicted of the murder of a taxi-driver, received presidential clemency.

Criticism from abroad was harsh. A liberal Swedish newspaper wrote: "28 November 1972 is a day of shame for the nation-state of France, which often holds itself up as a model of an enlightened country in our times". Sweden had abolished the death penalty for all crimes that same year. While abolition was gaining ground in the rest of Europe, the guillotine and the death penalty continued to make history in France.

However on 21 January 1977, the unofficial moratorium on executions in the United States ended, following the death by firing squad of Gary Gilmore, by his wish, four days earlier in Utah.

In the same year, Amnesty International held a conference in Stockholm, following six preparatory seminars in Paris, Hamburg, New York, Colombo, Ibadan and Port of Spain. The conference highlighted the fact that the death penalty was not only used for political ends in a great many cases but was also, by nature, a political weapon. In conclusion, the conference adopted a declaration expressing the position of Amnesty International on the death penalty and setting out an action programme against capital punishment. At the end of the Stockholm conference, Robert Badinter, an active participant in the proceedings, said:

> The great merit of Amnesty International is not to treat the abolition of the death penalty as an isolated issue that could be resolved without constant and fervently fighting against violations of fundamental human rights, of which the right to life is simply the first.

France changed presidents and Valéry Giscard d'Estaing refused clemency three times. Despite serious reservations about his guilt, Christian Ranucci was executed on 28 July 1976, followed by Jérôme Carrein on 23 June 1977, and Hamida Djandoubi – the last person to be guillotined in France – on 10 September 1977.

Between 1978 and the presidential elections in 1981, the parliamentary debate was backed by a study group in favour of abolition, formed in the National Assembly by parliamentarians of all tendencies. Abolitionist movements, led by all the groups in the French section of Amnesty International, urged politicians, including deputies, senators and current and future presidential candidates, to back the abolition of the death penalty.

The election campaign following Valéry Giscard d'Estaing's term in office provided an opportunity for broad debate on capital punishment, and abolition became a campaign issue.

By becoming a state party to the International Covenant on Civil and Political Rights on 4 November 1980, France had already committed itself to no longer applying the death penalty to persons aged under 18 years at the time of the offence or to pregnant women. Ratification became effective on 29 January 1981 and was published in the Official Gazette on 1 February 1981.

In 1980, with thirteen European states already having opted for abolition, Valéry Giscard d'Estaing went for a second term in office saying: "I feel a deep-down aversion to the death penalty", but at the same time: "I feel that such a change can only be made in a society at peace with itself whose members feel secure. And for as long as that peace is not felt, it would be going against the profound sentiments of the French people". Not to go against the profound sentiments of the French people or not to go against the opinion polls? That was the question, since the polls continued, and the majority did not want abolition.

195

But in a television programme on the presidential election campaign entitled *Cards on the table,* the candidate François Mitterrand expressed his own belief:

> I will not hide my thoughts on the question of the death penalty any more than on the other issues. And I have no intention of publicly fighting this issue pretending to be what I am not. In my deepest conscience, which is in harmony with that of the churches, the Catholic church, the Reform churches, the Jewish faith, all the great humanitarian movements, both national and international, in my conscience and in my heart of hearts I am against the death penalty (...) I am standing for election as the President of the Republic and I am seeking a majority of the votes cast by the French people and it is no secret wish on my part. I say what I think, what I stand for, what I believe, what constitutes my spiritual ties, my concern for civilisation: I am not in favour of the death penalty.

The outcome would show that elections are not won by following opinion polls but by putting forward values in line with one's beliefs, by taking a political stand: on 10 May 1981, François Mitterrand was elected President of the Republic.

Legislation was quick to follow. The new president commuted a death sentence passed on 28 October 1980 on Philippe Maurice, who was branded a "thug, cop-killer and hostage-taker" by the press but, fourteen years later, completed a thesis while in prison, drawing praise and congratulations from the examining panel. However, French prosecutors still asked for the death penalty: three death sentences were passed in May 1981.

On 9 July, following the European Parliament's adoption of several resolutions in favour of abolition on 18 June 1981, France's new Justice Minister, Robert Badinter, announced that he would be proposing the abolition of the death penalty.

On 17 September the French National Assembly began its examination of the abolition bill. It was an historic moment indeed when, at five in the afternoon, Robert Badinter took the floor and made a speech that would go down in the annals of the Chamber:

> Mr Speaker, my honourable colleagues, I have the honour, in the name of the Government of the Republic, of asking the National Assembly to abolish the death penalty in France.

The vote, on 18 September, was clear-cut, the only remaining unknown being the final count: Article 1 abolishing the death penalty was carried with 369 votes in favour and 113 against. The bill was passed with 363 votes in favour and 117 against.

A few worries remained as the bill still had to be voted by the Senate. Following debate on 30 September 1981, the upper house of French parliament definitively passed the legislation abolishing the death penalty, with 160 votes for and 126 against.

So France finally abolished the death penalty for all crimes, whether in ordinary or military law, by Law No. 81-980 of 9 October 1981, which entered into force on the following day and stated, in Article 1: "The death penalty is abolished." The six French prisoners awaiting their death sentence were granted clemency.

France then underpinned its legislation with an international commitment, by ratifying Protocol No. 6 to the Convention for the Protection of Human Rights and Fundamental Freedoms (the European Convention on Human Rights), undertaking not to re-introduce the death penalty in peacetime other than in the event of denunciation of the protocol in the conditions stipulated in Article 65 of the Convention. Ratification was registered by the Council of Europe on 17 February 1986.

Now, at the beginning of this new millennium, the Council of Europe's forty-five member states have all signed Protocol No. 6 abolishing the death penalty and forty-three of them have ratified it. As the Council of Europe has frequently stated, all its member states are firmly opposed to the death penalty because they believe that such a punishment is totally inconsistent with human rights and the rule of law.

In accordance with this principle, in 1994 a Swedish member of parliament, Hans Goran Franck, submitted a report to the Council of Europe Parliamentary Assembly proposing a new protocol to the European Convention on Human Rights abolishing capital punishment once and for all. Protocol No. 13 to the Convention for the Protection of Human Rights and Fundamental Freedoms concerning the abolition of the death penalty in all circumstances, was approved by the Council of Europe's Committee of Ministers on 21 February 2002 and opened for signature and ratification in Vilnius on 3 May.

In the words of the Organisation's Secretary General, Walter Schwimmer:

> The Council of Europe was already proud to have banished the death penalty in peacetime on a continent where more than 800 million people live. With Protocol No. 13, it opens the way to abolishing this barbaric punishment in all circumstances. We hope that this will be a decisive step towards a universal abolition of the death penalty and we shall spare no effort in achieving this.

That same day – 3 May 2002 – the Council of Europe press service announced that thirty-six states had signed the protocol. By 12 April 2003 there were eleven ratifications and a further twenty-nine signatures. It entered into force once the tenth ratification had been lodged.

The Council of Europe was set up to foster stability in Europe by promoting democratic values and respect for human rights. Its focus on the death penalty dates back to 1957 and it drew up the first international treaty for the abolition of the death penalty in peacetime. It now obliges every country seeking membership to undertake, before accession, to abolish the death penalty – a requirement supported by all the Organisation's bodies.

The European Union has adopted a broad policy aimed at promoting the abolition of this form of punishment throughout the world. At the Nice European Summit in October 2002 the European Parliament, the Council of the European Union and the European Commission solemnly proclaimed the Charter of Fundamental Rights, described by Robert Badinter as the European Union's moral foundation. Under Article 2 of the charter: "Everyone has the right to life. No one shall be condemned to the death penalty, or executed." By leading the campaign for abolition, Europe is exporting the universal values on which it is founded. The European Parliament frequently passes resolutions calling for universal abolition, pleading for clemency or requesting protection for individuals who might be executed. The Council of Europe's Parliamentary Assembly has called on the United States and Japan to establish a moratorium on executions.

Much remains to be done, however, in the world as a whole, and once again it was the Council of Europe and the European Parliament that hosted the First World Congress Against the Death Penalty, in Strasbourg from 21 to 23 June 2001.

Organised by the association Ensemble contre la peine de mort (Together against the Death Penalty), the congress brought together a whole host of partners, non-governmental organisations, law specialists and media. Over 110 speakers from all over the world took part in the workshops held at the Council of Europe.

At a formal sitting in the assembly chamber of the European Parliament, Nicole Fontaine, President of the European Parliament, Raymond Forni, President of the French National Assembly, and Lord Russell-Johnston, President of the Parliamentary Assembly of the Council of Europe, were joined by the parliamentary speakers of some twenty countries in launching an appeal for a universal moratorium on executions.

And as we wait and hope for that moratorium to be taken up in every country in the world, the words of Robert Badinter during the congress must never be forgotten:

> Like all human rights, the right to respect for one's life is universal and inalienable. Our common fight against the death penalty will only end, therefore, once it has been abolished by the last state to engage in this practice. Then, and only then, we will have carried out our duty. Then, and only then, we will have secured victory for the just cause that we champion. There can be no justice that kills. That is the absolute commandment. There can be no justice that kills without renouncing itself. That is why the abolitionist cause will always press on until it has ultimate victory, because it is the cause of humanity and justice.

The Russian Federation and the death penalty

Anatoly Pristavkin
Adviser to the President of the Russian Federation

Without going into the details of my country's recent and distant past, I should like at the outset to point out that the internationally-held stereotype to the effect that Russia has always actively used capital punishment to inspire fear in its citizens is not entirely fair. It is well known that the first attempt to prohibit the death penalty following the extreme cruelty of Peter I's reign was made by his daughter Elisabeth; indeed, this was the first such attempt in Europe. Even in the nineteenth century, which we consider cruel, only about 300 people were officially executed.

The 1917 Bolshevik coup d'etat, known in Russia as the October Revolution, brought its own harsh changes and a new order in legal procedure and punishment. For almost the entire twentieth century, capital punishment was part of life across a huge and powerful state. It is unlikely that genuine statistics exist on the use of the death penalty during the Soviet era. I am not referring to political repression, for which the number of victims is in the millions. It has been suggested that 640 000 people were executed for criminal activities between 1921 and 1954, on the basis of court judgments – something like 20 000 a year. Later, from 1962 to 1990, another 24 000 were executed. It would appear that the figures have been revised downwards, since punishment statistics were classified as secret. After 1992, when the Pardons Commission, Russia's first such body, began its work (I was asked to chair it by Boris Yeltsin), the number of executions fell to a few people each year.

Unless the above figures are taken into account, it is impossible to understand Russian society's profoundly unhealthy state, nor the reasons for its unwillingness to accept any attempt to put an end to use of the ultimate sanction. In the 1990s, I attended debates in the Russian Federation Parliament on the draft law to introduce a moratorium on the death penalty. At that time, one in seven Duma members voted to adopt the law. The communist members voted decisively in favour of the death penalty.

The accession of the Russian Federation to the Council of Europe in January 1996 has played an exceptionally positive role in humanising public consciousness. At that time, we undertook not to apply the death penalty, until such time as Protocol No. 6 to the European Convention on Human Rights was ratified by parliament. Russia has not applied the death penalty for the last seven years, and already hope is slowly dawning that we can continue to live in a society without state-organised mass killing. What is striking, though, is that every step towards a better Russian penitentiary system, every move towards reform of the justice system and, in particular, every proposal to outlaw the death penalty provokes vociferous public debate and mobilisation by the so-called hawks, demanding even harsher punishments. Their main argument is that the annual crime rates are rising, especially the figures for serious crime involving violence, and that the number of murders has risen. The public, terrified by the growth in crime, thus sees no other solution but to return to the firing squad.

Of course, such calls are also heard from time to time in other European countries, for example during the French presidential elections. The example of the United States, Japan and various other countries, where the death penalty has been maintained on the statute book is also often referred to.

In Russia, the latest campaign for the return of the death penalty began two years ago, with the newspaper publication of a letter from Professor Dobrenkov of Moscow University, whose 17-year-old daughter had been killed by gangsters. About a hundred well-known Russian figures added their signatures to his appeal, which was entitled "To the people and the president". It read:

> The fatherland is in danger. Russia is on the verge of self-destruction. The enemy is at the gate, and its name is crime. A wave of murders and serious crime has swept across the country... Criminals have unleashed open terror against every citizen, and are holding society in a state of complete fear...

He then concluded:

> *In order to satisfy the West's political demands and despite the people's will* (my emphasis – A.P.), a moratorium on the death penalty for particularly serious crimes against the person has been introduced in Russia... The decision to impose a moratorium on the death penalty was not simply mistaken, but pernicious. It has turned out to be a major tragedy for society...

This appeal, extremely persuasive at first sight, was signed by: Osipov, President of the Russian Academy of Science; Tadzhuddin, Senior Mufti of Russia and the European countries of the Commonwealth of Independent States; Zhores Alferov, Nobel prize-winner for physics, and many famous artists, writers and parliamentarians. Unfortunately, one of Russia's leading writers, Alexander Solzhenitsyn, came out in support of the death penalty, saying that "Russia can put an end to terrorism only by restoring the death penalty". Even the Russian Orthodox Church acted evasively, refusing to take a stand or to judge the numerous calls for the death penalty as they deserve.

Of all those who signed the "appeal", only one person was, in my opinion, sincere: the grief-stricken father. The others, who are now encouraging President Putin to reinstate the death penalty (and their number includes dozens of principals from the country's leading universities) are not naïve enough to be fooled. They cannot fail to understand that a reinstated death penalty would not affect the guilty, but, just as in the past, would have an impact on the socially unprotected sections of society, those who cannot "buy themselves out of trouble" and would suffer penal consequences while others go unpunished. Opponents of the death penalty are asked for evidence. There is ample evidence, in thousands of cases: for example, practically every person whom we recommended for a pardon during the decade that the Pardons Commission existed (1992-2001). These were not the terrorists or leaders of organised gangs described so eloquently in our press, but shepherds, homeless people, boiler stokers, etc. Of course wicked people do exist, appalling murderers and maniacs, but such individuals do not account for the millions of prisoners who continue to fill our penal colonies and prisons. Life imprisonment, which is now the alternative to the death penalty, is an excruciating punishment in our current conditions, and worse, since it is long and drawn out. Our opponents know this very well. An article on this problem was called just that: "A living death sentence".

A recent visit by a parliamentary delegation, headed by the Minister of Justice, to a colony for former death row prisoners, that is those whose death sentences have been commuted to life imprisonment, gave a first-hand insight into the unbelievably difficult conditions in which these lifers exist. No radio, no newspapers, no opportunities for family visits. Incarcerated in former monastic cells on a lonely island in the northern forests, their letters beg us to reinstate the death penalty. Even after all they had seen, our parliamentarians have postponed ratification of Protocol No. 6 for an indeterminate period, and certainly until after the next round of elections. Their personal popularity was much more important than the fear of discrediting their country and their president. Of course, there are exceptions amongst the members of the State Duma.

Pavel Krashenninik, Chair of the Duma Committee on Legislation, described this stand by the Duma as a blow to Russia's prestige in European society and exploitation of our citizens' dissatisfaction and unhappiness about how the state is tackling crime.

The reader cannot fail to notice that an old totalitarian-era phrase was used in the above-mentioned "appeal" by Professor Dobrenkov, which incidentally had wide repercussions across society; it referred to the West's pernicious influence. In this context, of course, the reference is to the Council of Europe. Our press also does not hesitate to use such arguments. Thus, one popular columnist, in an article on "The right to execution" (what a headline!) waxes lyrical about the fact that the Council of Europe "forbids us" from re-introducing the death penalty. However, according to the same writer, the Council of Europe "pleads for these same murderers, and also for the Chechen separatists…".

Moreover, the Chechen trump card is used by other supporters of the death penalty. After an explosion in Mineralniye Vody (a town in the North Caucasus), the governor of Stavropolskiy Kray and the regional parliament demanded that terrorists be shot. The head of the Don Cossack forces suggested that the death penalty be introduced for those organising and participating in terrorist acts. According to the Cossacks, "our society has not matured sufficiently to call itself a democracy. We should base ourselves on the constitution of the United States, in which the death penalty is permitted". Senior military officials responsible for "anti-terrorist operations" in Chechnya have also spoken out in favour of restoring the death penalty. General Troshev, an adviser to President Putin, is an active advocate of capital punishment.

Indeed, the situation is truly paradoxical: the chairperson of one of the regional pardons commissions (these commissions were established by presidential decree in the Russian Federation's regions, replacing the single centralised commission which I chaired), announced at his commission's first meeting that he considered the death penalty to be necessary. Fortunately, he is still an exception. But one can imagine the kind of decisions such a regional commission would take on pardons if the death penalty were now to be re-introduced.

We can evaluate the extreme passions stirred up by this issue simply by examining the headlines of articles published in the Russian press: "The right to execution", "G. Zyuganov and S. Baburin want death", "The fight for death, not for life", "Lawful execution", "Invitation to an execution", etc.

A columnist in the *Rossiya* newspaper recently stated that as, of 1 July 2003, Europe had definitively rejected capital punishment and wrote:

> I am willing to put a fully accurate figure on the minimum number of people in our country who support complete abolition of the ultimate sanction: 150. This is the number of persons condemned to death, waiting for a final decision on their fate…

Of course, there are in fact rather more people who support prohibition of the death penalty, although their voices are not always heard. In response to the letter "To the people and the president", an appeal to the State Duma was published (organised by the present writer at the initiative of members of our former pardons commission): "Abolishing capital punishment in Russia through legislation". The statement was signed by leading writers, painters, academicians, professors, artists and leaders of voluntary organisations, such as Lyudmila Alekseyeva, President of the Moscow Helsinki Group, among others.

Yavlinskiy's party, Yabloko, has taken an authoritative position in this argument. According to one of its leaders:

> The issue of capital punishment has been blown out of all proportion, especially by armed structures attached to government ministries, and the objective is to distract public attention from the extremely poor quality of the law-enforcement agencies' work. Before criminals are punished, they must be found and evidence of their guilt must be produced. The law-enforcement agencies are not succeeding in this area. Rather than improving the quality of their work, they prefer to turn the issue around, claiming "we wanted to maintain the death penalty". In reality, we must choose one of two options: either we are part of the Council of Europe and we abolish the death penalty, or we withdraw from the Council. We must not sit on the fence.

Oleg Mironov, Plenipotentiary for Human Rights, sees the issue as follows: "The point of politicians is that they are able to take decisions which run counter to the public's wishes. Russia would find herself outside civilised European society if the Duma were to defy international standards".

For the full picture, the opinion of one more person must be given. As the reader will understand, his is not an unimportant view.

I quote:

> If the hypothesis that we suffer most from the evil existing within ourselves is true, then we can say that by making punishment harsher – and the death penalty is in fact not punishment, but rather vengeance on the part of the state – then, by increasing the severity of punishments, the state is not eliminating cruelty but merely reproducing it again and again. The state ought not to assume a right that can belong to the Almighty alone – taking life from a human being. As a result, I can firmly state that I am against restoration of the death penalty in Russia.

These words were uttered by Vladimir Putin, the Russian President.

Among the ten or so important and vital questions that perturb society, surveys show that the re-introduction of the death penalty lies in fifth place. Consequently, it is essential to organise long-term educational and ideological work, press campaigns and debates, and especially to revitalise the work of the courts and law-enforcement agencies, which are currently unprofessional and exceptionally corrupt, in order to resolve this matter once and for all. Political and economic stabilisation and, more generally, improvement of overall living standards will play a key role in this process. That being said, the *Rossiya* journalist quoted above correctly points out that the arguments about whether or not it is time for us to join international civilisation by outlawing the bullet, electric chair or gallows from judicial practice have already been overworked to the point that they are repellent to Russians, owing to their complete futility. He concludes:

> It sometimes seems that if there is one thing on which a moratorium must be placed, then it is on this debate, which has no practical import whatsoever in our particular social conditions.

I could not agree with him more.

The present situation of the death penalty in the United States

Hugo Adam Bedau
Professor in Philosophy at Tufts University

In the new millennium, the death penalty continues to hold the United States in its grip and it is impossible to predict how soon that grip will weaken, much less disappear altogether. Let us begin by looking at some of the major factors supporting the current status of the death penalty:

- The Supreme Court's ruling in 1976 that the death penalty as such does not violate the Constitution remains intact. Circumstances under which the current members of the Supreme Court would decide to reverse the decisions of a generation ago are difficult to imagine.

- The *de jure* moratorium on executions from 1968 to 1976 spared the lives of hundreds of death row prisoners, but it led to few lasting improvements in the statutory or constitutional protections of due process of law and equal protection of the law in death penalty cases; and did little to create an informed body of public opinion against this form of punishment.

- The annual number of executions has grown remarkably in recent years: from 1 in 1981, 18 in 1986, 14 in 1991, 45 in 1996, to 85 in 2000 – the most since 1951. There is no evident reason to expect this number to decline or even hold steady in the near future. Correspondingly, the number of prisoners on death row (more than 3 700 in the spring of 2003) has never been greater.

- Today, appellate review by the federal courts of state court convictions and sentences in capital cases is fraught with impediments, thanks to congressional efforts and Supreme Court rulings aimed at bringing finality (at the cost of fairness) to appellate litigation in capital cases.

- No member of the current Supreme Court is on record opposed to the death penalty on the ground that it violates the 8th amendment prohibition of "cruel and unusual punishment" – or on any other constitutional ground.

- No state legislature in recent years has abolished the death penalty.

- No state supreme court in recent years has judged the death penalty to be inconsistent with the state's own constitution.

- No state chief executive in recent years, with one major exception, has commuted the sentences of his state's death row prisoners on the ground that the death penalty is in violation of human rights – or, for that matter, on any other ground. The exception is former Governor George Ryan of Illinois, who early in 2003 extended clemency to all 171 of the state's death row prisoners.

- No established public voice has caught and held the nation's attention as a critic of the death penalty; both presidential candidates in the recent general election (2000) supported capital punishment.

- The nation's politics continue to be distorted and corrupted by the stranglehold the death penalty has on elective and appointive officials. The worry is widespread that the surest way to end one's political career is to become known as an opponent of the death penalty.

- Juveniles (persons under 18 years of age) are still liable to be sentenced to death and executed in some states.

- In the mid-1990s, Congress enacted new federal death penalty statutes, including a few involving no homicide. These laws also empowered the federal government to pre-empt state jurisdiction, thus enabling the prosecution of a crime as a death penalty case in states (such as Michigan and Massachusetts, among others) that have abolished this penalty.

- Federal judges appointed by the current Republican administration are not likely to find many reasons to rule against convictions and death sentences in the capital cases that come before them for review.

- The effort to obtain a nationwide moratorium on executions, to provide an opportunity for careful study of the administration of the death penalty, is stalled (as of early 2003) both in Congress and in more than a dozen states where such measures have been proposed.

- Public opinion polls continue to show majority support for the death penalty for murder.

- Early in 2001, the execution of Timothy McVeigh was the first under federal law in thirty-seven years and was carried out by the recently elected Republican administration of President George W. Bush, known for his support of the death penalty during his tenure as Governor of Texas, during which he presided over more executions than any other governor this century. For the first time in decades, the nation witnessed an execution that dramatically publicised support for the death penalty in the executive branch of the federal government.

Arrayed against these facts are a variety of considerations that encourage a somewhat more optimistic view for those who favour abolition.

Public opinion – a mile wide but an inch deep

Common knowledge has it that a large majority of the American public supports the death penalty (as noted above). But the truth is more complex. First, survey research shows that a majority (63%) of the public currently accepts the death penalty; this is the lowest public support in twenty years. Second, the same research shows that the public is evenly split (46% to 45%) in its preference for the death penalty over long-term imprisonment. For reasons not entirely clear, this sharp contrast between what the public professes to accept and what it professes to prefer has not been effectively communicated to politicians, whose chief reason for opposing abolition is the belief that the electorate demands it.

Elusive support for the death penalty

For various reasons peculiar to American history, the death penalty today is largely a relic of the system of racial injustice and anti-black violence that runs like a bloody wound through the nation's social fabric. The death penalty system is manifestly strongest in the old Confederacy (virtually co-extensive with the so-called Bible Belt) in the deep South. There is little visible support for this form of punishment in the nation's major metropolitan newspapers or among academic social scientists. Political commentators have been divided on the issue, but for reasons to be mentioned below are increasingly vocal in expressing doubts about the system. Whereas the law journals and book store shelves overflow with every kind of criticism of the death penalty and its flaws, there are no recent books and few articles arguing the case for capital punishment. Opponents of the death penalty have long ago won the battle of words – and of research, too.

The Capital Jury Project

Most research against the death penalty in the United States during the previous century focused on one or the other of two main topics: deterrence and racism. Social scientists argued persuasively that there was no convincing evidence of the superior preventive efficacy of executions. They argued even more persuasively that the death penalty system as it actually operates, especially in the South, reflected the historic racism of the larger society. This research, conducted in the 1980s, established the race-of-victim factor: persons convicted of killing a white victim were 4.3 times more likely to be sentenced to death than those convicted of killing a non-white victim.

207

A wholly new line of research was inaugurated in 1990 with the creation of the Capital Jury Project. Underway in fourteen states, the aim of the project is to study how capital jurors make their life or death sentencing decisions. Based on in-depth interviews with a thousand former capital jurors, the chief question to be answered is whether capital trial juries conform to or violate the standards laid down by the Supreme Court in a series of decisions since 1976. Results to date suggest that jurors typically do not fully understand the instructions from the trial judge, and that even when they do, they do not comply with them. For example, four out of ten jurors indicated that they believed they were *required* to vote for a death sentence if they found the murder was "heinous, vile, or depraved". But the law states that such a finding is only one of several sufficient conditions of a death sentence and did not by itself (as these jurors believed) make a death sentence mandatory.

This research is significant for at least two reasons. First, it forces one to conclude that the "guided discretion" in death penalty sentencing endorsed by the Supreme Court in 1976 has not worked out in practice as intended. Second, it bolsters criticism of the system based on the actual experience of former capital trial jurors who have given first-hand testimony about how they discharged their awesome responsibility in deciding between a punishment of life in prison or death.

Supreme Court justices express their doubts

The Supreme Court has not (as of this writing) ruled in favour of the constitutionality of any of the non-homicidal state and federal death penalty statutes. Instead, since 1976 the Supreme Court has without exception ruled unconstitutional such non-homicidal statutes, and it is by no means certain that it will soon alter its path in a new direction. Since 1976 several members of the Supreme Court – most recently Justice Harry A. Blackmun (1908-99) and Justice Lewis F. Powell (1907-98) – have concluded that the death penalty as administered in the United States is an unconstitutional violation of due process of law, equal protection of law, and is a cruel and unusual punishment however administered.

In the summer of 2001, Justice Sandra Day O'Connor, not an opponent of the death penalty as such, voiced her concerns about the capacity of the nation's courts to administer a fair and effective system of capital punishment. She even went so far as to say that the current system "may well be allowing some innocent defendants to be executed". Doubts of this sort have proved in the past to be the preface to a refusal altogether (in Justice Blackmun's words) to tinker any further with "the machinery of death".

Miscarriages of justice

By far the most influential and troubling aspect of the death penalty in the United States today is the demonstrable failure of the system to convict and sentence only the guilty. Incontrovertible evidence of innocent men being wrongfully convicted and saved from execution only by the diligent efforts of persons outside the system, such as journalism students, family members, newspaper reporters, dramatically points up the problem. No one can seriously believe that all such errors have been detected in time to avert the execution of someone actually innocent. At the conclusion of a recent federal death penalty case in Massachusetts, the trial judge Michael A. Ponsor observed:

> [A] legal regime relying on the death penalty will inevitably execute innocent people...Mistakes will be made....

The extensive publicity given to many such cases, especially in Illinois, prompted Governor George Ryan to institute a moratorium on all executions in the state pending review and remedy of the procedures and practices involved in capital cases. Of the many factors that can weaken national support for the death penalty, this is unquestionably the most influential.

Maladministration of the death penalty

Lawyers familiar with the way the death penalty system actually works at present in the United States have amply documented the outrageous practices, unfair rulings, the abuse of discretion, tolerance of injustice in many forms – above all, the problems arising from poverty and race – that occur far too often and are typical of the system at its worst. Recent research at Columbia University Law School has shown that between 1973 and 1995, "[appellate] courts found serious, reversible error in nearly 7 out of 10 of the thousands of capital sentences [investigated]". After state appellate courts threw out 47% of the death sentences they reviewed, due to grave flaws, subsequent federal appellate review found "serious error undermining the reliability of the outcome in 40% of the remaining sentences".

One important step toward mitigating these failures would be the Innocence Protection Act, a bill filed in Congress early in 2001 with bi-partisan support. If enacted, the bill would institute a wide variety of procedural changes affecting the administration of the federal death penalty. While not advancing the cause of abolition directly, this piece of legislation (like the moratorium) would make prominent and enduring the concern over fairness in the death penalty system. If, as most abolitionists believe, it is functionally impossible to have a fair death penalty system, that lesson would effectively be taught by the efforts to comply with the requirements of the act.

Incompetence and unavailability of defence counsel

Standards for counsel representing a capital defendant vary from state to state and are often remarkably low. The Supreme Court ruled in 1984 that a plea for re-trial based on a claim of ineffective assistance of trial counsel would not succeed unless it were shown that counsel failed to provide "reasonably effective assistance" and that but for counsel's errors a different outcome was probable. In 1996, Congress ended federal funding for post-conviction defender organisations, leaving appellate litigation in capital cases to be financed entirely by the states, with enormously varied results. In 2000, the Supreme Court ruled that counsel who slept on and off during trial could be said to have provided inadequate representation only if the defendant could show that his counsel while dozing had missed important aspects of the trial proceedings. Since a convicted defendant's successful appeal depends on the skill and devotion of his counsel, it is deeply troubling to learn from a report in *The New York Times* that in the summer of 2001,

> ... [d]ozens of inmates on death row lack lawyers for their appeals, in part because private law firms are increasingly unwilling to take on burdensome, expensive and emotionally wrenching capital cases...

Moratorium

Beginning in 1987 the American Bar Association (ABA) has advocated a variety of proposals designed to provide better protection for capital defendants, but without much evident effect. In 1997, however, the ABA's House of Delegates recommended a nationwide moratorium on the death penalty, to enable a thorough review of the administration of capital punishment with an eye to revisions in longstanding practices that would reduce, if not eliminate, the risk of erroneous convictions, sentences, and executions.

In the 1980s, there was little interest outside confirmed abolitionist circles for such a death penalty moratorium; in 2001 the subject has been widely debated and in several cases nearly enacted by popular demand. The great merit of the moratorium movement is that it promises heightened scrutiny of the workings of the system by persons not hitherto deeply concerned with it one way or the other. It also empowers informed abolitionists to persuade fence-sitters that the longstanding complaints registered against the system are not exaggerated and they are not isolated and infrequent occurrences.

Muted political support

While it remains true that the presidential candidates in 2000 supported the death penalty, they did it in a relatively muted manner. The chief effect was largely to remove the death penalty from the campaign –

probably a good thing, since the typical modern political campaign has never been a helpful forum for debate and public education on this issue. Whereas in the general election of 1988, Republicans loudly criticised the Democratic presidential candidate for his opposition to the death penalty, Republican strategists in 2000 made no effort to boast of their candidate's conspicuous support for the death penalty. Sensing that the public would not respond favourably to portraying Governor George W. Bush as "tough on crime", proved by the record number of death sentences carried out during his term of office (152), Republicans let the death penalty become virtually a non-issue.

The irrationality of death penalty support

During the previous century professed support for the death penalty rested chiefly on belief in its superior preventive powers: it would deter crimes that no less severe punishment would, and it would prevent crimes through incapacitation in a manner superior to imprisonment. Or so death penalty supporters alleged. In any case, if the death penalty were to be used for various crimes and not only murder (as indeed was the case until the 1970s), its defence would have to rest mainly on its preventive (deterrent and incapacitative) powers. But by the end of the century, with the death penalty confined to homicidal crimes, the deterrence argument had largely been abandoned, owing in part to the lack of convincing empirical support. (In early 2000, only 8% of those who supported the death penalty did so on the ground that they believed it to be a deterrent and "sets an example." Four years earlier, the nation's leading professional criminologists announced their conclusion that the death penalty was not a superior deterrent to long prison sentences.)

Instead of prevention, retributive considerations are the chief support on which defenders of the death penalty now rely: murderers deserve to die. (As the then governor of Florida put it in 1989, "I believe in the death penalty for one who has taken someone else's life.") From an empirical point of view, this proposition is difficult to argue for or against – except to note that unalloyed retributivism is not so widely shared as some would believe. If trial courts, prosecutors, governors, and legislatures believed it, they would favour mandatory death penalties, they would oppose plea bargaining (avoiding a death sentence by confessing to the crime, or by giving testimony against one's co-defendants), and they would oppose clemency except where the defendant could prove he was innocent. In actual practice, nothing of the sort happens. The Supreme Court has ruled against every form of mandatory death penalty it has reviewed, prosecutors would be unable to do their job if they abandoned plea bargaining, and trial courts bring in a death sentence in only a fraction of the cases where in theory it would be appropriate. The rarity of commutations is the sole remaining stronghold of retributive considerations. In short, retribution in the form of "a life for a life" is daily subordinated to other considerations by those who nominally support the death penalty and have the responsibility to administer it. This is very unlikely to change in the near future, and these compromises with retribution point up the frailty of any rational foundation on which to rest support for the death penalty.

The execution of McVeigh

In the spring of 2001 it was bruited about across the nation that the terrorist bomber, Timothy McVeigh, was a poster boy for the death penalty. He murdered 168 men, women and children, and wounded hundreds of other victims – and throughout his imprisonment he showed no remorse for what he had done. How could one bear the thought of McVeigh alive and well in prison when he had brought so much harm to hundreds and endless suffering to scores of families? As Vice-President Dick Cheney said a few weeks before the execution, "I think if there ever was a man who deserved to be executed, it's probably Timothy McVeigh".

Running against this line of thinking were the perhaps surprising views revealed by survey research. Only 18% of respondents thought that executing McVeigh would be an effective deterrent to future acts of terrorist violence and murder. At the other extreme, 28% thought executing him might make him a martyr in the eyes of others who shared his anti-government views. Respondents were not asked whether they thought death by lethal injection was a suitable retribution for killing 168 innocent people.

The truth is that McVeigh is a poster boy for abolition. First and foremost, his crime was a rarity, one that made him unique among the thousands of prisoners now on America's death rows. Nothing of any permanent value about the practical realities of the death penalty today in the United States can be learned from the McVeigh case because his crime is so atypical. So was his trial. Unlike most of those on death row, McVeigh received excellent counsel at trial and would have done so on appeal as well, if he had not rejected post-conviction appeals. Few seriously believe his sentence and execution will serve as a deterrent. How can anyone believe that his execution – essentially painless, calm and clean – is adequate retribution for his crime? If neither deterrence nor retribution is a manifest product of his death, what really is the point? (Much the same can be said of terrorist attacks generally.)

"Closure" or reconciliation?

The point of an execution, we are often now told, is "closure", which is understood to mean relief from the suffering endured by the surviving family members, a relief they believe they can find only in knowing their loved one's murderer is dead, or – better yet, in actually witnessing his death. On this view, the preventive powers of the death penalty as well as the moral claims made on behalf of retribution are subordinated to its alleged emotional and psychological benefits. In recent years in the United States the annual criminal homicide rate of around 15 000-18 000 deaths yields some 100 000 immediate family members who are potential seekers of closure.

What they find, often enough, however, is something quite different. Sister Helen Prejean, author of *Dead man walking* (1993), has served as a spiritual counsellor to many families of prisoners on death row and has also been confronted by closure seekers. As they witness the trial and appeals and perhaps testify at the sentencing phase of the trial, she has noted that "they learn new details of the crime, and with each new turn of the trial and its aftermath the media call them to get a reaction." This is hardly a recipe for "closure," since it feeds the anger and keeps alive the resentment so many survivors have toward the murderer.

Taking a completely different approach is Murder Victims Families for Reconciliation (MVFR), founded in 1976. A growing national organisation, it has impeccable credentials: Its members, too, know what it is like to survive the murder of a loved one. They believe that nursing their anger and hatred serves no good purpose – indeed, the very opposite. MFVR has brought its message of reconciliation to many legislative hearings, media events, and execution vigils across the nation. Many other abolitionist organisations are active in the United States today (the National Coalition to Abolish the Death Penalty, also founded in 1976, has sixty state affiliates and has sixty other regional and national organisations affiliated with it). MVFR, with its uniquely brave and impressive message, may well be the most persuasive and exemplary in the years ahead.

International human rights law

Bit by bit, opposition to the death penalty on the ground that it violates the human rights of the prisoner is making headway in the United States. Despite the refusal of the federal government to sign or ratify the Second Optional Protocol to the International Covenant on Civil and Political Rights, aiming at the abolition of the death penalty, or even to ratify the covenant without reservations, these and other provisions of international human rights law have increasingly become part of the debate in the United States over the death penalty. This influence was evident in the Supreme Court's decision in 2002 forbidding the execution of anyone who was mentally retarded.

Execution of the mentally ill, execution of persons who committed a capital crime under the age of 18, and enactment of new capital crimes – each of these is still done in various US jurisdictions, each violates international human rights law, and each has come under increasing criticism. More argument and agitation on this ground can safely be predicted. They are bound to have an impact, however indirect, on the complacency with which the death penalty is accepted.

Conclusion

In the summer of 1972, when the Supreme Court ruled that the then prevailing administration of the death penalty was "cruel and unusual punishment," several experienced observers of the death penalty scene in the United States (including this writer) believed that a major and irreversible step toward total abolition had been taken, and they predicted that there would be no more executions in the nation. In the nearly three decades since then, forty states and the federal government have re-enacted death penalty statutes and sentenced more than 6 000 convicted murderers to death; two dozen of these jurisdictions have carried out more than 700 death sentences. So much for ill-advised predictions.

At present, the death penalty in the United States is undergoing the most extensive criticism and re-evaluation in its history. This attention is bound to lead to dissatisfaction and a change of mind in many of its current supporters, especially those who want a death penalty but want fairness in the way it is administered as well. How that growing discontent can be channelled into effective political opposition to the death penalty remains to be seen. There are no unambiguous signs that this is taking place or is about to take place. With the passage of time, the irony of the present situation – the United States often boasts of its concern over human rights violations elsewhere in the world (and rightly so), yet the courts, the legislatures, and the people fail to see such violations where our practice of the death penalty is concerned – is bound to be sobering. One can only hope that awareness of this fact and a willingness to act on it to rid the nation of the death penalty will come sooner rather than later.

The death penalty in Japan

Yoshihiro Yasuda
Lawyer and anti-death penalty activist

Japan, like other countries, has a long history of applying the death penalty. However, in the 346 years between 810 and 1156, at the instigation of the emperor, who was impressed by the Buddhist notion of compassion, not one execution was carried out. This was the Heian period, a period of peace centred on aristocratic life at the court, when no major wars were fought. But with the burgeoning of the warrior class, the death penalty was re-introduced. The death penalty took extremely cruel forms, varying from garrotting and beheading to ritualistic methods. *Seppuku* (forced suicide by cutting one's stomach open with a sword) was at times regarded as the most honourable form of capital punishment.

The Meiji Restoration (1868) symbolised the beginning of Japan's modernisation process. After the introduction of a west European-style penal system, the death penalty was applied by hanging. The death penalty remains in force to this day, although there was a de facto temporary suspension of three years and four months between 1989 and 1993. Between 1945 and 2000, as many as 623 people were executed. The Supreme Court continues to rule that the death penalty violates neither the Constitution of Japan nor the International Covenant on Civil and Political Rights (ICCPR).

The government views the death penalty as a matter relating to the penal system, and not as a human rights issue, and declares that it will maintain the death penalty in the future.

On 31 March 2003, there were seventy-two inmates on whom the death penalty had been imposed in first and second trials, but whose sentences were not at that stage final, and the number is on the rise. These people are in danger of having final judgment passed against them without sufficient opportunity for defence. And there are another fifty-six inmates for whom the death penalty is already final. They are strictly isolated from society and horribly mistreated in an inhumane environment. Indeed, they live in fear of death, without any opportunity to defend themselves.

Execution is carried out in strict secrecy, and no information is disclosed. As a result, the mass media rarely report on the death penalty situation, and there are few opportunities for public debate on the pros and cons of the penalty. Nor has abolition of the death penalty been taken up as a serious political issue by the political parties or the Diet (parliament).

There is a deep-rooted belief in Japan that the state or the emperor holds the power to determine life. In other words, a person's life belongs not to him or herself, but to the public. There is also a widely held view that ending one's life is the most sincere way of taking responsibility in society. The most severe penalty in atonement for a misdeed is death. Therefore, the death penalty is regarded not as a human rights issue, but as a means of accepting responsibility and thereby atoning for one's sin. Politicians, judges, prosecutors, and even lawyers, regard the death penalty as a matter of crime and punishment. Abolition of the death penalty remains a minority cause.

The number of executions carried out over the last twenty years is shown below:

Year	1983	1984	1985	1986	1987	1988	1989	1990	1991	1992	1993
Number of executions	1	1	3	2	2	2	1	0	0	0	7

Year	1994	1995	1996	1997	1998	1999	2000	2001	2002	2003
Number of executions	2	6	6	4	6	5	3	2	2	

No executions were carried out in the first three months of 2003.

Japan's legal order and the death penalty

Constitutional provisions on the death penalty

There is no direct reference in Japan's Constitution to the death penalty. Provisions that relate to the death penalty include: "... all of the people shall be respected as individuals. Their right to life...shall, to the extent that it does not interfere with the public welfare, be the supreme consideration in legislation and in other governmental affairs... no person shall be deprived of life...except according to procedure established by law ...cruel punishments are absolutely forbidden."

The first provision is quoted by both sides, those who argue that the death penalty is constitutional and those who claim that it is unconstitutional. The second provision is cited as a ground for condoning the death penalty, and the third as proving that it violates the Constitution.

Crimes punishable by the death penalty

At present, the following crimes are punishable by death.

These are, under the Penal Code:

- civil war-related crimes (which are punishable by death or imprisonment for life);

- inducement of war with a foreign power (death);

- assistance to an enemy (death, life imprisonment or a prison sentence of not less than two years);

- arson of occupied structure (death, life imprisonment or a prison sentence of not less than five years);

- damaging or destroying a building by flooding (death, life imprisonment or a prison sentence of not less than three years);

- derailment of a train resulting in death or injury (death or life imprisonment);

- endangering traffic and thereby destroying or derailing a train resulting in death (death or life imprisonment);

- causing death by poisoning drinking water (death, life imprisonment or a prison sentence of not less than five years);

- murder (death, life imprisonment or a prison sentence of not less than three years);

- robbery resulting in death or murder (death or life imprisonment);

- robbery and rape resulting in death (death or life imprisonment).

Under special laws, the following five crimes are punishable by death:

- use of explosives (death, life imprisonment or a prison sentence of not less than seven years);

- causing death as a result of a duel (death, life imprisonment or a prison sentence of not less than three years);

- causing death as a result of an air crash (death, life imprisonment or a prison sentence of not less than seven years);

- causing death by hijacking an aircraft (death or life imprisonment);

- killing a hostage (death or life imprisonment).

The last three crimes on the "special laws" list were first defined in the 1970s.

Legal provisions concerning the implementation of the death penalty

The Penal Code stipulates that the death penalty shall be carried out at a prison through hanging. A person who has been condemned to death has to be confined in a prison until the punishment is carried out. The Code of Criminal Procedure stipulates that the death penalty shall be carried out on the orders of the Minister of Justice, and that such an order shall be given within six months of the date when the judgment becomes final. The Code of Criminal Procedure also stipulates that such execution shall then be carried out within five days, in the presence of a public prosecutor, a public prosecutor's assistant and a warder. There is no provision, however, as to who shall perform the execution. The provision that the order for execution is to be issued within six months is not complied with.

The Prisons Act states that the treatment of prisoners sentenced to death is to be the same as that of other detainees, that the death penalty shall be carried out in the prison grounds and that no executions are to take place on national holidays, at the end of the year or at new year. It also states that, after a prisoner has been executed by hanging, his/her death is to be confirmed, but that strangulation is then to be continued for another five minutes before s/he is released from the rope. However, there is no legal provision with regard to the place of execution (other than that it will take place at a prison) or to the instrument to be used for execution.

The Criminal Compensation Act states that the state shall pay appropriate compensation, as determined by a court, not exceeding 30 million yen (approximately €234 800), if a prisoner is wrongfully put to death. Where loss of property is incurred, additional compensation of not more than 30 million yen can be paid. In other words, it is assumed that the death penalty may be carried out as a result of a mistaken judgment.

Legal provisions concerning grounds for non-application of the death penalty

The Juveniles Act stipulates that the death penalty shall not be carried out on a person who was under eighteen years of age when the crime was committed. There is no such exception for senior citizens. In 1993, Hideo Deguchi was put to death at the age of 70. Over the last ten years, two people have been executed at the age of 69. And Haruno Sakamoto was 73 when the high court handed down its judgment in his case.

Where persons with mental disabilities are concerned, the Penal Code stipulates that a person who is insane must be found not guilty. The death penalty may be reduced to life imprisonment for an act committed by a person of weak mind. The Code of Criminal Procedure provides for a stay of execution only if a prisoner is deemed insane at the scheduled time of execution or if a female prisoner is pregnant, execution then being deferred for as long as these situations prevail.

A request for a "re-opening of proceedings" (re-trial after the confirmation of a sentence) or for a pardon has no legal effect in terms of a stay of execution, as an application for the "re-opening of proceedings" or a pardon are not among the stipulated grounds for suspending an execution.

Legal provisions concerning the defence of those sentenced to death

No special defence rights are guaranteed for those suspected or accused of crimes punishable by death or for persons who have been sentenced to death. They are treated in the same way as suspects in other cases. The situation is as described below.

The court does not assign a public counsel prior to indictment. There is no public counsel system before the indictment stage for a person suspected of a crime punishable by death. Furthermore, since public counsel is appointed separately for each stage of the legal proceedings, an appellant is without a lawyer after an appeal, unless either another public counsel is appointed or the accused appoints his/her own. A person accused of a crime punishable by death has no right to appoint or to dismiss a public counsel. S/he also has no means of dismissing an idle lawyer.

Once the penalty has become final and binding, the state has no provision for a defence system. Therefore prisoners do not have lawyers. The state does, however, have a defence system for when a request is made for proceedings to be re-opened (re-trial). However, the lawyer has no privileges and may not meet the prisoner without supervision by a prison officer. His/her visiting hours are as restricted as those of non-lawyers. There is no provision for a public counsel system. The reasons for re-opening of proceedings (re-trial) are severely restricted to instances such as: "when clear evidence has been newly discovered that, in regard to a person found guilty, a 'not guilty' verdict or acquittal should have been announced." For this reason, a judgment is rarely given for proceedings to be re-opened (re-trial).

A prisoner may request protection under the Habeas Corpus Act, but the conditions for such requests to be granted are extremely strict, one example being "when it is evident that the alleged danger to the prisoner is clearly in violation of laws and regulations". Particularly when applied to detention by the court (detention of a death row inmate), which is presumed to be lawful, there is no remedy available.

There are two types of pardon, a general amnesty under a Cabinet order and an individual pardon. A person on death row may petition for an individual pardon, but this is not an entitlement, so no appeal is possible if his/her petition is refused.

In criminal cases there are at least nominally three levels of court proceedings: district court, high court, and Supreme Court. In reality, however, the high court is usually the scene of subsequent proceedings in which the court of appeal reviews the original judgment, while the Supreme Court, in principle, rules on constitutional matters and on the consistency of case-law. In practice, therefore, there is only one fact-finding court.

Appeals are not automatic, having to be initiated by the accused who may have been sentenced to death at either the first or the second trial. If there is cause for dissatisfaction over a lower court ruling, both the prosecutor and the accused have the right of appeal, so the accused, who may have avoided the death penalty or have been found not guilty, may again face the fear of a possible death sentence.

The death penalty system, its imposition and application

From arrest to indictment

Following arrest, a suspect may be held for a maximum of seventy-two hours. If further time is necessary, s/he may be detained for a maximum of twenty days. The Prisons Act stipulates that detention shall be in a prison, but a police detention unit may be used instead. In most cases, therefore, the suspect is detained at a police station (known as a substitute prison or *daiyo-kangoku*) immediately after arrest.

A substitute prison may have mixed or solitary confinement. In any case it consists of a small space only just large enough for a person to lie down in behind the bars. It is equipped with a toilet but contains no furniture. Detainees are prohibited from keeping their own possessions or receiving any food from outside the institution. In most cases the court will ban visits, so a suspect is not allowed to see his/her family or communicate by mail. The suspect is taken out of his/her cell and forced to make confessions, being subjected to day after day of harsh interrogation behind closed doors, from early morning to late evening.

Almost half of death row inmates were indicted after interrogation without the presence of a lawyer at the police investigation stage. For the last few years the Bar Association has adopted a system of assigning lawyers on a shift system, so that, if requested by the suspect, a lawyer will be dispatched free of charge within twenty-four hours. The lawyer, however, may not be present during the police interrogation, and may only talk to the suspect for fifteen to thirty minutes at a time, if the court has ordered a ban.

In Japan, once indicted, 99.8% of accused persons are found guilty. This is because a written statement, especially a suspect's confession obtained during the investigation rather than from testimony in court, is considered major evidence on the basis of which guilt can be proved. A criminal investigator, therefore, focuses on extracting a confession from the suspect by detaining him/her for interrogation after arrest. The suspect is therefore detained in poor conditions in a substitute prison and forced to confess under duress, subject to uncertainty and fear, and often open to assault and intimidation. A person suspected of a capital crime may receive threats such as, "you will receive the death penalty if you don't confess", or promises such as, "if you confess I will ensure that you escape the death penalty". The very existence of the death penalty is at times used as a means of forcing a confession. So a prosecutor, enjoying absolute discretion, has almost complete power over the life and death of the suspect.

The right to silence is guaranteed by the Constitution, and it is laid down that the suspect should be notified of this right prior to interrogation. If a suspect exercises this right, s/he may become the target of criticism and suffer disadvantages, such as being refused bail after indictment. Most suspects, anxious to escape the ordeal of detention and interrogation, end up signing self-incriminating statements. These usually cover subjective facts, such as the suspect's motives, whether or not s/he had murderous intent or whether or not the crime was premeditated.

In this situation many false charges are laid. Sakae Menda and three others, while on death row, successfully appealed for their proceedings to be re-opened (re-trial), and were then cleared of the false charges which had been laid against them. Two inmates who died in prison were in the process of requesting a re-trial, having consistently proclaimed their innocence. They were 95 and 81 years old at the time of their deaths. Since 1945, eight persons have been sentenced to death by the lower court and then declared not guilty by the higher court. False charges are eight times more common in respect of crimes punishable by death than in other cases. Twenty-six of the current fifty-five prisoners on death row are requesting re-trial on account of false charges. In one such case, the first court found Masaru Okunishi not guilty. Because a prosecutor appealed, he was then sentenced to death at the second trial, and the judgment was declared final by the Supreme Court. He is requesting the re-opening of the proceedings. Another man, Iwao Hakamada, suffered mental disturbance in the process of requesting the re-opening of proceedings (re-trial).

The mass media have a tendency to quickly accept the guilt of a suspect merely because s/he has been arrested, and to publish his/her photograph and personal data, including name, profession and address. The suspect is at that stage condemned by the court of public opinion. Where incidents have attracted public interest, the suspect and his/her family thus become targets of public condemnation even before being brought to trial.

Trials

In 1948 the Supreme Court ruled that, since the Constitution allows for the death penalty, that penalty does not represent cruel and inhumane punishment and is therefore constitutional. Since then it has consistently found the death penalty constitutional. Lower courts follow this ruling. No attempt has been made to review it.

Of the seventeen crimes punishable by death, one, the crime of inducement of war with a foreign power, is punishable only by death. For other crimes, it is the judge who chooses between death and another penalty. However, in the context of the death penalty, there is no provision in law on how a case is to be assessed; it is left to the discretion of the presiding judge. Furthermore, the Supreme Court has indicated only an abstract standard:

> It is approved in cases of serious culpability, and when capital punishment is deemed unavoidable for the purposes of general prevention, and because of the need to maintain a balance between the crime committed and the punishment.

It is thus the court that decides between life and death, a decision determined especially by the judge's attitude and views on life and the efforts of the defence counsel. It is not unusual for the death sentence to be handed down at the first trial, then reduced to life imprisonment on appeal, or for the opposite to happen, a sentence of life imprisonment in the first trial being changed to the death sentence at the appeal stage. In the extreme case of Norio Nagayama, the rulings kept changing: the death penalty was imposed at the first trial, life imprisonment at the second, then the Supreme Court overturned that sentence and referred it back to the lower court, where the death penalty was again imposed, and this was subsequently declared final by the Supreme Court. At his first and second trials, Shozo Nishiyama was sentenced to life imprisonment with forced labour, but the Supreme Court overturned this and referred the case back. It is also reported that there are discrepancies between regions.

Most people sentenced to death are found guilty of murder or of murder during burglary. The following table shows the incidence of heinous crimes, the numbers of people sentenced to death at their first trial, the numbers of those whose death penalty has been confirmed, and the numbers actually executed between 1971 and 2000.

Period	Murder, burglary resulting in death and injury, burglary and rape (heinous crimes)	Number of persons receiving death sentence at their first trial	Number of confirmed death sentence	Number of prisoners executed
1971-1980	41 352 (100)	58 (100)	43 (100)	69 (100)
1981-1990	35 780 (87)	60 (103)	40 (93)	14 (20)
1991-2000	42 367 (102)	43 (74)	40 (93)	39 (57)

The adversarial system is not part of criminal procedure in Japan. Anyone accused of a capital crime is seldom granted bail and must remain in detention throughout the trial. There are numerous cases where the accused has had to appear in court without sufficient access to counsel. Evidence collected by the police or the prosecution is in principle not disclosed to the defence counsel. In court the accused cannot sit with his/her defence counsel. During trials of capital crimes it is customary for the prosecutor to call victims and bereaved family members to the stand when demanding the death penalty.

Treatment of prisoners

Facilities

Prisoners, when bail is not granted after indictment, are transferred from their place of temporary confinement to a prison, where they are kept in solitary confinement pending final judgment. The size of the solitary confinement cell is approximately five square metres, and each contains a toilet and a washbasin. There is a small desk, but nowhere to store bedding or personal belongings, and hardly any room to move about.

Most prisons are unheated, and most inmates therefore suffer from chilblains and cracked skin on their hands and feet. No prisons have air-conditioning so inmates are forced to suffer unbearable heat and humidity. Furthermore, most death row prisoners are confined in a special cell designed to prevent them from taking their own lives. These cells are under video surveillance, so prisoners are monitored round the clock. Half of the window is fixed and cannot be opened, and the other half opens onto an iron plate with pin-sized holes. Airflow is about one two-hundredth of that in an ordinary cell, while the amount of light is about two-sevenths, making the environment especially unpleasant. Except when bathing, taking exercise or receiving visits, prisoners spend all their time in this cell, even eating their meals there.

Communication with the outside world

Prisoners are allowed to communicate with the outside world only through letter writing and receiving visitors, including their lawyer. No telephone or fax communications are allowed. Visits are limited to one a day (except those by lawyers, whose visiting time is unlimited) between 9 a.m. and 5 p.m., in a designated visiting area. Visiting time is restricted to between five and thirty minutes, at the warder's discretion. All visitors, including lawyers, are separated from prisoners by an acrylic screen. If a visitor other than a lawyer comes, a warder is present throughout the visit taking notes.

There are no restrictions in respect of the addressees of letters, but only one letter (of no more than seven pages) per day may be sent. Prisoners may receive letters from any source, but outgoing and incoming mail is carefully censored, and any inappropriate phrases are rewritten or blacked out. The same applies to books.

The court has power to suspend visits or the writing and receiving of letters to/from persons other than a lawyer. The suspension applies even to family members and friends. Prisoners may have with them only a limited number of items, including the materials they need for their own trial.

The use of writing materials is strictly controlled. This, combined with lack of access to a computer or copying facilities, very much hampers prisoners' activities for their own defence.

Everyday life, meals, exercise and medical services

From when s/he is woken up in the morning until bedtime, the prisoner's day is strictly ordered. Refusal to submit to this regime results in punishment, often entailing the use of restraining devices such as leather handcuffs, confinement in a linoleum-covered "protection cell" *(hogobo)*, and beatings by prison warders over a two-day period. The same kind of punishment is also inflicted on inmates on whom the death sentence has been passed and declared final. Nagoya Prison officials are even reported to have beaten a prisoner to death in February 2003.

The prison controls the amount of light in the cells, and prisoners may not turn off the light before lights-out or turn it back on afterwards. Meals are served three times a day in the cells, breakfast at 7.40 a.m., lunch at 11.50 a.m. and supper at 4.50 p.m. This unnatural pattern involves three meals squeezed into a period of nine hours. Exercise outside the cells is limited to thirty minutes, twice weekly in summer and three times a week in winter. The exercise area measures about two metres by five. Prisoners are provided with a skipping rope, but are not allowed to wear shoes, being forced to go barefoot or to wear thin-soled slippers.

Three baths a week are allowed in summer, and two in other seasons, lasting no more than fifteen minutes each time. When not receiving visitors, exercising or bathing, prisoners are confined to their cells. Between waking up and the inspection that takes place after supper, they are not allowed to walk around their cells, but must remain seated in a set position. They are absolutely forbidden to speak, sing or utter any sound. Those who so wish may do light work (on a voluntary basis). Through this they may earn a maximum of 5 000 yen (approximately € 39) or so a month, although this has recently been severely restricted.

Many prisoners suffer lower back pain, caries, pyorrhoea, weakened sight and neurosis as a result of lack of exercise, vitamin deficiency and lack of medical services.

Treatment of death row inmates

A prisoner whose death sentence has been confirmed is kept in solitary confinement in the prison where execution is to take place. Conditions in terms of prison cell, exercise, bathing, medical services and voluntary work are the same as those of a defendant. Communication with the outside world, however, is restricted just to close family members. A prisoner awaiting execution is not allowed to write for newspapers or magazines. S/he is allowed to receive mail only from approved people and is not even told of the existence of any other mail addressed to him/her. Although fourteen years has gone by since the confirmation of Toshiaki Masunaga's death sentence, permission has not been granted for his adoptive mother and his brothers to visit him. Masaharu Harada, a brother of the victim murdered by Toshihiko Hasegawa, is not allowed to visit the offender on death row, although he was able to meet him before confirmation of the death sentence. The request by Mr Gunnar Jansson, Chair of the Council of Europe Parliamentary Assembly's Committee on Legal Affairs and Human Rights, to meet Misao Matsumoto was not granted in March 2001, even though the prisoner (on death row) also wished to meet him. These severe restrictions are applied ostensibly to keep the condemned person's mind at peace, but in fact they are meant to deny any hope of life and to force him/her to accept death. A death row inmate is often estranged from his/her family, so there are many instances in which an execution takes place without the prisoner having made any contact with the outside world. If s/he so wishes, s/he may receive a monthly visit from religious advisers, whose presence the condemned person may request at his/her execution.

In these harsh conditions, and facing the fear of death, many prisoners on death row develop mental disorders. In 1993 Tetsuo Kawanaka was executed despite suffering from schizophrenia at the time. Iwao Hakamada (now 63), reportedly innocent from the very first stage of the investigation, now suffers from severe mental illness after almost thity-six years of detention. He is now unable to recognise his brothers or to understand that he is on death row. Similarly, Tsuneki Tomiyama (now 85), who is also allegedly innocent, is in a critical condition after thirty-nine years of detention, coupled with the effects of advancing age.

Right of defence

Requests for the re-opening of proceedings (re-trial)

As already explained, the stringent criteria laid down make appeals almost impossible. Sakae Menda and three others had spent twenty-eight to thirty-four years in prison before they were declared innocent after repeated requests for re-trial. In 1999, however, Teruo Ono was executed even as he was in the process of requesting re-trial.

Applications for a pardon

Only three people have been granted a special pardon since 1945. Since 1975, no death row inmate has received a pardon. The pardon decision is communicated verbally to the prisoner and not relayed to his/her lawyer. In 1995 Shuji Kimura was informed that his request for pardon had been rejected and, notwithstanding his request at that juncture to consult his lawyer, he was executed shortly afterwards.

Executions

Executions are held once or twice a year, with several taking place on the same day. Those executed will have spent six or seven years on death row since receiving the death sentence. It is the Minister of Justice who is responsible for deciding who should be executed, when, and in which order. In recent years, in order to avoid debate in the Diet, executions have been scheduled outside sessions of the Diet, although this is not something for which the law provides.

Notice of execution is not given in advance to either the inmate or his/her family or lawyer. Executions usually take place in the morning. One hour prior to execution, the condemned person is suddenly summoned, informed and taken to the place of execution. There is no opportunity to bid farewell to his/her family or call his/her lawyer to request legal assistance. Thus death row prisoners live in daily fear of death until the morning is over.

At the place of execution, they may ask to say farewell to their religious advisers, and may even be given a few minutes to write a will. Then their hands are handcuffed together behind their back, a blindfold is put on, they are led to the scaffold, and their knees are bound together. As soon as the noose has been placed round a condemned person's neck, a signal is given, and several guards push buttons, one of which opens the trap door on which the person is standing, causing him/her to fall to his/her death. In the basement below a doctor waits to confirm death.

After the execution, the family is informed and given twenty-four hours to claim the body. The executed person's belongings are returned to the family, but not his/her diary of the days prior to the execution, as the family is told that no such document exists.

Present trends

Public opinion

The death penalty, according to the government, is retained because the majority of citizens support it. In fact, a government opinion poll conducted recently showed support for capital punishment to be increasing. This is thought to be due to incidents such as the nerve gas attack by the Aum sect on Tokyo's metro.

	1956	1967	1975	1980	1989	1994	1999
In favour of retention	65 %	70.5 %	56.9 %	62.3 %	66.5 %	73.8 %	79.3 %
In favour of abolition	18 %	16 %	20.7 %	14.3 %	15.7 %	13.6 %	8.8 %

These findings are based on a questionnaire that put two questions: "Are you in favour of abolishing the death penalty in any circumstances?" and "Do you consider the death penalty unavoidable in certain circumstances?". Those who replied yes to the first question were recorded as favouring abolition, and those who agreed with the second as retentionists. The figures are not an accurate reflection of public opinion.

The fact is that opinions about the future of the death penalty are now very evenly divided between the two sides.

	1967	1975	1980	1989	1994	1999
In favour of retention	43.4 %	43.8 %	48.4 %	51.1 %	39.3 %	44.8 %
In favour of immediate, gradual or conditional abolition	36.2 %	29.3 %	24.7 %	26.1 %	42.8 %	38.8 %

While Japan does have a crime victim compensation system, it lags far behind the West. Many victims endure great hardship without remedy. The recent rise in the numbers of heinous crimes committed has increased support for keeping the death penalty.

227

The number of murders per 100 000 population in a few major countries is as follows.

	USA	UK	Germany	France	Japan
1988	8.4	2	4.1	4.6	1.2
1993	9.5	2.6	5.3	4.9	1
1998	6.3	2.7	3.5	3.7	1.2

The attitude of the government

The government states that it will be retaining the death penalty. In 1993 and 1998, the Human Rights Committee of the International Covenant on Civil and Political Rights recommended that the government of Japan take measures towards abolishing the death penalty and improving the treatment of those on death row. The government has not taken up this recommendation, but on each occasion promptly responded by carrying out outstanding executions. At a joint seminar in Tokyo in May 2002 attended by representatives of the Diet Members' League for the Abolition of the Death Penalty and of the Council of Europe, on the subject of the abolition of capital punishment, Justice Minister Mayumi Moriyama indicated that she has no intention of abolishing the death penalty. According to Moriyama, the question of whether the death penalty should be retained or abolished hinges on domestic uniqueness. Japan has a culture in which one atones for one's sins with one's life.

The Japanese Government has a record of opposing any proposed United Nations resolutions on the abolition of the death penalty. In fact, it actively lobbies against the adoption of such resolutions, and Japan's is an insistent and powerful voice in favour of retaining the death penalty.

The attitudes of the Diet and political parties

The Diet is extremely non-committal about abolition. Bills on abolition of the death penalty have already been presented to the Diet four times, in 1901, 1902, 1907 and 1956. All were dropped. No other bills have been presented subsequently. On a few occasions, members of the Diet concerned about the death penalty have put questions to the Ministry of Justice, but the Diet has never held a serious debate on the merits of the issue. No special committee has ever been appointed.

There are eight political parties, three of which pledge in their manifestos that they will abolish the death penalty. All three are minor parties, and none of them treats it as a major policy issue. In other words, no political party is actively working to abolish the system. However, some members formed an all-party Diet Members' League for the Abolition of the Death Penalty in 1994 (this had 122 members, one-sixth of the entire membership of the Diet, as of 31 March 2003). The league is planning to submit a bill which would impose a moratorium on capital punishment by the end of 2003.

Under this bill:

• an ad hoc committee would be set up to discuss the possibility of abolishing the death penalty within three years;

• in the meantime, a moratorium would be imposed;

• a new sentence of life imprisonment without parole would be introduced to fill the gap between the death penalty and life imprisonment with parole.

Trends in legal circles

Japan's Supreme Court has consistently expressed its opposition to the abolition of the death penalty, or at best adopted a passive position. In its view, the question of retaining or abolishing the system is a matter for the legislature, not for the judiciary.

The Public Prosecutor's Office appealed to the Supreme Court in a total of five cases in which life imprisonment was imposed in 1997 and 1998, arguing in favour of an expansion of the application of capital punishment. The cases concerned included four in which the courts of first and second instance had ruled in favour of life imprisonment, and one case in which the crime was punished by the death sentence in the court of first instance, but by life imprisonment in the court of second instance.

The Japan Federation of Bar Associations (JFBA) used to oppose the abolition of the death penalty, but is now calling for commutation of the death penalty and drawing attention to the inhumane treatment of death row inmates. Having issued public statements calling for a moratorium following every execution, the JFBA, in November 2002, proposed a moratorium law and a fundamental review of capital punishment. However, it has not yet come out in favour of abolishing the death penalty. This suggests that, even among those in the legal profession, many are strongly in favour of retaining the system. Only 0.3% of Japan's 18 000 lawyers are willing to defend prisoners sentenced to death.

Mass media

In the first half of the 1990s, during the period when implementation of the death sentence was first suspended and then restarted, the mass media showed deep concern about the death penalty, calling for a national debate on the merits of the system. However, after routine application of the death penalty and a series of Aum incidents in 1995, the number of articles debating the merits of the system declined drastically. Even the Council of Europe's June 2001 resolution calling on the Government of Japan to abolish the death penalty was covered by only a limited number of newspapers, and only a small amount of space was devoted to it.

A move towards abolition of the death penalty

A movement begun by enlightened citizens in the early years of the twentieth century died out with the emergence of militarism. Again, after the second world war, some prison staff, scholars and intellectuals initiated a movement in 1955 to try to abolish the death penalty. However, the movement petered out without achieving its objective, following the death of its central figure. In the 1980s Amnesty International's Japanese Section set up a Network Centre Against the Death Penalty, and some groups of citizens initiated a movement to abolish the death penalty. An association of death row prisoners was set up, called A Grain of Wheat, and a prisoner on death row, Masashi Daidoji, is a leading figure in this. In 1989, the United Nations adopted the Second Optional Protocol to the International Covenant on Civil and Political Rights, aiming at the abolition of the death penalty. These initiatives provided momentum. In 1990, Amnesty International's Japanese Section, together with individual citizens and private organisations, lawyers, politicians, members of religious groups and some condemned prisoners, organised Forum 90 to support ratification of the Second Optional Protocol, and this has played a central role in the movement. The momentum has grown in religious and academic circles. The National Council of Churches of Japan, the Anglican Church and the Tendaishu Buddhist sect have declared their commitment to abolition of the death penalty. Some of the academicians of the Penal Code Society have issued a declaration. However, these efforts have not succeeded in influencing broad public opinion or in achieving a political outcome. The anti-death penalty movement is demanding not just the end of the death penalty itself, but also the introduction of life imprisonment as an alternative penalty, the suspension of the carrying out of death sentences and more humane treatment for prisoners on death row.

In 1993, an Asia Forum for Abolition of the Death Penalty was established by groups from Hong Kong, the Philippines, Taiwan, Korea and Japan, but this has not succeeded in becoming a substantial force. However, no executions have been carried out under President Kim Dae Jung, and more than half of the members of Korea's Parliament are in favour of abolition. The second Asia Forum for Abolition of the Death Penalty took place in Seoul in November 2001, and an initiative is under way in Korea to introduce a bill on abolition of the death penalty. In Taiwan, the Minister of Justice has said that he wishes to abolish the death penalty within three years.

Conclusion

Japan carries out the death penalty in total secrecy. Neither the prisoner's lawyer nor any member of his/her own or the victim's family may witness the execution. The place of execution is not open to the public. No exception is made for members of the Diet or the press. On the grounds of the protection of privacy and the mental state of the prisoner, no information is disclosed other than the execution date and the number of executions carried out. Prison staff are sworn to secrecy even after retirement. Discussion of the death penalty is taboo.

The death penalty in Japan is unjust, cruel and abnormal. A person suspected of a crime that is punishable by death is harshly interrogated in poor conditions, without adequate opportunity for defence. As a prisoner s/he is harshly treated and in nearly every case is sentenced to death during unfair court proceedings. On death row, s/he is kept in isolation and subjected to further inhumane treatment, kept in daily fear of execution, and with no opportunity for defence. This in itself is an act of barbarous and uncivilised torture.

Unfortunately, there is little possibility of improvement in the near future. However, there are individual citizens, private organisations, lawyers, politicians and members of religious groups who continue to seek change.

In the twenty-three years of my career as an attorney, in an attempt to avoid death sentences and to prevent executions, I have defended eleven cases of persons charged with capital crimes. Two cases were re-tried, in three of my cases I averted the death penalty, and one case ended in execution. I am one of the founding members of Forum 90.

Appendix I

Protocol No. 6 to the Convention for the protection of human rights and fundamental freedoms concerning the abolition of the death penalty, as amended by protocol No. 11

Strasbourg, 28 April 1983

Headings of articles added and text amended according to the provisions of Protocol No. 11 (ETS No. 155) as from its entry into force on 1 November 1998.

The member States of the Council of Europe, signatory to this Protocol to the Convention for the Protection of Human Rights and Fundamental Freedoms, signed at Rome on 4 November 1950 (hereinafter referred to as "the Convention"),

Considering that the evolution that has occurred in several member states of the Council of Europe expresses a general tendency in favour of abolition of the death penalty;

Have agreed as follows:

Article 1 – Abolition of the death penalty

The death penalty shall be abolished. No-one shall be condemned to such penalty or executed.

Article 2 – Death penalty in time of war

A State may make provision in its law for the death penalty in respect of acts committed in time of war or of imminent threat of war; such penalty shall be applied only in the instances laid down in the law and in accordance with its provisions. The State shall communicate to the Secretary General of the Council of Europe the relevant provisions of that law.

Article 3 – Prohibition of derogations

No derogation from the provisions of this Protocol shall be made under Article 15 of the Convention.

Article 4[1] – Prohibition of reservations

No reservation may be made under Article 57 of the Convention in respect of the provisions of this Protocol.

Article 5 – Territorial application

1   Any State may at the time of signature or when depositing its instrument of ratification, acceptance or approval, specify the territory or territories to which this Protocol shall apply.

2   Any State may at any later date, by a declaration addressed to the Secretary General of the Council of Europe, extend the application of this Protocol to any other territory specified in the declaration. In respect of such territory the Protocol shall enter into force on the first day of the month following the date of receipt of such declaration by the Secretary General.

3   Any declaration made under the two preceding paragraphs may, in respect of any territory specified in such declaration, be withdrawn by a notification addressed to the Secretary General. The withdrawal shall become effective on the first day of the month following the date of receipt of such notification by the Secretary General.

Article 6 – Relationship to the Convention

As between the States Parties the provisions of Articles 1 to 5 of this Protocol shall be regarded as additional articles to the Convention and all the provisions of the Convention shall apply accordingly.

Article 7 – Signature and ratification

The Protocol shall be open for signature by the member States of the Council of Europe, signatories to the Convention. It shall be subject to ratification, acceptance or approval. A member State of the Council of Europe may not ratify, accept or approve this Protocol unless it has, simultaneously or previously, ratified the Convention. Instruments of ratification, acceptance or approval shall be deposited with the Secretary General of the Council of Europe.

Article 8 – Entry into force

1   This Protocol shall enter into force on the first day of the month following the date on which five member States of the Council of Europe have expressed their consent to be bound by the Protocol in accordance with the provisions of Article 7.

---

1. Text amended according to the provisions of Protocol No. 11 (ETS No. 155).

2   In respect of any member State which subsequently expresses its consent to be bound by it, the Protocol shall enter into force on the first day of the month following the date of the deposit of the instrument of ratification, acceptance or approval.

Article 9 – Depositary functions

The Secretary General of the Council of Europe shall notify the member States of the Council of:

a.   any signature;

b.   the deposit of any instrument of ratification, acceptance or approval;

c.   any date of entry into force of this Protocol in accordance with Articles 5 and 8;

d.   any other act, notification or communication relating to this Protocol.

In witness whereof the undersigned, being duly authorised thereto, have signed this Protocol.

Done at Strasbourg, this 28th day of April 1983, in English and in French, both texts being equally authentic, in a single copy which shall be deposited in the archives of the Council of Europe. The Secretary General of the Council of Europe shall transmit certified copies to each member State of the Council of Europe.

Appendix II

Protocol No. 13 to the Convention for the protection of human rights and fundamental freedoms, concerning the abolition of the death penalty in all circumstances

Vilnius, 3 May 2002

The member States of the Council of Europe signatory hereto,

Convinced that everyone's right to life is a basic value in a democratic society and that the abolition of the death penalty is essential for the protection of this right and for the full recognition of the inherent dignity of all human beings;

Wishing to strengthen the protection of the right to life guaranteed by the Convention for the Protection of Human Rights and Fundamental Freedoms signed at Rome on 4 November 1950 (hereinafter referred to as "the Convention");

Noting that Protocol No. 6 to the Convention, concerning the Abolition of the Death Penalty, signed at Strasbourg on 28 April 1983, does not exclude the death penalty in respect of acts committed in time of war or of imminent threat of war;

Being resolved to take the final step in order to abolish the death penalty in all circumstances,

Have agreed as follows:

Article 1 – Abolition of the death penalty

The death penalty shall be abolished. No one shall be condemned to such penalty or executed.

Article 2 – Prohibition of derogations

No derogation from the provisions of this Protocol shall be made under Article 15 of the Convention.

Article 3 – Prohibition of reservations

No reservation may be made under Article 57 of the Convention in respect of the provisions of this Protocol.

Article 4 – Territorial application

1.   Any State may, at the time of signature or when depositing its instrument of ratification, acceptance or approval, specify the territory or territories to which this Protocol shall apply.

2.   Any State may at any later date, by a declaration addressed to the Secretary General of the Council of Europe, extend the application of this Protocol to any other territory specified in the declaration. In respect of such territory the Protocol shall enter into force on the first day of the month following the expiration of a period of three months after the date of receipt of such declaration by the Secretary General.

3.   Any declaration made under the two preceding paragraphs may, in respect of any territory specified in such declaration, be withdrawn or modified by a notification addressed to the Secretary General. The withdrawal or modification shall become effective on the first day of the month following the expiration of a period of three months after the date of receipt of such notification by the Secretary General.

Article 5 – Relationship to the Convention

As between the States Parties the provisions of Articles 1 to 4 of this Protocol shall be regarded as additional articles to the Convention, and all the provisions of the Convention shall apply accordingly.

Article 6 – Signature and ratification

This Protocol shall be open for signature by member States of the Council of Europe which have signed the Convention. It is subject to ratification, acceptance or approval. A member State of the Council of Europe may not ratify, accept or approve this Protocol without previously or simultaneously ratifying the Convention. Instruments of ratification, acceptance or approval shall be deposited with the Secretary General of the Council of Europe.

Article 7 – Entry into force

1   This Protocol shall enter into force on the first day of the month following the expiration of a period of three months after the date on which ten member States of the Council of Europe have expressed their consent to be bound by the Protocol in accordance with the provisions of Article 6.

2   In respect of any member State which subsequently expresses its consent to be bound by it, the Protocol shall enter into force on the first day of the month following the expiration of a period of three months after the date of the deposit of the instrument of ratification, acceptance or approval.

Article 8 – Depositary functions

The Secretary General of the Council of Europe shall notify all the member States of the Council of Europe of:

a. any signature;

b. the deposit of any instrument of ratification, acceptance or approval;

c. any date of entry into force of this Protocol in accordance with Articles 4 and 7;

d. any other act, notification or communication relating to this Protocol.

In witness whereof the undersigned, being duly authorised thereto, have signed this Protocol.

Done at Vilnius, this 3 May 2002, in English and in French, both texts being equally authentic, in a single copy which shall be deposited in the archives of the Council of Europe. The Secretary General of the Council of Europe shall transmit certified copies to each member State of the Council of Europe.

Appendix III – Table showing abolition in Council of Europe member, candidate and observer states

STATES	DATES OF ABOLITON (D/M/Y)		Date of last execution (year)	Protocol No. 6 to ECHR[1] date Entry into force (D/M/Y)	Statute	Protocol No.13 to the ECHR[2] Entry into force (D/M/Y)
	Peacetime	Wartime				
Albania	Constitutional Court decision 10.12.1999		1995	01.10.00	Abolitionist	signed
Andorra	1990 in the Constitution		1943	01.02.96	Fully abolitionist	01.07.03
Armenia	August 2003: entry into force of new Criminal Code replacing the death penalty with life imprisonment 9 September 2003: full abolition of the death penalty		1991	01.10.03	Fully abolitionist	
Austria	1968		1967	01.03.85	Fully abolitionist	01.05.04
Azerbaijan	10.02.1998		1993	01.05.02	Fully abolitionist	

1. Protocol No. 6 to the European Convention on Human Rights (ECHR) concerning the abolition of the death penalty in times of peace.
2. Protocol No 13 to the European Convention on Human Rights (ECHR) concerning the abolition of the death penalty in all circumstances.

Country			Year	Date	Status	
Belgium	Law of 1996		1950	01.01.99	Fully abolitionist	01.10.03
Bosnia and Herzegovina	1995			01.08.02	Abolitionist	01.11.03
Bulgaria	10.12.1998		1989	01.10.99	Fully	01.07.03 abolitionist
Croatia	The 1990 Constitution abolished the death penalty when Croatia was still part of the socialist Federal Republic of Yugoslavia		1973	01.12.97	Fully abolitionist	01.07.03
Cyprus	18.02.1999	2002	1962	01.02.00	Fully Abolitionist	01.07.03
Czech Republic	The death penalty was abolished in the Czech Republic in 1990 when it was still part of the state of Czechoslovakia.		1988	01.01.93	Fully abolitionist	signed
Denmark	- First 1930 - Re-established following the second world war - Re-abolished in 1978		1892 1950	01.03.85	Fully abolitionist	01.07.03
Estonia	Law of 13.05.1998		1991	01.05.98	Abolitionist	signed
Finland	1949	1972	1944	01.06.90	Fully abolitionist	signed
France	Law of 09.10.1981	(particularity of Constitution Article 16 for President)	1977	01.03.86	Fully abolitionist	signed
Georgia	In Criminal Code of 11.11.1997		1995	01.05.00	Fully abolitionist	01.09.03

Germany	Basic law West Germany 24.05.1949 East Germany: July 1987		1949 1981	01.08.89	Fully abolitionist	signed
Greece	16.12.1993	Maintained	1972	01.10.98	Abolitionist	signed
Hungary	Constitutional Court decision 31.10.1990		1989	01.12.92	Fully abolitionist	signed
Iceland	Constitution 1928		1830	01.06.87	Fully abolitionist	signed
Ireland	1990		1954	01.07.94	Fully abolitionist	01.07.03
Italy	01.01.1948	25.10.1994	1947	01.01.89	Fully abolitionist	signed
Latvia	18.03.1999		1996	01.06.99	Abolitionist	signed
Liechtenstein	01.01.1989		1785	01.12.90	Fully abolitionist	01.07.03
Lithuania	In law 22.12.1998		1995	01.08.99	Fully abolitionist	01.05.04
Luxembourg	20.06.1979		1949	01.03.85	Fully abolitionist	signed
Malta	1971	21.03.2000	1943	01.04.91	Fully abolitionist	01.07.03

Moldova	December 1995	1990	01.10.97	Fully abolitionist	signed
Netherlands	1982	1952	01.05.86	Fully abolitionist	signed
Norway	1979	1948	01.11.88	Fully abolitionist	signed
Poland	Criminal Code 06.06.1997	1988	01.11.00	Fully abolitionist	signed
Portugal	1867 / 1976	1849	01.11.86	Fully abolitionist	01.02.04
Romania	1989 (Article 22 of Constitution)	1989	01.07.94	Fully abolitionist	01.08.03
Russian Federation	February 1999. Constitutional Court ruled that the application of the death penalty is unconstitutional until jury trials are available throughout the Federation.	1996 moratorium on executions introduced	signed	De facto abolitionist	
San Marino	1865	1468	01.04.89	Fully abolitionist	01.08.03
Serbia and Montenegro	2002, (when it was still part of the Socialist Federal Republic of Yugoslavia)	1992	signed	Fully abolitionist	signed
Slovakia	1990 (when Slovakia was still part of Czechoslovakia)	1988	01.01.93	Fully abolitionist	signed

Slovenia	1989, (when it was still part of the socialist Federal Yugoslavia)	1991 (article 17 of the Constitution)	1957	01.07.94	Fully abolitionist	01.04.04
Spain	1985	1995	1975	01.03.85	Fully abolitionist	signed
Sweden	1972		1910	01.03.85	Fully abolitionist	01.08.03
Switzerland	1987	1992	1944	01.11.87	Fully abolitionist	01.07.03
"The former Yugoslav Republic of Macedonia"	Constitution 1991			01.05.97	Fully abolitionist	signed
Turkey	August 2003		1984	01.12.03	Abolitionist	signed
Ukraine	Constitutional Court decision 29.12.1999		1997	01.05.00	Fully abolitionist	01.07.03
United Kingdom	1969	1998	1965	01.06.99	Fully abolitionist	1.02.04

APPLICANT STATES	Abolition in Peacetime	Abolition in Wartime	Date of the last execution	Statute	Second optional Protocol to the ICCPR[3]
Belarus			Retentionist		
Monaco	Constitution 17.12.1962		1847	Fully abolitionist	Party to Protocol No.2

OBSERVER STATES	Abolition in Peacetime	Abolition in Wartime	Date of the last execution	Statute
Canada	July 1976	10.12.1998	1962	Fully abolitionist
Japan				Retentionist
United States				Retentionist
Mexico	abolished	maintained	1937	Abolitionist

3. Second Optional Protocol to the International Covenant on Civil and Political Rights (ICCPR) aiming at the abolition of the death penalty (United Nations)

Sales agents for publications of the Council of Europe
Agents de vente des publications du Conseil de l'Europe

Council of Europe Publishing/Editions du Conseil de l'Europe
F-67075 Strasbourg Cedex
Tel.: (33) 03 88 41 25 81 – Fax: (33) 03 88 41 39 10 – E-mail: publishing@coe.int – Website: http://book.coe.int